Embodied Collective Memory

The Making and Unmaking of Human Nature

Rafael F. Narváez

University Press of America,® Inc.
Lanham • Boulder • New York • Toronto • Plymouth, UK

Copyright © 2013 by University Press of America,® Inc.
4501 Forbes Boulevard, Suite 200, Lanham, Maryland 20706
UPA Aquisitions Department (301) 459-3366

10 Thornbury Road, Plymouth PL6 7PP, United Kingdom

British Library Cataloguing in Publication Information Available

Library of Congress Control Number: 2012940016
ISBN: 978-0-7618-5879-9 (paper : alk. paper)—ISBN: 978-0-7618-5880-5 (electronic)

Cover photo by Rafael F. Narváez

Para las Alinitas y para Karen

Contents

Contents

Acknowledgments

This project was partly supported by the Elinor Goldmark Black Fellowship for Advanced Studies on the Dynamics of Social Change. Many thanks also to Veronica Alfaro, Maija Andersone, Karen Coleman, Yifat Gutman, James Jasper, and Vera Zolberg for comments and suggestions. I am particularly thankful to Jeff Goldfarb. Preliminary versions of some of the material have appeared in *Body and Society* (Narváez 2006).

Introduction

What Gets Left Out of History Books People don't sigh. There's no burping.—
Ellen D. Watson

Take the word *remember*: it comes from the Latin *re* (to pass back through) and *memor* (mindful, mind). "Remember" means passing a segment of time back through the mind. Logical as this seems, it is not, however, the only alternative. In Spanish, *recordar (re-cordis)* means passing a segment of time back through the heart, as though the past were thus sutured (Sanskrit *sutra*: string and memory aid) to the heart. Recall as well Marcel Proust's famous passage where the taste of a "little piece of madeleine" suddenly takes the narrator back to his childhood. Beginning on the tongue, the madeleine makes its way up to become a nostalgic memory, an abstraction, part of an identity. Proust then speaks of an "involuntary memory" and how it becomes a "voluntary" one, which implies that something buried and sensuous can become a conscious cognitive memory. "The past," he says, "is somewhere beyond the reach of the intellect and unmistakably present in some material object [or in the sensation that such an object arouses in us]" (in Benjamin 1968, 158). It seems to me that the French *souvenir* (*sub-venire*: "comes from below") is a Proustian word, in that it suggests that a memory can come from below, from the body, if we follow Plato, to then go "up" and gather around the abstractions of the mind.

But the English *remember* is a Cartesian verb. It appears to invoke a straight through faculty of the mind, where the Cartesian body — "this whole machine made up of flesh and bones," this "corpse" commanded by a "ghost" (Descartes 1988) — has little to do with remembering.

The verb *remembering*, that is to say, encourages the impression that memory is a Cartesian effect of the mind and underestimates the mnemonic

1

importance of the body. Lakoff and Johnson (1999) say that memory has been historically represented according to the "folk model of faculty psychology" as a kind of "mental entity" that inhabits the "Society of the Mind," where we find all the other (disembodied) faculties or citizens of the mind, perception, imagination, etc. "After several hundred years," they say, "a version of this folk theory of the mind [made-up of metaphors and stereotypes] is still influential in philosophy of mind, as well as in the cognitive sciences" (Lakoff and Johnson 1999, 410-413). This is also true of many writers on collective memory. Le Goff (1992), Olick and Robins (1988), and Olick, Vinitzky-Seroussi and Levy (2011) have spelled out the exceptions to this, but collective remembering is often understood in terms of disembodied psychical faculties.

Yet, any close look at the social order reveals a stream of collectively relevant bodily events — gestures, corporeal and phonetic rhythms, common affective idioms and emotional styles, shared perceptual and affective schemata, techniques of the body — which are largely *learned in a social context*, and thus consigned to habit, to bodily automatisms — to corporeal memory. Consider, for example, perceptual events. Biologically grounded as they are, and thus universal to an extent, percepts are not merely biological. They also involve elements of culture, cultural meanings that partake from the perceptual event. So that ears, for instance, "ethnic ears," as Alfred Tomatis says (1991), often "learn" local sound nuances and indeed become attuned to culturally significant sound frequencies and patterns. The percipient hears not only through vibrations and related nerve impulses, but, again, also through her culture. The nose, Katherine Ashenburg argues, is likewise "adaptable and teachable" (2007). Perception in general and vision in particular are "organized by historical conditions," as Walter Benjamin writes (1968). Even the experience of physical pain — biological, universal, and phylogenic as it is — may also vary with social location (Wall and Melzack 1996). As I will subsequently show, an entire constellation of bodily operations and events reflects, in different ways and degrees, aspects of the collective order, what bodies have learnt in various social contexts. And thus, along with ideas, values, and norms, these embodied elements also belong to the domain of collective memory.

Furthermore, even a glance at history lets us see that many of these learned bodily events are more or less synchronized, and that patterns of synchronization are framed by social frameworks. Bear in mind that, as neuroscientist Marco Iacoboni says, "We have an instinct to imitate one another — to synchronize our bodies, our actions, even the way we speak to each other" (2009, 109-110), an ability that indeed makes us human (Blackmore 2000), as it helps us empathize with others, develop an intersubjective emotional register, and garner a sense of self. (The self, we will see, is always and necessarily othered, and we glean the first glimpses of the self in the mirror of others, as Iacoboni [2009] and George H. Mead [1934] have shown.) This "instinct to imitate one another," Iacoboni adds, "to synchron-ize our bodies [is affected by] powerful *local* effects of mirroring and imita-tion [which contribute to] shaping a variety of human cultures that are often not interconnected with one another" (2009, 109-110, original emphasis).

A close look at the social order reveals, in other words, collectively rele-vant aspects of embodiment, embodied aspects of collective memory. This book discusses the ways in which social actors come to reflect social condi-tions and how these social conditions often become entangled, precisely, with gestures, with sentiments, with phonetics — with the bodies of individ-uals who bring these conditions to life. Embodied collective memory (ECM), I will argue, is a social structure that results from the transubstantiation of history in people, from the collective in-corporation of bequests given by the past. Writers such as Marcel Mauss, Pierre Bourdieu, Paul Connerton, Mich-el Foucault, Norbert Elias and others have already helped us understand this preservative tendency of embodiment. They have helped us see how social actors embody, enact and vivify the demands of culture, so that the present devolves as a vivification of the past, of tradition and history, and so that the prescriptions of the social order become, precisely, "naturally" entangled with everyday life, *organically* sedimented within the social order. But ECM is not merely determined by the past, by the "imagination of the dead," as Richard Rorty would say. It is also a site of possibilities. And embodied social actors often erode cultural norms inherited from their traditions, and thus create, even if not purposefully, new conditions of existence, for better and for worse. This book also deals with the ways in which social actors collectively detach themselves from what that past prescribes for their bodies (for example, from the values that previous generations ascribed to pre-marital virginity); so that, as they disentangle their everyday lives from the organic grip of tradition, they bring to life new collective practices, and indeed new collective futures.

The discussion that follows, I should clarify, does not suggest that people either embody elements of the past or of the possible, dichotomously, as many possibilities may, of course, fall in between. Yet, the theory I propose deals with social mechanisms whereby the past becomes sedimented in indi-vidual and collective bodies, while, on the other hand, also dealing with embodied mechanisms that lead to social change. Betty Friedan (2001) has provided examples that illustrate these ideas. She showed that, in the fifties, many housewives embodied tradition, in a literal sense, vividly reflecting the social code in their "feminine" gestures, corporeal and phonetic rhythms, affects, sartorial standards. But on the other hand, the Second Wave, led by Friedan, brought forth not only new ideas but also new "natures": new ways of vivifying and enacting femininity. Embodied social actors, that is to say, can usher in new ideas and collective discourses, and eventually new social structures, new laws, new collective identities and political agendas — new struggles for power among social forces.

Embodied collective memory, in summary, involves mechanisms that affect, at times decisively, the life and the social course of individuals and groups. As Pierre Bourdieu, Michel Foucault, and others have argued, bodies are very important instruments of social order, and of social control. To be sure, bodies are necessary channels of social and political domination. Gender domination, for example, is particularly effective when, precisely, the gestures, desires, ways of occupying space — when the bodies of men and women reflect and thus legitimize gender ideologies. But bodies, as I argue, are also channels of disorder, sites where people, for better or for worse, undo the organic grip that culture and tradition often have upon everyday life.

In Chapter One I argue that, although there are exceptions, most researchers on collective memory have neglected the idea that collective mnemonics involve embodied aspects and practices. The corpus of Collective Memory Studies has helped us better understand how social groups relate to time, especially to the past, but it has taken little notice of how *embodied* social actors collectively relate to time, especially to the future. This book tries to fill this vacuum, as well. And, to do so, I begin by reviewing some old and somewhat forgotten ideas from the French sociological tradition. This review shows that key aspects of subjectivity, indeed key human categories of understanding such as time and space, emerge through social and historical conditions. Maurice Halbwachs shows, for example, that memory, this center of the self, is not just an individual construct, but something profoundly permeated by collective experiences. On the other hand, with Marcel Mauss we see a parallel idea: that the body itself is not merely an individual thing either, but something that partakes from collectivity, as bodies reflect the demands of tradition, of the collective order and its boundaries and hierarchies.

More generally, the French School helps us see that subjectivity and indeed individuality are not the exclusive domain of individualistic psychology, neurology, or of philosophies of consciousness. We see that, instead, individuality is also a key theme for sociology, as the individual is always connected to collective processes. What transpires from this review of the French sociological tradition is that both memory and the body, often thought to be quintessentially individualistic constructs, belong not only to biology and psychology, but also to sociology and consequently to history. The body and memory are here shown to be depositories and crucibles of historical meaning, whose potentialities, though born in nature and framed by it, are largely realized through culture.

In subsequent chapters I argue that the ideas bequeathed by the French School were more fully integrated and developed by Pierre Bourdieu at the end of the twentieth century. Bourdieu helps us further see that social action is not always rational or cognitive, but also embodied, naturalized, "intuitive." We see that collective "intuitions" (e.g., "feminine intuitions"), and attendant actions and interpersonal interactions, are often framed, propped, nudged by objective social conditions. Bourdieu provides an important sociological perspective that has helped us better understand the ways in which mental schemata are connected to bodily schemata and how both are connected to social, economic, and ideological frameworks. He shows that processes whereby social conditions become in-corporated are in fact full of political implications; for example, related to the embodiment of gender ideologies and hierarchies. He shows that embodied social actors often share naturalized compasses and orientations that can help them move toward certain futures while foreclosing others. Collective futures, we see here, are sometimes sedimentations of the past, and can devolve from arbitrary demands that often govern, for instance, gender, race, class, and the lives of men and women who fall within the gravitational range of related ideologies.

Here I also discuss Bourdieu's theory of "symbolic violence," which indeed helps us see that the embodiment of the past, the vivification of inherited symbolic orders can result in the most complete forms of social domination. This theory speaks about the in-corporation of unfair social cosmologies, about the incarnation of the "fundamental principles of the arbitrary content of a culture [that are thus situated] beyond the reach of consciousness" (1977, 94). Symbolic violence, Bourdieu argues, involves a naturalized expression of history, a collective embodiment of hierarchical structures and parallel modes of censorship. Bourdieu shows, for example, that even the most arbitrary of gender ideologies may become naturalized, embodied, transubstantiated in social actors, and that these collective processes can "naturally," organically sustain related social hierarchies, and provide different scales of opportunities for social actors (Bourdieu 2001).

Bourdieu argues that both the dominating and the dominated contribute to establish a collective order that is very hard for social actors to question, to interrogate from an objective vantage point, precisely because of its "natural" and "evident" organic harmony. He says that the mechanisms that keep the social order in motion are often hard to question precisely because they are in-corporated by the dominated person herself, and because, through the embodied social actor, they are woven into the social organization. These social mechanisms, that is to say, emanate from people's bodies: they are entangled with collectively relevant affects and intuitions, with the dominant common sense, with cultural norms that are enacted through gestures, smiles, corporeal rhythms, phonetic patterns that become consolidated through everyday social rituals. These social processes thus seem to emanate from nature itself.

Symbolic violence means, in other words, that it is hard to take an objective distance, cognitive or affective, from the objective social forces that, once embodied, sustain our "nature": our desires, affects, aspects of perception, our bodily memory, individual and collective. It is through symbolic violence that unfair political requisites are performed "intuitively" and silently by dominated social actors. Here, unfair social mechanisms can be experienced not only as normal but also as necessary by the person who is burdened by them. And here, even collective minutia such as shared gestures and socially rooted affects can help foreclose alternative futures for individuals and groups. We also see that Bourdieu's theory of symbolic violence helps us understand key questions pertaining not only to processes of engenderment, as suggested, but also to race and class, which, I argue, are also aspects of ECM, vivifications of cultural dynamics and symbols.

Bourdieu is thus interested in the ways in which external conditions creep up into bodies, and pays much attention to the ways in which these objective conditions, as they become part of "nature," thus become invisible for us. Yet, I also argue that Bourdieu's perspective, helpful such as it is, is also limited and limiting. He is not a historical or cultural determinist, as critics argue, but his theory overemphasizes the mechanisms whereby external conditions influence embodied individuals. Though he blazed a trail of sobering political realism, Bourdieu's suspicions against the purported transparency of the social world precluded him from understanding changes that stem from the pre-social, and also bodily, aspects of individuality. These are changes that stem from the corners of human nature that, as Freud and others have shown, can take us past social conventions and therefore past social possibilities. Bourdieu failed to take a position with respect to the (meta-historical) agencies that Freud (and Nietzsche) ascribed to the *id* (German *Es*, the "it" part of us), a psychosomatic agency that, Freud suggested, is in constant conflict with the agents of culture and indeed in conflict with norms and the law. This, I suggest, is the heel of Bourdieu's Achillean sociological project.

Hence, in an attempt to go beyond Bourdieu's model, I consider psychoanalytical theory. First, I show that psychoanalysis has fallen out of favor among many important critics; and that even powerful writers, such as Karl Popper, have pointed out the errors of this theory, including Freud's early biologistic biases, which suggest that raw human nature often determines aspects of psychology and culture. These helpful criticisms have allowed us to see, for example, that, despite Freud's entrenched humanism, the early Freudian model is limited by the idea that personhood and subjectivity are, to an extent, residues that issue from a largely impersonal psychosomatic "apparatus." (In the appendix I also discuss the critical reception that psychoanalysis has had, overall, and point out some of its important problems, but also some of its possibilities.) Yet, these helpful skeptics have also discouraged us from seeing the indispensable points made by psychoanalysis, Freudian and post-Freudian. In particular, they have made it hard for us to grasp the idea that aspects of human nature, leaning on psychosomatic agencies, constantly resist the claims of culture; so that cultural mechanisms that attempt to colonize human nature tend to run into resistances, negotiations, compromises, and slips. The tip of this resistive iceberg is easy to see if, for example, one takes a glance at the history of religious institutions and their constant efforts to encroach upon the slippery domains of sexuality and gender.

Drawing upon this rather Nietzschean psychoanalytical perspective, I show that socialization can result in a radical, even pathological suppression of individuality, and of embodied aspects of individuality, as those related to sexuality (the notion of the closet, for instance, may provide an initial glimpse into this sort of cultural encircling). But we also see that disruptions of cultural patterns, small or big, individual or collective, sporadic or accumulative, are not only possible but are in fact a constant in history, as shown paradigmatically by the history of sexuality, an element of embodied collective memories. This history let us see that just as culture modifies the biological order, the demands of this "lower" order can in turn modify culture, and the structures of the family, dominant norms, the law, etc. In summary, I show that Bourdieu's notion of "habitus" (embodied schemata of dispositions and intuitions that often reflect the structures of social order) is rooted in an unstable structure associated to the id. "Lower agencies," in the Freudian idiom, constantly "push" (*Trieb*) against the expectations of tradition and of the past.

Hence, we move from the notion of "somatic compliance," suggested by Bourdieu, to the notion of somatic resistance, and to the idea that embodied social actors often build new normalities, new standards, new ways of being, new cultural schemata. I argue that embodied individuals and groups often create potential spaces, new contexts of possibility where inheritances from the past are, by degrees, reappropriated. Collective memory, as Halbwachs argued, often involves a reassembling, a reorganizing of the past. Similarly with embodied collective memory, which also involves dynamics whereby history is reassembled at the level of "nature." Social actors are not always "grafted" or "inscribed," as the middle Foucault said (1977), by structures and institutions, as if embodiment were something "made out of formless clay" (ibid., 135). As they reconstitute the bequests of the past, social actors can in fact change the flow of historical time, even if by small degrees at a time; for example, at the level of social institutions, such as those of the family, the law, the church.

These are some the basic ideas that underpin the following chapters. I should also clarify that the theory I propose deals only with a certain range of social dynamics, and that it is not a grand theory of social change. But within its analytical scope, this book casts light, let me insist, on processes leading to social change and to social sedimentation; and it also offers a pragmatic perspective about these processes, showing that the embodiment of culture and traditions can have good, bad, and mixed consequences. When consigned to the domain of embodied collective memory, traditions may ground identities and communities, providing coherence and stability for them. But on the other hand, when naturalized, traditions can also overshadow the individual, encroach upon the deeper corners of her nature, and even remove her truer sense of self. Likewise, I also suggest that the processes whereby culture and the past cease to have a grip on embodiment need to be seen pragmatically. When social actors remove tradition from the domain of embodiment, they may thus remove the organic sense of integration with the past and with others who share a similar history, which may create anomic drifts and collective anxieties. Yet, removing the "imaginations of the dead" from the domain of life can also open new possibilities for individuals and communities.

The main axes of this book are thus the French School (Bourdieu included) and psychoanalytical theory, but I also draw from other theoretical and empirical sources, including phenomenology, neurology, and history. And the examples I provide to illustrate the various aspects of embodied collective memory also go beyond the empirical cases typically discussed by the French School and by psychoanalysis. I discuss, for instance, the history of gestures, of food and nutrition, the psychology of sensations such as pain and cold, the sociology of emotions, of scatology, the changing social parameters of embarrassment, and sexuality, gender, and race — all of which are aspects of embodied collective memories, constructs rooted in biological as well as social processes.

In the end, this book deals with the life of the past and the life of the possible. It provides a perspective on bio-socio-psychological processes that bring the past and/or the forthcoming to life. It clarifies the role that social actors play in these processes, even if beyond cognitive intent, through automatisms or through strategic and aggregative disruptions. This book deals, ultimately, with human nature, and how it is constantly being made and unmade, for better and for worse. How do we create it, and with what consequences? Which social groups participate in these processes more actively, and which groups tend to be excluded? Can we control these processes? Which forms of embodied memory can hinder us, which ones can give us good roots into the past, and which ones can help us act and think mythopoeically, so that we can thus imagine and construct our own future, new symbols, sentiments, pleasures, schemata of perception?

Chapter One

The French Sociological Tradition

In our daily lives the forces of history are present.—Jeffrey Goldfarb

THE FRENCH SCHOOL

Collective Memory Studies have been very useful in helping us understand commemorative rituals and events; or how social groups understand time, especially the past; or how, more generally, social actors come to partake from shared symbolic universes. But encouraging age-old platonic biases with respect to the body, most writers on collective memory have also discouraged, as suggested, the idea that collective memory involves embodied dimensions and practices that work "below" and beyond consciousness. Most of these approaches have also discouraged us from thinking about the ways in which embodied social actors collectively relate to social space as well as to time, particularly to the past and to the future. In this chapter, expanding upon the French School of Sociology, I show that collective memory involves mental as well as bodily schemata, both of which are connected to social frameworks, and that this sort of embodied perspective can provide a distinctive understanding of how social groups relate to time. This perspective, I suggest, can help us understand how collective pasts become sedimented in individual and social memories, in individual and "social bodies," and how the past thus becomes vivified (in the present), so that social groups "naturally," "intuitively" march toward inherited futures. (In subsequent chapters I will show that an embodied perspective can help us understand how social actors detach themselves from the past and hence bring to life new collective practices, new imaginations, and new futures.)

Here I focus on the three main figures of the French School, Emile Durkheim, Marcel Mauss, and Maurice Halbwachs, who have provided founda-

9

tional theoretical premises, "shoulders of giants," as Newton may say, upon which we can have an initial glimpse into the links that connect collective memory to the body, to social frameworks and to time. These writers indeed established a turning point in epistemology, gradually shifting the focus of attention from mentalism to embodiment, particularly through Mauss' theory of the techniques of the body (discussed subsequently). Though Emile Durkheim, the founding father of French sociology, was indebted to Descartes and Plato, the school that he founded ultimately managed to step out from the dominant Cartesianism, from disembodied Platonism, from the sway of the Kantian "Copernican" revolution, and from the *a priori* subject that, Kant argued, transcended the senses, culture, and history. Kant, Descartes, and Hegel continued to be the dominant figures of this end of the century, but many and lasting changes were nonetheless portended by Durkheim and the Durkhemians;[1] and this school indeed became the locus of a long lasting impulse increasingly concerned with what Heidegger, after Husserl, called the "problematic of embodiment."[2]

Durkheim, one may argue, in fact pioneered a sociological critique of the body; at least in that his theory of effervescent rituality began to clarify the idea that this form of intensely bodily activity injects meaning and cohesion into social groups. He argued that the embodied social actor, inserted in this kind of periodic effervescence, thus participates in the production and reproduction of social meaning, social renewal, cohesion, and creativity. The key Durkheimian idea, let me insist, is that, because of their effervescence, these rites are highly embodied and that they indeed lean — almost anaclitically, to use Freud's language — on the interactions of intensified bodies.[3] Durkheim suggests, that is to say, that social order and cohesion can become more and more sedimented as bodies come together to collectively, periodically, and effervescently experience, enact, and feel the prescriptions embedded in the social order.

In turn, following Durkheim, Mauss and Halbwachs put together a theoretical framework to account more fully for what Durkheim's theory left mostly abeyant: social order "in between" the peak moments of effervescent rituality: Mauss through a theory of habitual bodily practices, and Halbwachs through a theory of collective memory. Both students of Durkheim showed that embodiment and memory are profoundly embedded in social practices; that they are largely created by social practices; and that they also serve as vehicles of social reproduction (though, as I will subsequently show, they also serve as vehicles of social renewal and creativity).

Durkheim's theory of morality and of the "schools of morality" (e.g., 1973) did give us a picture of social order in times of "calm." But what Aristotle calls an "efficient" causal account, a "mechanical" account telling us just *what* pivots, what moves, and sustains the socio-moral order in times of calm, was better developed by his two students. By Mauss, first, who showed that although embodiment was at its peak in effervescent rituality, the "techniques of the body" were sedimented first and foremost through everyday rituality, through the ordinary social practices and habits of social actors. Social order, he argued, is carried at the very level of the body and is also expressed everyday in and through the techniques of the body. Walking, for example, because it carries not only biological but also cultural markers (the rhythm of a peasant woman, for instance, tends to be different than that of a middle class woman), can thus leave a trace of meaning befitting certain social positions and cultural contexts. Walking, learned everyday through imitation, through occupation, through social positioning, can thus signal and enact social meaning. To be sure, anticipating Michel Foucault, Mauss suggests that history and society, social ranks included, were inscribed upon our bodies and were thus daily performed by us, a theme that I will subsequently develop in detail.

Similarly with Halbwachs: although he thought that collective remembrances gather strength through rituality (for example, through commemorative rituals), he also emphasized how they are sedimented through everyday collective rituals and practices, to thus become "organically anchored" within the everyday life and the flux of the social world. Collective memory, he implied, also carries social order, as collectively shared reminiscences are linked to mores, beliefs — to social practices, in general. Halbwachs in fact makes his famous distinction between history and collective memory, where history belongs to a dead past and collective memory lives organically in the present. Collective memory means, that is to say, that the past is organically connected to the collective order, and thus anchored within the present. It means that the past is thus actualized, acted out and re-*presented* by the individual and by the social group. (And so "person" here has the almost performative sense of *per-sonare*, "to speak through the mask": a mask that is given by a collective past and worn and performed individually in the present, a mask that is thus present and past, individual and collective, unique and common.)

As I will show, Halbwachs discusses memory (emphasizing the mind) in terms that are very compatible with Mauss' discussion of *habitus* (emphasizing the body). And both theories complement the bigger Durkheimian framework, which speaks of the two poles of *homo duplex* — precisely, body and mind, as though Halbwachs and Mauss were respectively theorizing the operations of the higher and lower poles that, Durkheim says, fundamentally characterize the human experience. But let us go back to Durkheim, who provides the foundations to these ideas.

Emile Durkheim

Durkheim was a rationalist in the Cartesian tradition. As he writes,

[W]e remain the land of Descartes…No doubt, Cartesianism is an archaic and narrow form of rationalism. . .But if it is necessary to transcend it, is even more necessary to conserve its principle…of distinct ideas which is at the very root of the French spirit and the root of all science. (in La Capra 1972, 8)

From the Cartesian tradition he inherited, in particular, a *homo duplex* (again, mind-body) way of thinking. The person, he thought, was one part body, biology, sensory experience, desire, desire for things, things individually valued, the "vulgar impressions," related "states of consciousness" — egotism. And another part, "the soul," the carrier of moral conscience and conceptual awareness, enabled the person to rise above egotism and to join in the social order; an order that, as in Freud, is and has to be endowed with some kind of supra-individual moral meaning. The body here is closer to individuality and egotism and the soul closer to collectivity and gregariousness.

For Durkheim, the body is in fact the pre-social element of *homo duplex*. But, importantly, although *individuated*, the embodied element is not *separate* from the social order. It is instead profoundly embedded in it, so that these "vulgar impressions," the "sensory experience," indeed the desires of the lower pole arise from everyday interactions with external things. Somewhat as in Freud, again, the individual and the supra-individual order, for Durkheim — the egotistical body and the "soul" attached to the "collective soul" — are separated *and* also linked. The former things are the substratum of the latter ones and there is tension and an energetic economy in between. The body, for Durkheim, is the substratum of consciousness in that individual consciousness emerges only as the egotistical demands of the body are overcome. Only thus the individual enters into the domain of collectivity to acquire a "soul" that largely reflects the "collective soul." For Durkheim, collective consciousness, the collective soul that touches the individual soul, is akin to the Freudian super-ego in that both are the representatives of external, supra-individual demands, law, morality — culture.

Durkheim thus speaks of the "empire" that society "holds over consciousness, which is often contrary to our most fundamental inclinations and instincts" (1965, 237). Again, collective consciousness is necessarily released through the overcoming of the egotistical demands of the body, which is also its substratum. In fact, for Durkheim, because collective consciousness does transcend the purely individual sphere, it has historically been misperceived and misrepresented through magical and theological languages of transcendence. Collective consciousness, he implies, is a sort of social prototype of things transcendent and immaterial, which naturally leads to notions of divinity and otherworldliness.

Philosophically, this is also the precise point at which Durkheim moves away from Kant and the dominant Kantian idealism: for the French sociologist, structural categories of sensible intuition and understanding are supra-individual, phylogenetically — but not transcendental, as in Kant. They are historical instead. Though concerned with universals and giving us a framework inclusive of enlightenment rationalism and positivism, Durkheim thought, against Kant's a-priorism, that mental categories — *are not subjective, universal, and God-given endowments*. Durkheim thought, instead, that they are constituted historically, by the very fact that we have to reach others, and through the social (and historical) bonds that human beings need to establish (Durkheim and Mauss 1963). "The fundamental notions of the mind," Durkheim writes, "the essential categories of thought are products of social factors" (1965, 170). Even categories such as time and space, for instance, are, for Durkheim, socially constructed. I will soon discuss this idea in detail, but let me presently say that, for these French sociologists, notions of space are effected by territorial morphology, and time by the "rhythm of social life" (1965, 488).[4] Hence, though the idea of temporality is universal, ideas about the meaning and nature of time, as chrono-ethnologists also argue, can vary historically and culturally.

To be sure, for Durkheim, categories of thought live and die with social groups. Durkheim and Mauss said in fact that our mental categories *in toto* emerge from the morphology of historically attained social bonds; "logical relations," they said, "are, thus, in a sense, domestic relations" (1963, 84). Meaning in general, for Durkheim, is ontologically attached to our relations to things and to the types of links we create with other people. "Ontologically," that is to say (Greek ὄντος, "being"), because the very nature of meaning — what meaning IS — is connected to the nature of things, to what things are, and to the types of connections that we establish with the world. So that as the world changes, meaning changes with it. Even morality, for Durkheim, is "closely akin to material things because [it is] conceived of in tangible forms" (in Janssen and Verheggen 1997, 294).

It is also instructive to compare Durkheim's historicistic approach against David Hume's empiricism (against which Kant built his idealistic model). For the Scot, recall, the categories of the mind come from hypotheses infinitely tested through human experience, a process that gives us a causal understanding of the world. Durkheim would agree with this or any phylogenic approach to the human mind; but in contrast to Hume, Durkheim focused on the experience of *homo socialis*, which by its intrinsic nature *must* form larger units, fellowships, etc., and therefore must have *shared* — that is: social — forms of thought and understanding (*societas* means unity through shared understandings). Hence, Durkheim's ideas about the mind, and about the subject, in general, are very different from Hume's. The Scot's perceptionism made him believe that individual selves "are nothing but a bundle or collection of different perceptions" (in Russell 1972, 662). By contrast, for Durkheim, individual selves do not result primarily from the interactions between the percipient and the world, the senses and external factors, but primarily from interactions among social actors. For him, human beings mirror the *social* world, and thus become othered, onto- and phylogenetical-ly, and invested with the (socio)logic that structures the social organization. Thus, rather than being a "bundle of perceptions," the Durkheimian subject is generally well-structured, grounded, ordered. Fundamentally defined by the collective order, he is endowed with a structuring capacity that already con-tains categories of understanding — acquired phylogenetically through the social life of the species.

With all this, and under the banner of The French School, a fledgling historicist sociology progressively began to conquer academic territory oth-erwise under the sway of the Kantian "subjectivist turn." Neither partaking from Kant's rationalism, nor going back to Kant's empiricist competition ("irrationalism" for Durkheim 1965, 27), the French School began to call our attention to how the subject is subjectified in profound ways by objective and historical conditions.

The Body and Collective Effervescence

Again, the cognitive dimension was very important for Durkheim (a cogni-tive dimension that, however, was historical and so to speak "sociologiz-able," more amenable to scientific sociology than to speculative philosophy). But one can hardly say that Durkheim was a cognitivist thinker. "To live," he said, "is above all things to act, to act without counting the cost and for the pleasure of acting" (in Janssen and Verheggen 1997, 295). Indeed, as Janssen and Verheggen (1997) have said, besides the "cognitivist" Durkheim there was an intuitivist and non-rationalist Durkheim who placed his stakes in collective effervescence, and in its concomitant — non-deliberative, non-mentalist — effects in social meaning. As Connerton also says, "Durk-heim . . . does indeed have a non-cognitive performative account" (1989, 103).

Durkheim, as we began to see, was interested in the various ways in which social representations (beliefs, meanings, ideas about the world) are disseminated into the social world by effervescent — thus intensely affect-oriented and highly bodily — collective rituals. He thought that meaning itself hinges, to an extent, on, precisely, periodic bodily effervescence; an idea that in fact opened a new pathway for social epistemology by positing human nature not as a fundamentally mental reality but as an (act)ual, experi-ential, ritual, and indeed intensely bodily reality. When he writes about effer-vescence, Durkheim seems to have in mind a strong sense in which social order leans on embodiment, such that the lower pole of *homo duplex* be-comes, indeed, an active substratum of social order.

The idea is that, for Durkheim, the key moment of meaning is the act. And key instances of social action tend to involve rituality. And ritualistic social action involves not always rationalistic social actors but also embodied actors who are more and more "embodied" as the ritualistic momentum increases. The peak moment of rituality, "ritual effervescence," indeed has the effect of lifting consciousness into abeyance — much as extreme pain or extreme exhilaration, often the basic ingredients of effervescence, tend to suspend the workings of consciousness. Against Descartes — for whom affects and passions are "thoughts of the soul" that obey "movements of the spirits" and need not have an embodied dimension (e.g., Descartes 1988, 229) — Durkheim's ideas about effervescence in fact highlight the embodied and collectively shared dimension of affect. These ideas thus highlight the social construction of affect but also the affective, non-deliberative, highly embodied construction of social meaning. Categories of meaning stem not only from the interactions of rationalistic social actors, but also from the interactions of intensely embodied social actors.

For Durkheim, social meaning and social cohesion are in fact largely constructed by way of ongoing ritual acts, which, again, get their strongest impulse during the effervescent ritual: a peak social moment that can harrow meaning into the very skin of the participants of the rite, often literally. A vivid example of this is the funerary rites of the Australian aborigines, who severely wound each other during the funeral, the widow of the deceased burning her breast, her thighs, arms, and legs. The Kurnai in North America "would gash themselves with sharp stones and tomahawks until their heads and bodies streamed with blood" (Durkheim 1965, 439). The effervescent ritual, highly corporealized, is thus an important moment when social order is constructed and reconstructed, and when meaning is pierced not only into the individual body but also into the social body. To a degree, collective representations, the symbolic order, thus rest on the experiences of, and the interplay between, intensified bodies. The body for Durkheim was more than a mere metaphor for social life. Janssen and Verheggen have said that for Durkheim, "the body is *the* ultimate substratum for society" (Janssen and Verheggen 1997, 297 original emphasis). They show that the Durkheimian social order is created through collective acts and representations whose function is "penetrating the individual's conscience," "imprint[ing]" its own characteristics "on the members it comprises" — while, however, also "shap[ing] the body and vice versa" (ibid., 298).

THE HIGHER AND LOWER POLES OF HOMO DUPLEX

Durkheim showed that collective effervescence constitutes a spindle of social meaning whereby inherited symbolic universes are vivified, shared, and legitimized. But as Lewis Coser points out, collective effervescence begs the question of meaning produced during times of social calm (in Halbwachs

1992, 25). As suggested, Durkheim's ideas about the "schools of morality" provide insights about the construction of meaning during the moments of "calm," but without, however, providing a comprehensive theory. Coser says that Halbwachs' theory of collective memory further filled and fed "the apparent void between periods of effervescence and ordinary life" (in Halbwachs 1992, 25).

For Halbwachs, to be sure, the glue that holds social groups together is constituted in part by collective memory, which is a synergist of social meaning and action, and of individuality and collectivity. Groups, he shows, have collectively relevant experiences and related viewpoints that traverse individual lives. Constellations of social meanings and events irradiate their particular colors through the glasses of individual consciousnesses and identities. We thus partake from the stakes and the memories of our milieu. We thus feel this or that collective grief, and this other sense of pride, or of normality. Thus we come to think of a "we" and a "them." Halbwachs implies, in fact, that even our most intimate, "individual" memories can be structured by social frameworks, and can thus take on a collective slant or degree of importance. In Chapter Twelve we will see that the experiences and thus the memories associated with sex, for example, intimate as they are, are nonetheless invested with the various spirits of various times and places. The Greeks, the Victorians, the knights and ladies of the twelfth century, for instance, experienced sex in similar but also very different ways, such that their repertoires of sexual memories were differentially invested and mediated by their respective worlds.

To be sure, Halbwachs often speaks with an ontological undertone that tacitly speaks of *being*, my *being*, what I *am* — which is not separate from my memories. Think of severe forms of memory loss: what one *is*, our coherence, affects, and ties to the world can vanish hand in hand with our memories. As an Alzheimer patient loses the names of his friends, the meanings attached to her flag and church, her Shakespeare — she therefore unties her ties to the world. She progressively retreats from the world. Her sense of self vanishes along with her memories, which vanish along with the world. Thus, if we were to reconstruct this disappearing self, we would have to reconstruct the world that disappeared with it. What Halbwachs implies is that, as loss of memory brings non-being into us, acquisition of memory, by contrast, brings us into being, into my mode of being, into what I am, which largely predicated by what the world is. In contrast to the Alzheimer patient, as the child develops a memory, she becomes progressively attached to the world, and rooted in certain objective conditions and forces that govern her world: gender, class, race — culture, in general. Hence, as memory is permeated by the collective order, her being is permeated by collectivity, by time and place. Memory, that is to say, shelters us from radical loneliness, in that we *are*, ontologically, part of a collective, individuated but not separate.

"Collective memory," in other words, does not mean that we all share the same repertoire of memories. It means that memory is individual (only I know certain aspects of my life) but cannot be individuated, and that it is indeed profoundly affected by social frameworks. Memory is thus uncanny: it partakes from opposites: it is what makes me an individual and it is also the glue that irretrievably attaches me to the collective order.

Note also that, much as Durkheim, Halbwachs also speaks of time not as a Kantian or mathematical thing, but as something that is also subjective and lived. In fact, Durkheim's idea that time involves collective and historical experiences was taken by Halbwachs who, turning from Bergsonian individualism to Durkheimian collectivism, made it the spindle of his theory. Collective memory, for Halbwachs, is not only a vivification of social spaces, but also a collective vivification of time, particularly of the past, a past that is thus lived in the present.

Perhaps, as Coser says (in Halbwachs 1992, 25-28), Halbwachs overemphasized the role that the present has over the past, suggesting that we constantly impose present imperatives upon the past. And thus, perhaps he underestimated the *presence* of the past: how the past flows unto the present to impose its character; how we presently carry our past. And here is where we have to turn to Mauss and to the problem of embodiment. An embodied perspective, as I argued, not only complements Halbwachs' ideas about collective memory, but can also help correct his presentist slant. On the one hand, an embodied perspective can help us see that social actors can "naturally" carry, in their bodies, the strong presence of the past; for example, when traditional forms of engenderment become incarnate in us. But on the other hand, embodiment also helps us see how social actors relate to the future; how they disentangle themselves from the requisites of the past, of tradition, and thus open their lives unto new possibilities. I will subsequently stop to fully discuss this idea, but for now let me provide an example: feminism. Think of the modalities of embodiment that the feminist waves bequeathed to modernity: new sexual, gestural, affective, sartorial standards. These new features of embodiment imply breakages with, and the creation of, embodied traditions, where nonconforming bodies began to call forth elements of the future, including new laws, new gendered divisions of labor, a new cultural logic, new traditions, and hence also new struggles and anxieties. Feminism, in short, opened up new futures for embodied social actors and groups.

Mauss' theory of embodiment and Halbwachs' theory of collective memory, in any case, can only be understood side by side. They are complementary pieces of the puzzle that, under the leadership of Durkheim, the French School tried to put together to address the old Hobbesian question of order and the questions of meaning and action. Again, whereas Halbwachs was concerned with the higher pole of the Durkheimian *homo duplex* (minds that reflect and enact dynamics of social ordering), Mauss was concerned with the lower pole (bodies that reflect and enact dynamics of social ordering). As I will show, Mauss and Halbwachs are indeed in constant dialogue with one another, a dialogue about the synergy between social frameworks, minds, and bodies, and about the ways in which social frameworks impinge upon individual minds *and* bodies — to trigger *individual* meanings, experiences, and actions. To be sure, what is further suggested by the conversation between these writers is that the question of individuality is not first and foremost a question for an individualistic psychology, or for biology, or for philosophy of consciousness, but for sociology, and more generally, a question about how collective and historical processes sediment mental and corporeal aspects of individuality.

Mauss' ideas on habitual bodily practices (1973) involve original insights that, like Halbwachs' theory of collective memory, also account for meaning in "between" periods of collective effervescence. Like Halbwachs' theory of memory, Mauss' theory of the techniques of the body also speaks of meaning produced across mundane and minute rituals in everyday life. Drawing from Aristotle, he is interested in cultural practices that operate at the level of habit — or more precisely, of *habitus*. As he says,

> For good many years I have had this notion of the social nature of 'habitus' . . . The word translates infinitely better than 'habitude' (habit or custom), the hexis, the 'acquired ability' and 'faculty' of Aristotle [habitus] does not designate those metaphysical habits, that mysterious '*memory*.' In [habitus] we should discern techniques and the work of collective and individual practical reason. (Mauss 1935, 6, my emphasis)

For Mauss the body itself belongs not only to biology but also to sociology and consequently to history. For him, the body is a crucible of social meaning whose potentialities, though born in nature, are ultimately realized through culture. In his oft-quoted *The Techniques of the Body*, Mauss sets up a whole taxonomy of bodily techniques (by gender, by age, by "output," and by type of transmission of the technique), which are sub-classified into techniques of birth, of infancy, of adolescence, of adult life, which are still more complexly sub-categorized. Under the Techniques of "Care for the Body," sub-division of "care of the mouth," for example, he writes the following:

> [C]oughing and spitting technique. Here is a personal observation. A little girl did not know how to spit and this made every cold she had worse. I made inquiries. In her father's village and in her father's family in particular, in Berry, people do not know how to spit. I taught her to spit. I would give her four sous (coins) per spit. As she yearned to have a bicycle, she learned to spit. She is the first person in her family who knows how to spit. (1935, 16)

Harkening back to Plato's *techne* but also forerunning Alasdair MacIntyre's Aristotelian view of tradition (e.g., 1988), Mauss says that a technique is an act "that is traditional and efficacious (and you see in this respect that is no different from a magical, religious or symbolic act). It has to be *traditional* and *effective*. There is no technique and no transmission if there is no tradition" (Mauss 1935, 8, original emphasis). The body here is the first realm of technology; a technology that is traditional and works efficaciously within a certain social order.

Importantly, here Mauss is one step ahead of Durkheim, his uncle, as he begins to show that the body has dimensions that are clearly not pre-social. With this renewed theory of the social role of the body, the nephew in fact gave a greater impulse to the objections that Durkheim had posited against philosophies of the agent that were based on an idealist, radical autonomy of consciousness. Indeed, in the spirit of the Neo-Pythagoreans (Galileo, Kepler) who contested the dominant deductionism and the teleological biases of scholasticism, Mauss posited a new non-teleological, inductionist, and embodied framework for sociology. "[W]e must proceed," he said, "from the concrete to the abstract and not the other way around" (ibid., 3). And so he opened up a new epistemological approach dealing with the relationship between nature and culture, and the concrete and the abstract. Henceforward, questions about human nature — now outside teleological, a-prioristic, rationalistic and subjectivist frameworks — increasingly began to be formulated from the point of view of the historical crisscrossing of biology, psychology, and sociology.

The French School thus provided something of a *Novum Organun* for the social sciences, which was embodied in Durkheim's treatise on method (1982), *and* in Mauss' tiny but important essay on Total Man; "total" insofar as it was inclusive of biology, psychology, and sociology (e.g., 1923). Here a sort of "total sociology" was insinuated and passed on to us, which was "totally" heedful of psychology and biology (an idea that has been overlooked, to an extent, by mentalisms of various sorts).

Again, there are striking parallels between Halbwachs' theory of memory and Mauss' theory of the body. If Halbwachs says that "It is in society that people...acquire their memories" (1992, 38), Mauss implies that it is in nature that we acquire the body, but it is in society that the body is released in its potentiality (e.g., 1935). If Halbwachs suggests that our memories vary along with the variations of the social order, Mauss suggests that our bodies vary with social time and space. Our bodily techniques and habitus, Mauss says, "vary not only just with individuals and their imitations; they vary especially across societies, educations, proprieties, fashions" (1935, 6). If Halbwachs, according to Patrick Hutton (1993), shows that "memory is only able to endure within sustaining social contexts...[because] individual images of the past are provisional," Mauss shows that the body is also sustained by specific social contexts, in which tradition and technique are rehearsed. Halbwachs shows that memory is a marker and a yardstick of social and historical differentiation; and Mauss similarly shows that the body is a marker and a measure of social differentiation (thus anticipating Norbert Elias and Pierre Bourdieu, two key writers that I will discuss soon).

If against the grain, Halbwachs says that memory is a non-individualistic creation, Mauss, against the grain, says that the body is largely a non-individualistic social construction, as well. Individual memory, for Halbwachs, cannot function but through "shared interactions." For Mauss, the body is the product of social interplay. Halbwachs says 1) that "the life of the child is immersed in social milieus through which he comes in touch with a past stretching back some distance. The latter acts like a framework into which are woven his most personal experiences" (1992, 68); and 2) that, "collective memory provides the group a self-portrait that unfolds through time, since it is an image of the past" (ibid.). Mauss could have written these sentences having in mind the ways in which the body is incorporated in society and tradition. To paraphrase Halbwachs adding Mauss' language: the "most personal experiences" of the child are the "most personal [bodily] experiences in touch with a past stretching back some distance. The latter acts like a framework into which are woven his most personal experiences." Here habitus is the structure that "provides the group a self-portrait that unfolds through time, since it is an image of the past." According to both Mauss and Halbwachs, we perceive our bodies and our memories, as unique, autonomous, and original — despite their entrenched social nature (and again Bourdieu and Elias are anticipated).

In general, Mauss and Halbwachs speak with an ontological ring suggesting that socially inflected bodies and memories have very much to do with what one *is* and with how and why one is. Here one can infer indeed that human beings are, fundamentally, socially inflected bodies and memories.

The continuities between Halbwachs and Mauss are not coincidental. As we will also see, memory and the body are largely assembled by socio-historical apparatuses. Much later, Paul Connerton (1989) in a sense subsumed the work of both students of Durkheim into an integrated theory of embodied collective memory. Against the "current orthodoxies," Connerton says that, "Every group...will entrust to bodily automatisms the values and categories that they are most anxious to conserve. They will know well the past can be kept in mind by habitual memory sedimented in the body" (ibid., 102). Memory, he suggests, is not only "inscribed" through the construction and display of cultural texts like printed media, etc., but is also "incorporated" in bodily practices, in various aspects of embodiment. Collective memory is thus not only about conscious commemorative practices but, at a different level, is also a dimension of a socialized body. The culturally integrated body is, in other words, a dimension of collective memory.

The lesson that we take from the French, in summary, is that, to twist a phrase by Nietzsche, cognitive memory recollects the historical "I" while the body *does* the historical I.[5] Collective memory is not inscribed on the body as a dead letter, but it is vivified by "it"; and, thus embodied, memory becomes, as Halbwachs wanted it, "organically" integrated into the world. "Organically," that is to say, not only because embodiment is an integral part of the social "organization," but also in a more literal sense, in that culture is hence transubstantiated in the materiality of bodies, their movements, pleasures, rhythms, gestures, and indeed in such embodied dimensions as perceptual schemata, in scatological habituses — in a constellation of embodied features (the nature of which will become apparent in subsequent chapters). Bodies are mnemonic media for the social order. Peter Burke (1989) has determined certain means of transmission of collective memory: oral history, written records, visual records, commemorative spaces, and actions (e.g., rituals). Bodies are also means of transmission of collective memory whereby tradition and the past are vivified. And precisely because bodies are media of transmission of memory, they can also be sites where embodied collective memories are rendered lifeless — and, therefore, where tradition and culture is rendered discontinuous.

In the next chapter we turn to Pierre Bourdieu, arguably the most important heir of the French School, and a writer who continued to develop the theory of the relationship between the body and the social order, and, without naming it, the theme of embodied collective memory, though with an added phenomenological dimension.

NOTES

1. And by other contenders against idealist rationalism; particularly by the "Masters of Suspicion": Marx's Hegelian critique of Hegel; Nietzsche's critique of idealism; and Freud's Cartesian critique of Cartesian reason.

2. The word *Leiblichkeit* (corporeality, embodiment) stems from Husserl's distinction between *Leib* and *Körper*, lived body and physicality (e.g., 1999). Later, Heidegger would say, "We don't 'have' a body, rather we 'are' bodily" (1991). We are not speaking, at this point in the history of embodiment, of body as a thing, but of "bodying" as an intrinsic component of life as lived. Later still, with Bourdieu, sociology becomes "embodied" in the sense of subsuming Durkheimian objectivism and Husserlian phenomenology (e.g., 1990b).

3. Anaclisis: to lean on, to stem from. Drives, for Freud, lean (anaclitically) on corporeal sources from which they aim at objects, including mental objects and social cathexes, which are the sublimated expressions of the sources (e.g., Laplanche and Pontalis 1973).

4. For Kant (1965), time and space are "pure forms of sensible intuition": "Time is not an empirical concept that has been derived from any experience"; and space "can be intuited a-priori."

5. In Zarathustra Nietzsche says, "'I' you say, and are proud of the word. But greater is that in which you do not wish to have faith — your body and its great reason: that does not say 'I,' but does 'I'" (1978).

Chapter Two

Pierre Bourdieu

THE PERSON AND THE SOCIAL WORLD

Raphael's masterpiece, The School of Athens, depicts none other than Philosophy itself. At the vanishing point of the scene, a graying, bare-footed Plato is talking to a younger, poised Aristotle. The teacher, wearing red and white, perhaps fire and air, is pointing up, "unto the heavens." The student, wearing blue and brown, perhaps water and earth, points toward the world, toward nature, toward the observer of the fresco herself. Both philosophers are surrounded by men who represent knowledge, some of whom are closer to Plato and some closer to Aristotle. Anticipating Alfred Whitehead's semiserious suggestion that the history of Western philosophy has been only a series of footnotes to Plato, the scene captures an idea that is widely accepted today: the history of thought in the West has been largely framed by vertical (idealistic, Platonic) and horizontal (materialistic, Aristotelian) axes. The young Raphael thus depicted not only Philosophy but, more precisely, the ontological and epistemological coordinates wherein the "question of first order" (matter or spirit?) had been fought about for thousands of years. This question, which was also a guiding question for the French School, is still with us today. As I discuss below, it is in fact at the center of Bourdieu's project.

The history of western philosophy, to be sure, has been vastly influenced by a small family of powerful dichotomies: ideality/materiality, spirit/flesh, mind/body, verticality/horizontality. Stemming primarily from Plato, but also from Paul, Augustine, Descartes and others, such dichotomous thinking has in fact sustained our everyday notions of "superior" and "inferior" things, of things celestial and mundane, eternal and temporal, spiritual and bodily. These age-old dichotomies have encouraged us, heirs of the Western Tradition, to see these "opposite" terms as separate (mind separate from body; idea separate from matter), and as clearly ranked (mind higher than body; spirit higher than matter). Our age, at least as ushered in by Rene Descartes, was in fact borne on the wings of these ideas. Modernity was set in motion as we became convinced, beyond all doubt as Descartes would have it, that the world of ideas (mind, ego, the subject) was radically sundered from the world of matter (the body, the external world, the object). Descartes in fact convinced us that we are part subject and part object and that to be human is to partake from two radically different natures: the mind, a "ghost in the machine," "the captain of the ship," the soul; and the body, a "corpse" and a "machine." He convinced us that, while the body belongs to the physical order, extends in space, is divisible, and obeys physical laws — the soul, by contrast, is a thinking substance that is *detached from matter*, something that doesn't extend in space, that is indivisible and not determined by physical laws.

This "folk theory of the mind," as Lakoff and Johnson might say, has been extraordinarily influential, and even the French School, as we saw, began by assuming some of these ideas ("we remain the land of Descartes," Durkheim says). Ideas that reveal themselves particularly in Durkheim's dichotomous, high/low understanding of *homo duplex*, and in the notion that the person begins as a pre-social creature whose egotistical, natural, and low impulses eventually adapted to the higher requirements of the external social world. Of course the Durkheimians didn't stop at this Cartesian point; and, as we also saw, they asked new questions, provided new answers, devised new methods — opened different windows onto the relationship between nature and culture, matter and spirit, embodiment and consciousness.

And these new perspectives were in turn enlarged and brought to their logical conclusion by Pierre Bourdieu, a writer who managed to leave not only a mark on the history of French sociology, particularly in the area of embodiment, but also on the history of contemporary Western thought. Against age-old habits of thought, Bourdieu began his polemic by indeed abandoning all Cartesian dichotomies, body/soul, verticality/horizontality, subject/object, internal/external.[1] As Loïc Wacquant says, "The unsettling character of Bourdieu's enterprise stems from its persistent attempt to straddle some of the deep-seated antinomies that rend social science asunder [e.g., subjectivism/objectivism] by honing a set of conceptual and methodological devices capable of dissolving these very distinctions" (1992, 3). His sociology, Bourdieu himself suggests, "has done away with a series of very socially powerful oppositions individuality/society, individual/collective, conscious/unconscious, interested/disinterested, objective/subjective" (1998, viii).

To be sure, as he contested the idea that the ego and the world are separated by a radical gap, Bourdieu helped us conceive not only of a new kind of subject, but also of a new kind of spatial order. Whereas for Descartes space meant separation between subject and object, for Bourdieu it meant continuity — an almost Heideggerian continuity between the person and the world,[2] an initial idea that is important for us to examine in some detail before discussing Bourdieu's model.

A New Embodied Subject

In fact, let me insert a small digression at this point, to discuss precisely the ways in which Bourdieu's phenomenology calls to mind Heidegger's spatiality, particularly Heidegger's notion of "being-in-the-world" (1996), which suggests an "ontological" continuity between my (mode of) being and the mode of being of the world where I *am*.[3] For Heidegger, recall, an "ontological solidarity," as Sartre says, indissolubly ties the personal world to the world, such that there is never a real separation between these seemingly sundered terms. Of course the subject and the object, me and the world, are divided "ontically" — that is, from the point of view of the naked, Cartesian eye that sees me and the objects around me as separate *things*. But "ontologically," Heidegger says, I am not *and cannot be* separate from the world. My being, he implies, is always and necessarily contextual. It is always embedded in a world that lends me its own mode of being. *I am what I am insofar as I am in the world, and insofar as the world is what it is.*[4] *To be*, Heidegger says, is to be attuned [*Befindlichkeit*] to a world that transpires and unfolds through my [mode of] being. Only in death, only as a corpse, as a thing, I become finally detached from the world. Only then I am finally alone, as death cuts the threads that connect me to the world. But as a living thing I am, as in the scriptures, always *allone*.

Bourdieu, to use the Heideggerian idiom, is "attuned" to these ideas. He would agree with the suggestion that my very ontological status — that is, my Being, my way of being — partakes from the ontology of the world, from the mode of being of the world.[5] But in contrast to Heidegger, Bourdieu posited a *historically specific* continuity between the person and the world, between social actors and social worlds. Always the heir of Durkheim (and of Marx), he suggested that the mode of being of the person is tied to the mode of being of the *actual* world where this person IS. Bourdieu, that is to say, outlined a novel phenomenology that necessarily includes a "social physics": the economic, political, cultural forces operant in the actual world. Whereas Heidegger speaks of an a-historical "essence of being" that universally and perpetually expresses itself through us (through *Dasein*), Bourdieu speaks of social beings that tend to embody, vivify, and enact their historical time and social place.[6] Whereas Heidegger speaks of being-in-the-world, Bourdieu seems to have in mind the notion of being-in-the-*social*-world. He seems to suggest that I am what I am largely because I inhabit a matrix of socioeconomic forces, a social order burdened by class territories, racial parameters, engendered divisions of labor — objective boundaries and disparities of various sorts. These objective social elements, he implies, align in various ways to demarcate scenarios of possibilities wherein I find the key features of my mode of being.

Bourdieu indeed introduces us to a new and historically-oriented ontology, and to a paradigmatic shift that reorients our views on the nature of human nature. Standing on the shoulders of his own giants, Bourdieu argues that, as the external world tends to encroach upon the internal world, the constellation of external social conditions tends to be reflected by the person as a whole. The world tends to be reflected not only by my ideas and values, by consciousness or cognitive schemata, in general, but also by a corresponding constellation of *affective and embodied* schemata. The melody of speech, for example, mirrors external conditions; it varies across socioeconomic and cultural boundaries. Within a margin of error, my socioeconomic position may predict not only the domains of meanings I tend to inhabit, and the range of words associated with them, but also the phonetic, gestural, corporeal expressions that bring these meanings to life, and aspects of the affects and emotions that dynamize these expressions. My socioeconomic position may predict the words that I use — but also how I use them. It often predicts the cadences of these words, their rhythms and volumes, the temporal structure of speech, the patterns of pauses, the characteristic pitch, the stress in words, the degree of synchrony between word and gesture, and aspects of the affective register, of the Heideggerian "mood" that frames these words. These things are typically underpinned by objective conditions, such as those related to class, and by ideological conditions such as those related to gender, race, nationality, religion, etc. So that Cornel West, for example, speaks of the ways in which the African American "antiphonal, call-and-response styles, rhythmic repetition, risk-ridden syncopation" largely reflect historical circumstances. He implies that such embodied features are in fact *responses* to the history of marginalization undergone by African Americans in the U.S. and that they did not simply appear, out of the blue, as it were. Rather, these markers of blackness emerged mediated, in the Hegelian sense, by the spirit of the time (1999).

Importantly, not only speech and rhythms are affected by the social order. Rather, the larger array of embodied features is also affected by it. Behavior at the table, our ways of sitting, walking and standing, hand expressions, our repertoire of gestures, affective schemata, for example, are also in ontological complicity with the world. Back to West, he says that the same history of black marginalization has been expressed not only in speech, but in general patterns of embodiment. The "assaults on black intelligence, ability, beauty and character," he says, "required persistent black efforts to hold self-doubt, self-contempt and even self-hatred at bay"; and these efforts were manifested in "Selective appropriations, incorporation and rearticulation of European ideologies, cultures and institutions alongside an African heritage — a heritage more or less confined to linguistic innovation in rhetorical practices, *stylizations of the body* in forms of *occupying an alien social space* (hairstyles, ways of walking, standing, hand expressions, talking)" (ibid., 128, my emphasis).

Furthermore, and now stepping beyond the range of examples provided by Bourdieu, such things as modes of weeping, humor and laughter, modes of experiencing pleasure, carnal and Kantian, desires and libidinal investments, taste, the taste of the gullet and of the mind, our motivic structures, our visions of self and other, the way we see our own bodies, our ways of feeling — are all tied to the world, as I will subsequently discuss. On the one hand, such minutiae of embodiment as hair are affected by the world, such that hair — short/long: masculine/feminine: conservative/not-conservative — expresses various social structures that underpin the world. But on the other hand, not minutia but the core aspects of the embodied experience, such as the schemata of perception, for example, are also encultured. Four subsequent chapters are devoted to this idea, but now let me point out, for example, that the sound frequencies we are mostly attuned to — are indeed influenced by the cultural context, as Alfred Tomatis has shown;[7] so that Tomatis, as suggested, speaks of a variety of "ethnic ears," of "conscious ears" attuned to the world (1991). Of course, hearing is biological and universal but, back to Heidegger, it is also in-the-world. Likewise with other organs such as the nose, which is also "adaptable, and teachable," as Katherine Ashenburg says (2007), so that the aesthetics and the semiotics of scents also vary with time and place. Even the eyes are teachable, as Walter Benjamin may agree (1968). Optics is biological, evolutionary, phylogenic but, as I argue in Chapter Sixteen, vision is shot through with history. Furthermore, other central aspects of the body such as neural circuitry (Kishiyama et al. 2009), and spatio-temporal ability (Fausto-Sterling 1992) are also sensitive to, and can be modified by, socio-cultural and economic circumstances.[8] There is a sense in which the brain itself is in-the-world as well (see Sroufe et al 2005). Physical health, another major aspect of embodiment, is also related to social location; so that conditions such as asthma, diabetes, obesity, nutrition, relative risk of dying — an array of differences in morbidity and mortality — are related to socioeconomic status and to culture, which can have protective or detrimental effects (Bakker and Mackenbach 2002).

Back to Bourdieu, as an heir of the French tradition, he helps us understand the ways in which human beings — brain and viscera, body and soul — are ontologically and phenomenologically connected to objective social forces. The French School had already traced lines of continuity between mind and society and between body and society.[9] But Bourdieu amplifies and synthesizes these ideas, extends bridges to German sociology and phenomenology, Marx, Weber, and Husserl, primarily; and thus introduces us not only to a new theoretical framework — but to a new type of social actor and in fact to a new type of human being. With Bourdieu, Mauss' "total" sociology climbs to another level from which we can see how social forces cradle and nurse many aspects of the human experience (without always determining personhood as I will soon discuss).

To be sure, the Bourdieuan idea of personhood seems to be, in general and save exceptions, a question of progressively acquiring a second nature (habitus) that day after day seems to turn into nature itself (*hexis*). Back to gender, the characteristic ways in which the person feels and experiences masculinity or femininity, for example, involve, precisely, the naturalization of a social order, its traditions, codes, and hierarchies. Gender *is*, in fact, naturalized nature. Daintiness vs. roughness, spatio/temporal vs. verbal abilities, English vs. math, the predisposition for occupying more or less physical space, gestures of subordination vs. gestures of superordination — are largely outcomes of social forces (see also, Fausto-Sterling 1992; Argyle 2007). These aspects of embodiment, which often mark the deeper structures of gender, are also sensitive to the circumstances of class, race, national origin, religion — time and place, in general. The masculinity of the French nobleman of the Baroque period, for example, often involved a sense of delicacy and gentleness — a gentle-manliness —, which was a marker of culture and of social positioning, an expression of the intersection of history, class, and gender. By contrast, the peasant expressed his masculinity in very different ways: his gestures, his bearing, his hands, and rhythm could not be those of a gentle-man. On the contrary, the body of the peasant was at home in coarseness and roughness, and therefore the peasant's experience of masculinity was indeed different than that of the gentleman. Their masculinities spoke of a Bourdieuan phenomenology necessarily glued to a social physics, particularly to the forces of social stratification.

From Bourdieu we indeed get the sense that "private" dispositions, private views and affects — my private body, even — are in fact not *that* private, precisely because they are anteceded and cathected by socioeconomic forces. Privacy, for him, always bears the mark of the other, ontologically and philogenetically. Indeed, it is worth noting that here Bourdieu anticipates current perspectives in neurobiology, which, as suggested in the introduction, also tell us that, because our brain "is *built* for mirroring," as Iacoboni says, we cannot "even think of 'self' except in terms of the 'other'" (2009, 133). "Without self," Iacoboni adds, "it makes little sense to define an other, and without that other, it does not make a lot of sense to define the self" (ibid., 133). It is only because our brain mirrors others that we are able to create the neural maps at the root of the self (ibid.). Only thus we can develop a habitus and schemata of embodiment in general, and acquire characteristic gestures and motor mechanisms that bear the mark of the other. Bourdieu would agree with these ideas. He also implies that the self and the other are necessarily co-constituted, but he adds that this process takes place within certain social and cultural frameworks that encourage patterns of co-constitution; for example, within social frameworks demarcated by discourses that govern the relations between men and women.

To be sure, the Bourdieuan subject is not always trapped in a world that is not of his choosing. As we will see in the next chapter, this subject is not merely an effect of an unchosen world; and Bourdieu would agree with the idea that the self is, of course, not exclusively constituted as a mirror of the other or of the world. (Neurologically, the self needs endogenous input, which also constitutes it; and in this sense there is always a degree of individuality and uniqueness in every single person.) But at this point it is only important to underscore that what Bourdieu wants to emphasize is that individuality often involves an internalized exteriority, collective views that we often experience as very personal and even as intimate and unique. The Bourdieuan (and neurobiological) idea to keep in mind for now is that the self can never be constituted by internal input alone. And that absent *external* input, the development of the self is simply not possible. (Recall indeed the work of Rene Spitz [1946], who showed that absent contact with others, infants in fact die even if physical needs, food, warmth, etc. are met). Bourdieu would agree with the idea that even the familiar sense of ownership over the perspective behind our eyes is, in varying degrees, constituted by the other; so that, to borrow an image from W.E.B. DuBois, we often see the world and ourselves largely through the eyes of others, through the eyes of history, through the eyes of the spirit of the times. To borrow now from Christopher Bollas, we sometimes hear with "borrowed ears."

NOTES

1. Bourdieu's work thus brooked many resistances, as these dichotomies held sway among structuralists who believed in a separation and a conflictive relationship between individuals and autonomous social structures that operated behind our backs; and among theorists of agency who posited a radical area of willful independence in social actors, an agency that prevailed over and against the influence of external structures.

2. Bourdieu is perhaps the most acerbic critic of Heidegger, "the pastor of being and [of] his lesser clergy" (e.g., Bourdieu 1999), and of their attempt to render an a-historical critique of human nature. But beyond such disconnection, their phenomenological coincidences can be traced back to a common stem, Husserl; and indeed, Bourdieu's initial ideas seemed to have been influenced by Heidegger's conception of the relationship between the subject and the object (see e.g., Bourdieu and Wacquant 1992).

3. These ideas, as we will soon see, also anticipate current advances in neuroscience, particularly as these relate to research on mirror neurons. This neurological revolution has shown that the "existential phenomenologists," as leading neurologist Marco Iacoboni says, "were correct all along" (2009, 262). "[W]e have evolved," Iacoboni says, "to connect deeply with other human beings" (ibid., 272) and "to be . . . fundamentally attuned to other people" (ibid., 279).

4. Further, *to be*, Heidegger argues, means that I understand (*Verstand*) this world not only cognitively (the dimension that Durkheim emphasized) — not because I can name the things in

the world — but because I have an embodied awareness of the world, an awareness that is inexpressible through language, as the symbols of language only re-*present* things in the world, and are thus always one step removed from the underlying *presence* of things. Heidegger would argue that cognition, in general — and our Durkheimian categories of understanding, in particular — are thus one step removed from presence, from the world as such.

5. This is also a key idea from current neuroscience, as we will see soon.

6. Heidegger's ontology emphasizes a pre-sociological "power of essence," "power of the origin," first source, a sort of primordial drive in human beings, a force, in the sense of *Ursprung* and *Urquell,* which precedes action. The question of Being, for Heidegger, is not a question of "naïve anthropologizing" or naïve psychologizing. To be cognizant of being as such, he would say, one needs to transcend any such sociological perspectives. Bourdieu of course radically questions this position and posits a social ontology.

7. According to Tomatis measurements, the German ear typically recognizes between 100 and 3,000 Hz; the French between 1,000 and 2,000; the English between 2,000 and 12,000, etc. Slavs master foreign languages easily due to their broader range of hearing, from 100 to 8,000 Hz. This aptitude, he explains, is related primarily to hearing rather than to speaking.

8. Preadolescents who differ only in socioeconomic status exhibited significant differences in prefrontal cortex activity, an area critical for problem-solving, creativity, and behavioral and executive functions (Kishiyama et al. 2009). Children in poverty appeared to function at the same level as adults with cortical damage (e.g., caused by stroke). Similarly, as Fausto-Sterling (1992) has shown, male teenagers may outperform female teenagers in visual-spatial tests, but only until females are exposed to a larger number of everyday situations that enhance such abilities; situations that are often discouraged among females because of cultural biases around femininity and masculinity. These situations may result in differential levels of not only spatio-temporal but also mathematical skill. Fausto-Sterling shows in fact that boys and girls are equal at math up until the seventh grade, but then boys tend to outperform girls, going into fields such as engineering and science more often than girls, which largely reflects differential encouragements and resulting differences in acquisition of skill. Sroufe et al (2005) followed 200 children born in poverty, from birth to early adulthood. By late adolescence, 50 percent of participants qualified for some form of psychiatric diagnosis which was primarily an effect of the environment.

9. Recall that categories of understanding, for Durkheim, are ontologically attached to the nature of the social world, so that the nature of the mind partakes from the changing nature of our world. Recall, in fact, that the Durkheimian subject owes his subjectivity to a world that is expressed through his memory and through his very body, as Halbwachs and Mauss argued.

Chapter Three

Somatic Compliance, Somatic Deviance

Western culture has made us blind to the intersubjective nature of our brains
—Marco Iacoboni

THE ADAPTIVE SELF

Later on I will discuss the ways in which the Bourdieuan subject steps outside the givens of the social world, culturally, bodily, and existentially. But for now let me only say that what Bourdieu emphasizes is that taking this outward step is difficult, and that it can be socially and existentially wounding. This notion, incidentally, is not new. And here Bourdieu is merely following an age-old consensus among sociologists, which says that societies are always armed with seductive and/or repressive mechanism designed to elicit a necessary degree of conformity from social actors. Think of the raised eyebrow that targets impolite behavior, the law enforcing a normative order, the tacit and explicit norms that govern the social contract. To be sure, sociologists have shown that social actors who do not comply with the basic requirements of the social order are often taxed with obstacles and with at least a degree of anxiety. The history of gayness, for instance, shows that gay men and women have been burdened by a surplus of economic, social, and mental health problems (Meyer 2003) precisely because they resisted, in various ways and degrees, the demands of the heteronormative order.[1] In general, anyone who socially and existentially wards off the demands of the social order is likely to face retaliations, which, depending on the severity of the transgression, can handicap the person, socially, economically, and existentially.

It is also important to note that transgressive behavior tends to be avoided not only because of external pressures, but primarily on account of internalized pressures, as Talcott Parsons showed. Bear in mind that social frameworks, as Durkheim says, are tied to our "soul," to our memories and bodies, as Halbwachs and Mauss argued. And that, because the world is a key part of who we are, taking a distance from it involves a measure of self-distantiation, which can be wounding to the self and to our identity. As Durkheim showed, "anomic suicides" are preceded precisely by the collapse of our ties to the world. And in fact, the collapse of the normative order that undergirds the self, the breakdown of the world within, may precede physical death, as research on death spells, for example, has shown (Davis 1988).[2] Hence, even if we grant, with Durkheim also, that degrees of deviance are necessary for societies, deviance is typically carried out at a cost. Though the deviant person may deliver elements of social renewal and creativity, even the great deviants, from Mandela to Van Gogh, pay the price of non-compliance. Thus it is in general easier for social actors to internalize, to mirror, and to vivify aspects of the social order than to attempt to change them. In subsequent chapters I will discuss the resistive aspects of personhood, but at this point we need to make another pause to consider the phenomena of adaptation in some detail.

Very many social psychologists have experimentally showed that we indeed tend to adapt quite rapidly to new social environments, and that in doing so we may forsake core aspects of the self. Philip Zimbardo's famous prison experiment, for example (1971), showed that healthy psychology students altered central aspects of their self-system simply by pretending to be guards and inmates at a mock prison; and that these changes occurred almost immediately, such that the experiment had to be suspended by the sixth day because this sort of role playing, Zimbardo thought, could actually damage participants. Zimbardo showed that, when legitimized ideologically and institutionally, social roles (inmate, prison guard, and we may add: woman, Christian, etc.) can elicit not only compliance but also the *desire to adapt,* even if these roles go against the core ideas and values of the individual. Stanley Milgram's often quoted (and replicated *ad nauseam*) experiment about obedience famously showed that regular citizens, about 65% of study participants, were quite willing to apply potentially supra-lethal electrical shocks (450 volts) to "learners" (confederates in league with researchers) merely because they were told to do so (Milgram 1975). Solomon Asch (1951), another pioneer in this area of social psychology, demonstrated that study participants easily denied obvious visual evidence, simply to go with the decision of their peers.

Human beings are also easily primed. Save exceptions, we are easily cajoled into altering not only basic attitudes, values, norms, but also basic emotions and even bodily dispositions. Here are some examples: subjects wearing purportedly fake sunglasses cheated at higher rates than subjects wearing authentic glasses, as though the fakeness of the glasses were rapidly absorbed by the participants in this study (Gino et al. 2010). Subjects solving word puzzles with words stereotypically associated with elderly people walked more slowly from the researcher's office to the elevator than subjects whose puzzles involved neutral words (Bargh et al. 1996). Subjects asked to imagine characteristics of a professor scored higher in trivia pursuit questions than subjects asked to think about soccer hooligans (Dijksterhuis 2005). Study participants squeezing a soft ball were more likely to perceive gender-neutral faces as female, and those squeezing a hard ball were more like to perceive these faces as male (Slepian et al 2011). Participants holding warm cups of coffee were more likely to judge peers as friendly than those holding cold cups (Williams and Bargh 2008). Participants holding heavier clip-boards were more likely to judge the opinions of leaders as more important when compared to participants holding lighter clipboards (Jostmann 2009), etc. These types of reports abound. Ap Dijksterhuis has said that priming and imitation "can make us slow, fast, smart, stupid, good at math, bad at math, helpful, rude, polite, long-winded, hostile, aggressive, cooperative, competi-tive, conforming, nonconforming, conservative, forgetful, careful, careless, neat, and sloppy" (in Iacoboni 2009, , , 201). Eyal Press (2012) has argued, indeed, that the mystery is not why some people comply, but why some people manage to go against the flow.

Recall again that human beings, as members of an exquisitely social species, are in fact designed to mimic others (Blackmore 2000) and that mimicking generally occurs pre-reflectively. (Indeed, we begin mimicking only minutes after being born [Meltzoff and Moore 1977].) Our brain is not only "built for mirroring," as Iacoboni says (2009), but "[b]rains are capable of mirroring the deepest aspects of the minds of others, even at the fine-grained level of a single cell" (ibid., 34). The very faces of couples living happily together have "higher facial similarity (they look more like each other) after a quarter century of married life than at the time of marriage" (ibid., 115), a study that provides support for Merleau-Ponty's notion that we can somehow "live in the face of others." Furthermore, we also tend to mimic affects, sensations, emotions, "pain, laughter, smiling, affection, em-barrassment, discomfort, disgust, stuttering, reaching with effort, and the like, in a broad range of situations" (Hatfield et al. 1993, 22). We often live in the body of others. Again, the self is profoundly othered. It always co-arises with the other. It *in*corporates aspects of the world.

Fields, Capitals, and Embodied Collective Memories

Back to Bourdieu, inasmuch as we mirror external circumstances, insofar as our lives are framed, primed, and even guided by prevalent ideas, by the images and the mythoi of our world — our actions tend to legitimize and sustain this world. The social order, Bourdieu says, is constructed by the same social actors who are constructed by it. Inasmuch as the external world "seduces" us, he says, such external conditions tend to be sustained by our everyday wishes, ideas, visions, affects, gestures. Think, for example, of gestures of subordination and of superordination related to gender (Argyle 2007). They are underpinned by social structures, but these structures are also underpinned by them. The movements of women, for instance, are generally less expansive than those of men, and women therefore tend to occupy less physical space (ibid.). Women's bodies, in this sense, reflect the fact that society often allots less cultural and political space for them. But, again, these constrained and constructed bodies in turn send signals that contribute to legitimize and to sediment this cultural and political order. To insist on a key idea, the social order is constructed not only by means of ideas, norms, and symbols that circulate from person to person — but also by the messages that bodies themselves transmit to other bodies.

Let us also consider the example of class: when "correct" posturing at the table is mirrored by the child and subsequently embodied by the adult, the very movements and bodies of the child's parents serve as means whereby the expectations and norms of class are transmitted to the child and subsequently sustained by the adult. This form of collective communication from "body to body," Bourdieu says, can create an organic agreement — not only cognitive but also corporeal — among social actors, and between social actors and their world. Hence, embodied social actors can confer a certain organic substance, a rhythm to the Hegelian spirit of their world, a world that becomes alive through embodied traits that are collectively relevant — through an embodied collective idiom that expresses a shared historical idiom. Thus not only collective memories, as Hawlbachs says, but *embodied* collective memories structure key aspects of personhood as well as key aspects of the social world, conferring coherence and direction to the person and to the group.

Bourdieu's phenomenological merging of the individual and the collective order is easily visible in his ideas about "fields" (1987) and a brief account of this notion should cast the additional light needed to see important details underpinning his theory. Rather than speaking about the structures and effects of the larger social world, as Marxists often do, Bourdieu speaks of smaller, sometimes overlapping, and relatively autonomous social spheres that typically revolve around a set of socioeconomic conditions. These social spheres provide a gravitational center from which a set of ideas, dispositions, and collectively relevant habituses stem. These centers of social gravity are "fields," spheres of "play and competition" wherein somewhat autonomous regulative principles exert their influence on social actors within gravitational range.

Lest one think that the notion of fields refers to "subcultures" or social fringes, Bourdieu gives the example of the French academic system (1990a), a field populated by social actors who often see, understand, and experience the world through intellectual habituses rooted in their socioeconomic and cultural background. By means of correspondence analysis, Bourdieu shows that socioeconomic factors such as family background, place of provenance (Paris vs. provinces), etc. often correspond to the dispositions, interests — to the inclinations and temperaments of the theoreticians in the French academia. Of course there is never a one to one correspondence between social and personal circumstances, but such socioeconomic variables tend to underlie the theoretical temperament of French academics, in general, and thus tend to underlie the field of French academia.[3]

Likewise with any of us who partake from social affiliations, from tacit or explicit membership in the array of fields in our society. Certain professional bodies, religious communities, street gangs, etc. can also serve as examples of fields that sustain certain social orders. In such social spheres, one might also see correspondences between objective conditions (e.g., divisions of class, gender, occupation) and the various dispositions of social actors (e.g., intellectual but also corporeal or even affective and perceptual, as we will soon see). In these fields, objective conditions align to give shape to a *nomos*: regulative principles that help people organize their "visions and divisions," their orientations and experiences — including many aspects of their corporeal experiences. These objective socioeconomic factors tend to encourage social actors to chase after similar stakes, and therefore to inhabit similar existential domains; domains wherein they develop shared traits and, I argue, shared aspects of embodied collective memory that involve mental, affective, perceptual schemata. (In subsequent chapters we will see how ECM overlaps with the concept of "habitus," while also being fundamentally different from it.) As social actors "play" in these Bourdieuan fields — as they engage in everyday interactions and actions regulated by a shared *nomos* — objective socioeconomic forces emerge as subjective traits: as patterns of speech, as hairstyles, affects, personal visions — as aspects of an embodied collective memory.

Symbolic Capital

These social games are neither random nor perfectly concerted. Fields require a measure of order and systemicity but they also allow for struggle and competition, though such competition is mostly confined to the limits of the field and by the stakes operant in it. Bourdiean players are, in fact, constantly competing for the stakes or "capitals" of the field, which can be cultural, social, economic, bodily.[4] The French academics and the gang members in the examples above compete for markers of prestige and status — for cultural and symbolic capitals. These stakes endow individuals with collectively relevant motives — indeed with motivic structures that are internal and external at once, personal and supra-personal. For example, I may privately decide to buy this or that shirt, but my private decision is likely anteceded by the field or fields wherein I operate, and by social forces, in general: the market, peers, social class; institutions and discourses that encourage goals, stakes, ideas, and motives in me, which are also tied to my decision. (Bourdieu would in fact argue that free will is often anteceded by the will of the social world, and that free will is therefore never radically free, as it is also othered, as it cannot be private in any radical sense.)

Importantly, when any of the "species of capital" becomes symbolic capital (e.g., cultural and economic capital grants status and prestige to the social actor), the performance of the player is enhanced. The status of the player grows, and prestige and power follow. Think, for example, of the successful gang member or artist: when such a person comes to *embody* the very symbolic stakes of the social game — when he literally in-corporates the essence of a world that exerts powers over peers who chase after similar stakes — he typically becomes invested with the sort of authority that brings to mind the Roman notion of *autorictas*. This is a form of authority that is driven not by force or compulsion but by the aura that surrounds the possessor of *autorictas*. One may think not only of Gandhi or Warhol, for example, but also of the anonymous social agent, the gang leader, the churchgoer who manages to incarnate the mythoi, the collective beliefs, the stakes operant in his world. When this happens, his/her authority, Bourdieu would say, is not only *understood* by others, cognitively, but also *felt* by them, "from body to body." Such a person thus becomes a signifier that supports and reflects collectively relevant meanings and stakes. He/she becomes the epitome of the embodied collective memory that brings the field to life.

This possessor of symbolic capital and symbolic power may extract an intuitive sort of acquiescence from the dominated, inasmuch as others *feel* his/her ascendancy as part of the "normal" (and their unconscious nods, voice pitch, gestures may pre-reflectively and almost ethologically confirm their differential status). I grew up in a small town in the northern Peruvian sierras where, a couple of generations back, whites felt free to summon any Indian passing by when menial chores had to be done. "José" and "María" were the generic and dehumanizing names for any such man or woman: "Joseph, come here, I need you to get me some bread, please." As a token of appreciation, Josephs and Maries could get, but not expect, a couple of rolls of bread or a "thanks" and pat on the shoulder. No compulsion, other than 500 years of colonization and attendant processes of differential symbolic appropriation, drove these "normal" interactions between Whites and Indians. Five hundred years were expressed through these brief interactions between those who embodied symbolic capital (whose looks, clothes, ac-

cents, gestures, and bearing inherently expressed the prevailing social hierarchies), and those who embodied a sort of negative symbolic capital: the
markers of social submission (whose looks, clothes, accents, signaled a "naturally" lower position).

This is a key point for the theory of embodied collective memory. As we
will see in the next chapter, embodied collective memories sometimes sponsor subordinate and superordinate "natures," as the example above suggests.
In the next chapter I will discuss Bourdieu's theory of symbolic violence,
arguably the highest point of the French tradition, and one of the highest in
the sociology of embodiment.

NOTES

1. Bear in mind that, under sodomy laws, homosexuality was prohibited and was legally
punishable in the U.S. Even oral sex was a felony punished with jail, up to 2003.

2. Death-spells have the following elements: a member of a tribal community breaks a
social taboo; he is judged and found guilty; a sorcerer recites an incantation against the infractor, may point a bone toward him/her, and then, "A consensus is reached among all concerned
that the end is near, and the victim's friends and family retreat as from the smell of death. They
return, but only to wail and chant over the body of a person whom they consider already dead.
Physically the victim still lives; psychologically he or she is dying; socially he or she is already
dead" (Wade Davis 1988, 206). As Wade Davis reports, many deaths resulting from such spells
have been confirmed. The mechanisms that precipitate these deaths remain unclear, but they
seem to be psychogenic and sociogenic. While remaining within the community, the victim is
existentially removed from it, divested of his social roles, status, removed from normal contact
with others ("socially he or she is . . . dead"), and such social death often gives way to
supralethal psychological disturbances ("psychologically he or she is dying") that can antecede
physical death.

3. It is worth recalling, back to Plato and Descartes, what William James (2000) had
already said about these writers, and about idealism, in general. Anticipating Bourdieu, James
says that philosophy is largely an effect of the "temperament" of philosophers, which in turn is
often an effect of the philosopher's social position. Platonism, for instance, was in part the
result of Plato's temperament, which was partly the result of the Athenian's social position. A
scion of the Athenian aristocracy, Plato was unlikely to become attuned to the sort of stuff that
Spencer associated with "philosophical grossness": materialism, empiricism, randomness, and
the senses. Instead, Plato's aristocratic temperament — the merging of his social and intellectual habituses, as Bourdieu may say — was naturally geared toward "higher" things: idealism, the
notion of a higher-lower duality, and systemicity (which was not without consequences for the
history of western thought, as argued above).

4. Economic capital is often overarching and dominant because the tendency of the other
capitals is to be transformed, in the last account, into economic capital. Cultural capital, for
instance — that is, having mastery over the subtleties of the social game, having "a feel for the
game," etc. — is often cashed out by players; for example, when cultural acumen helps them
get a better paying job beyond the actual skills needed for the job, or when cultural capital
ushers them toward a profitable marriage, helps them get into a prestigious/profitable school,
and so on. This is not true, of course, of every situation or of every field, as some fields,
especially those related to the arts, may in fact define their stakes in opposition to accumulation
of economic capital.

Chapter Four

Symbolic Violence vs. Creativity

SYMBOLIC VIOLENCE AND RACE

Bourdieu's project reaches its culminating point with his theory of symbolic power and of symbolic violence (2001), a key, if limited, perspective for my theory of embodied collective memory. Before discussing symbolic violence, it is worth discussing first a mainstream perspective on social violence, the contrasting backdrop against which it will be easier to understand Bourdieu's ideas. Consider the sort of total violence exerted, for instance, by the institutions of slavery in the American South. The quote below belongs to Frederick Douglass, a runaway slave whose exploits eventually led him to become an advisor to Abraham Lincoln; a man who, by the end of his life, stood as one of the most influential spokesmen against slavery during the nineteenth century. Here, Douglass recalls one of his earlier memories as a young child living in a farm on Maryland:

> I have often been awakened at the dawn of day by the most heartrending shrieks of an own aunt of mine, whom [her master] use to tie to a joist, and whip upon her naked back until she was literally covered with blood. No words, no tears, no prayers from his gory victim seemed to move his iron heart from its bloody purpose. The louder she screamed, the harder he whipped; and where the blood ran fastest, there he whipped longest. He would whip her to make her scream, and whip her to make her hush; and not until overcome by fatigue, would he cease to swing the bloody clotted cowskin. This terrifying scene was the blood-stained gate, the entrance to the hell of slavery, through which I was about to pass. (Douglass 2003, 20)

Douglass bespeaks a childhood with "no shoes, no stockings, no jacket, no trousers, nothing on but a coarse linen shirt, reaching only to my knees," a time when his feet were so "cracked with the frost, that the pen with which I am writing might be laid in the gashes" (ibid., 37). He tells us that he and the other children on the farm were fed coarse boiled corn that "was put into a large wooden tray or trough, and set down upon the ground. The children were then called, like so many pigs, and like so many pigs they would come and devour the mush; some with oyster-shells, others with pieces of shingle, some with naked hands, and none with spoons. He that ate fastest got most; he that was strongest secured the best place; and few left the trough satisfied" (ibid., 37). He describes a society where it was easier for slaveholders to remember the names of their horses than the names of their slaves, a time when it was not unusual for farmers to father their own slaves, a place where preachers often spoke about the divinely designed nature of slavery.

The South, as we know, took every pain to take everything away from its slaves: parents and children, their sense of family, their ability to read and write. But in the case of Frederick Douglass, perhaps the only thing that this rapacious South couldn't take away was his "capacity for indignation," to borrow the phrase from Alberto Flores Galindo, a Peruvian historian interested in colonization and the nature of the colonized mind. "The slaveholders," Douglass says, strive to "darken the soul of the slave, for they know well he will look upon them as oppressors, and consider their system the vilest that ever saw the sun" (1846). Douglass managed to keep this capacity to "look upon them as oppressors," and it was this ability to understand — *and to feel* — such moral deficits, which allowed him to squeeze "drop by drop the slave out of himself and [to wake up] one fine morning feeling that real human blood, not a slave's, [was] flowing in his veins," if I may use the famous phrase by Chekhov (in West 1999).

By contrast, the theory of symbolic violence asks us to think, to borrow the image from Douglass again, of a benighted soul. Bourdieu asks us to imagine a form of social domination that can leave the appurtenances of life intact, home, property, even political rights — while removing the person's capacity to experience the indignities imposed by the social order *as indignities*. He asks us to bear in mind the ways in which the most "intolerable conditions of existence" can be experienced as natural, normal, commonsensical. Indeed, symbolic violence is not always bloody or blatant, and can be gentle at times, and seductive — while always deploying a more complete and often unassailable form of social domination. Embodied collective memories, I insist, can sustain "natural" social hierarchies, and can thus "darken the soul" of those who bring these hierarchies to life.

A Young Slave from Tennessee

Compare the narrative provided by Douglass, and its seemingly impossible obstacles, against the stories of the slaves who voluntarily joined the (Southern) Rebel Army during the American Civil War. Think about the lives of the slaves who risked their lives and limbs to defend slavery, the magnitude of *their* obstacles, and the extent to which slavery was, for many of them, an existential rather than a legal or political problem. (So that when the legal-political problem was solved, the embodied-ontological condition remained, and was often passed on, as inheritance, to subsequent generations.)

The *St. Petersburg Times* (Garry 2007) recounts the story of a "young slave from a Tennessee plantation named Louis Napoleon Nelson, who went to war as a teenager with the sons of his master." Louis Napoleon "cooked and looked out for the others." He foraged for food for his masters. "One time, he killed a mule, cut out a quarter and hauled it back to his comrades." On account of having memorized parts of the King James Bible, the slave served as an illiterate chaplain for mortally wounded confederate soldiers, laboring to absolve his oppressors and to grant them passage to heaven. He "saw action, fighting with a rifle under the command of Confederate General Nathan Bedford Forrest," a slave trader, a plantation owner, and arguably the first Grand Wizard of the Ku Klux Klan.

The South was defeated, Louis Napoleon Nelson found freedom, and he freely chose to live on the plantation for another 12 years. "Over the years, he went to 39 Confederate reunions," the *Times* reports, always wearing the woolly gray uniform of the Rebel Army, always recalling, with his former masters and comrades in arms, the bygone days of slavery in the American south. He died in 1934 under Jim Crow laws, when blacks were born in segregated and grossly inferior hospitals, educated in segregated schools, when they attended segregated churches, and when they were finally buried in segregated cemeteries. When Louis Napoleon died, the *St. Petersburg Times* reports, "The local paper ran an obituary that called him a 'darky.'" Before dying, he bequeathed his Rebel uniform to his grandson, a man who still dons the Rebel garb, who also participates in Confederate meetings, and who appears to regard Lincoln as a despot.

Implied by Bourdieu's theory of symbolic violence is that socially em-bedded agents often do and want certain things, and *will* in certain ways, because, as Heidegger would say, they have been thrown into a world that is not of their choosing. Again, the will of a person often bespeaks the will of their world, so that his "acts of cognition," Bourdieu says, are often "acts of recognition" that pre-reflectively legitimate the inherited social world. These acts of "miscognition" in fact reinforce the order of things. The theory of symbolic violence tells us that we sometimes feel in certain ways and want certain things because we are arbitrarily located under the regulating sway of social, economic, political forces; forces that, precisely because we embody them, are very hard to notice from our encultured vantage point. Symbolic violence is in fact a form of feeling, a mood, in the Heideggerian idiom, and may even involve exalted sentiments such as pride and love. Louis Napoleon

Nelson grieved for a grieving master. Durkheimian "altruistic suicides," sated with exalted feelings, often express radical forms of symbolic violence.

"What is alone of value in mental life," Freud said, "is rather the feelings. No mental forces are significant unless they possess the characteristic of arousing feelings" (Freud 1907, 49). Symbolic violence means that social forces can not only arouse feelings — but that these forces can sediment *affective memories* (not Bourdieu's term), whereby the dominant common sense is *felt* as common, and normality as normal. One can see the germ of this aspect of embodied collective memory in a young girl's delight in assuming a feminine play-role where passivity and fantasy close ranks against feelings of independence and power. But we may also see it in the adult who grows to inhabit a body that *feels* incompatible with power, a body that signals powerlessness in its carriage, through its tone of voice, gaze, its way of sitting, etc. Symbolic violence also means, to paraphrase Bourdieu, that we become ignorant of our own ignorance and of the social mechanisms that make it possible. This aspect of embodied collective memory is therefore hard to abandon, precisely because it is hard for us to see it, because it is already an aspect of our minds and bodies, an aspect of our "nature." As it is hard to get rid of one's accent, it is also hard to get rid of one's embodied idiom, which carries the accented language of time and place, even if this language bespeaks our own domination. This encultured idiom, when collectively enacted, sustains the broader discourses of domination. And it often bolsters social ranks; for example, those related to race, class, gender, and sexuality.

SYMBOLIC VIOLENCE AND GENDER

The example of Louis Napoleon Nelson is extreme; and symbolic violence can take more subtle guises. It is often exerted through the rhetoric of "normalcy," of "common sense," "good taste," "femininity," "good manners," the law, the rhetoric that often sustains *idola* in the Baconian sense. Take the 1950s, for example, and consider the women who carried in their gestures, in their sentiments and phonetic habituses, in their clothes and chores, the features of the normative consensus about gender. Recall the "feminine mystique," as Betty Friedan famously termed it (2001). Friedan showed that this dominant consensus told women that they had no higher glory that to seek fulfillment in their given roles as nurturers (ibid., 16). After all, nature itself — that is to say: God Himself — had endowed women with the vital capacity to nurture, and had thus designated a *telos,* a fate for them, which involved taking care of the family, the house, the chores, the laundry, the children, the husband. As many women found themselves inertially chasing after such a "biological" fate, they also found their lives and thoughts and movements revolving around kitchens, laundry rooms, gardens, parking lots.[1] To be sure, the mystique was not only a collectively accepted discourse about gender, but also a lifestyle that involved certain fashions, gestures, ranges of conversation and action, phonetic expressions — an embodied memory that provided compasses for the future. A woman interviewed by Friedan says this:

> I never had any career ambitions. All I wanted was to get married and have four children. I love the kids and Bob and my home. There is no problem you can even put a name to. But I am desperate. I begin to feel I have no personality. I am a server of food and a putter-on of pants and a bedmaker, somebody who can be called on when you want something. But who am I? (Friedan 2001, 21)

Friedan tells us that, as "The feminine mystique permits, even encourages, women to ignore the question of their identity . . . It makes [women] unable to *see* themselves"; so that, "An American woman no longer has a *private* image to tell her who she is, or can be, or wants to be" (ibid., 72, my italics). Friedan helps us see the extent to which women, to reiterate an important trope, saw themselves through the eyes of others, from a borrowed perspective, as though not quite owning their point of view.

For the most part, Betty Friedan's ideas have passed the test of time. Aspects of her theory have been criticized, particularly because she provides a mostly White middle class perspective on gender, leaving behind intersections between gender, class, and race. But in general it is easy to agree with her ideas, which in fact are largely commonsensical today. But, back to Bourdieu, the notion of symbolic violence provides a perspective that, though overlapping with Friedan's, opens a new window onto the problem of gender ideology. His theory helps us see that "ideologies" are not merely ideological. In fact, the concept of gender "ideology," Bourdieu implies, prevents us from seeing that collective discourses can penetrate the everyday rhythm of social life, life as lived, such that the lives of men and women become vivifications of "ideologies," of politics. To paraphrase Theodor Adorno, such life can become "the experience of its absence," a protracted "doxic experience," to borrow now from Husserl. Everyday ideas, wants, chores, can thus become aspects of ideological enactment, an aeskesis, a spiritual and bodily training that underpins such "natural" female characteristics as self-abnegation, for instance; characteristics that can mark the lives of women, their career choices, their levels of achievement, their role in history. James Joyce asks,

> What special affinities appeared to him to exist between the moon and woman? Her antiquity in preceding and surviving successive tellurian generations: her nocturnal predominance: her satellitic dependence: her luminary reflec-

tions: her constancy under all phases, rising and setting by her appointed times, waxing and waning: the forced invariability of her aspect: her indeterminate response to inaffirmative interrogation: her potency over effluent and refluent waters: her power to enamour, to mortify, to invest with beauty, to render insane, to incite to and aid delinquency: the tranquil inscrutability of her visage: the terribility of her isolated dominant implacable resplendent propinquity: her omens of tempest and of calm: the stimulation of her light, her motion and her presence: the admonition of her craters, her arid seas, her silence: her splendor, when visible: her attraction, when invisible (in Bourdieu 1990, 1).

Woman as the moon, pale and reflective; man as the sun, scorching and illuminating: this is ideology, but ideology that often becomes incarnate.

Friedan says that American women no longer had "a private image" to tell them who they were. But it is also important to understand that many women willingly eschewed a private, individual point of view, and that their own decisions and desires often reinforced their own sense of alienation. The point is not to unreflectively blame the victim, but to recall that sometimes the victim plays an important role in the process of victimization, particularly when such a person undergoes a farther-reaching form of violence capable of subjugating him/her in the most inescapable and effective way, as the example of Napoleon Nelson also suggests. Symbolic violence means that people sometimes *choose* to see the world and themselves through the eyes of others. It means that social actors can become attracted by a growing void in the self, and pulled by a tendency toward self-distanciation. Desire, as Freud argued, can turn against the self. It can blaze a trail toward the person's social and existential diminution. Bourdieu would agree. And indeed he would add that the person's desires can contribute to create not only her own heteronomic mode of being, but also her own oppressive world. He would say, in fact, that the desire of the oppressed is necessary to construct effectively oppressive social dynamics.

Consider anorexia nervosa, for example, which in a certain sense may be viewed as an extreme form of symbolic violence. When not attributable to neurochemical or biological deficits, this disease can be, at least in part, sociogenic. It can have a cultural etiology, related particularly to the constant stream of images and ideas broadcasted by the cultural industry, the media that speaks on behalf of the market and of power in general. When sociogenic, anorexia nervosa typically tells the story of women who desirously, even desperately, and mostly pre-reflectively, seek to embody a damaged ideal of the feminine.

Similarly with "bigorexia": Samuel Fussell's book, *Muscle* (1991), has provided an excellent portrayal of the world of bodybuilding, showing how some men — desirously, at times desperately, and largely pre-reflectively — may likewise come to embody physical and existential deficits; deficits that lurk under the paradoxical veneer of manly strength. In this autobiographical monograph, Fussell tells us the story of those athletes of bulk who, like himself, devote their lives to reaching the apex of "competitiveness." Such a "journey" often involves deficits that are not very different from symptoms associated with anorexia: spells of dizziness, possible thyroid problems, kidney malfunction, and liver-related effects including hepatitis, possible gallstones, increased possibility of cancer, nervous crying, half-comatose sleep, the "thousand-mile stare," isolation, diminished social bonds, nervous anger, premature baldness, bouts of diarrhea, acute acne, chronic rectal bleeding necessitating the wearing of Huggies, lower sperm count, increased body hair, "impoverishment of the span and intensity of relations with the other gender," "crater-like trenches of scar tissue [which competitive bodybuilders] dig in their behinds through repeated injections, which can create knots the size of a pomegranate that have to be removed by surgery every so often" (Fussell 1991, 167) — all of which, Fussell's colleagues tell him, "is perfectly normal . . . Big man, this is about *looking good*, not feeling good" (ibid., 167, original emphasis; see also, Wacquant 1995). As in anorexia, these deficits are largely sponsored by culture, by what we may call the new masculine mystique. These are encultured egos whose desires, much as those of the anorexic, are also proportional to their weaknesses.

Social actors, that is to say, are not only addressed by the arbitrariness of culture, but are often courted and seduced by it; and therefore they often espouse, quite willingly, such arbitrary demands and injunctions. Again, the "normality" of unfair social forces is often undergirded by the libidinal expenditures and investments of dominated social actors. Antonio Gramsci spoke of hegemony, and how the ethos of dominant groups often provides the guiding principles for the lives of the dominated. From Bourdieu we can further infer that this ethos can also serve as the framework through which the very "nature" of the dominated emerges.

SYMBOLIC VIOLENCE AND CLASS

One last example of symbolic violence is needed to show a particular characteristic of this seductive and depersonalizing form of embodied memory. As we may infer from Bourdieu, this form of violence often involves petty, everyday wants and a related sense of "busyness," in the Heideggerian idiom. Think, for example, of some of the upward-aiming anxieties that sometimes nudge members of the middle classes. Paul Fussell (1983) can help us see various elements of symbolic violence in these class-related anxieties.[2] He provides examples from shopping catalogues that aim to attract "discriminating people" and "people of refinement" from the American middle classes. These catalogues sell such items of distinction as drinking glasses emblazoned with fake heraldic blazons; "glasses [with] your own family name and coat of arms," which the shopper is encouraged to buy, on credit if needed, notwithstanding the important disclaimer in small print: "No genealogical relationship between your family and the persons who originally bore the coat of arms selected is intended or implied" (Fussell 1983, 118). Upward-aiming anxieties, as I suggested. Still reading these catalogues, Fussell says that,

> Practically all you need to know about the psychological circumstances of the middle class is latent in the "Champagne Re-cork" which Hammacher Schelemmer purveys. "'This unusual stopper,' the catalogue indicates, "keeps 'bubbly' sprightly, sparkling after the uncorking ceremony is over. Gold electro-plated." There you have it: at once the desire for grandeur and the need for prudence, the two contradictory motives at perpetual war in the hearts of those caught in the middle. (ibid., 118)

Fussell seems to think that these odd appurtenances speak of an "internal warfare"; and that they tell the story of folks who are constantly deploying anxious and petty armamentaria in an effort to wring a measure of prestige, the illusion of prestige, the hyperreality of prestige, on credit if necessary. "All these 'heraldic' . . . appurtenances," he generalizes, "register the depth and pathos of the feeling of unimportance which is the bugbear and stigma of the middle class" (Fussell 1983, 118). But back to the theory of symbolic violence, Bourdieu helps us see that such bibelots and wishes and things — do not only speak of small personal deficits (that pile up to give shape to the psychology and cosmology of the middle class, as Fussell implies). Again, desires are not merely given facts, as they are largely records of our experiences, syntheses of our interactions in the world. These bibelots — these petty tools of impression management and their attendant anxieties — record personal but also cultural problems. They trumpet private existential deficits, but these deficits are necessary for this kind of market economy to grow, because these lacks underpin many of the motives of the consumer. These lacks indeed help bolster a systemic need for social stratification. The notions of "refinement" and "discrimination," which are highlighted in the catalogue, already bespeak this systemic need.

Let me discuss, apropos of this idea, the role that the market often has in terms of encouraging cognitive, affective, and indeed bodily parameters in the consumer. At least since the times of Frederick Taylor and Elton Mayo, the free market has been, by design, tapping into buyers' wants and feelings, often effectively. (And it is getting better at it, so that today we may speak of "neuro-marketing," for example: the notion that marketers may elicit not personal but impersonal responses at the level of neurons themselves [Iacoboni 2009, 219-228]). Indeed, the growth of the market largely hinges on such measure of effectiveness. These market mechanisms are not always effective (and they may lead to desirable outcomes economic growth, more jobs, etc.) but they are often effective and, again, are not without risks. And these risks stem precisely the from a systemic need to create needs and feelings in the consumer, for her to tick in the direction of psychological, social, and economic investments and transactions. When and if the market manufactures the sense that I have a certain existential, social, psychological, bodily deficits, which I can mythically alleviate with products, it thus manufactures different forms of symbolic violence. Of course there is never a one to one correspondence between the needs of the market and my needs, or between marketing and feelings or habituses. (In fact, consumers often respond in ways that contradict the needs of social and economic forces, and can lead the market's tendencies and strategies. When the Second Wave of feminism crashed over the U.S., for example, the market began to cater to the needs of the "liberated woman," offering her, for instance, cars and cigarettes.) But the market is nonetheless designed to create at least some degree of correspondence between my desires and the needs of the economy (Hochschild 1979 and 2003), and between the economy and habitus. The market grows inasmuch as its interests become, to some degree, naturalized, consigned to embodied collective memory.

And, importantly, the correspondences connecting market needs to personal needs — do not always follow, as Adam Smith argued, the *strictly private* interests of consumers. Rather, they often follow private interests that are othered and underpinned by larger, extraneous, and even alienating economic interests. Adam Smith suggested that egotism and self-centeredness, as they provide motives for consumers which dynamize and underpin the free market, are necessary for the common good. But today self-centeredness is often other-centered, and has little to do with the actual needs of the "true self" in Winnicottian terms — the self that, to borrow again from DuBois, can see through his own eyes, not through the eyes of others. In this economic system, the self, its views, needs, and motives are often vehicles for the views, needs, and motives of others. The average American sees an average of two million TV commercials in a life span of sixty-five years, not counting exposure from the internet, buses, billboards, etc. (Herr 2008). The market may thus shape aspects of perceptual collective memories, and of the libidinal and affective motives that underpin them.

From the Latin *capita,* "heads," capitalism has the etymological sense of "something that gets into people's heads," as ideology, as mythos. Let me add that capitalism is also something that encroaches upon the senses, as it cradles and nurses a certain phenomenology of apperception and of self-perception, visions of self and others, which are key features of embodied collective memories. This economic system not only encourages dominated groups to see a certain order as normal and desirable, but to sustain this "natural" order, to invest their desires, aspirations, and modes of perception in it. As I suggested, this sort of hierarchical collective order tends to become natural precisely inasmuch as it emanates from people's bodies: from their eyes, affects, gestures, desires. Capitalism, to insist on a central point, thus sponsors various forms of symbolic violence that are expressed through various forms of embodied collective memory. [3]

A CRITICAL APPRAISAL OF BOURDIEU'S THEORY

Social Actors as Creating

Lest the reader conclude that Bourdieu's theory may lead us to a narrowly constructivist and deterministic theoretical space, it is important, by way of conclusion, to outline the ways in which the Bourdieuan subject is not only created but also creating.

The competitive properties of a field can allow for changes in its structure, in the distribution and positioning of the players, and in the stakes or capitals operant in it. The skilled (social) player can become endowed with the capacity — bio-psycho-social in nature — to achieve a better position within the structure and boundaries of the field, and can be successful in this sense. Indeed, exceptional individuals, by dint of a strong individual will, can single-handedly disturb the harmony of their fields. Baudelaire, for instance, managed to step outside the dominant literary, ethical, and aesthetic games (Bourdieu 2000). But to have such an impact, the author of the *Flowers of Evil* had to become a thereto unknown species. To create what Victor Hugo called the "new shudder" in the literary field, Baudelaire had to learn to navigate the everyday details of his life as an outsider; he had to learn to *live* differently, and had to wangle up new *intuitions* and visions from where his "accursed" (*maudit*) literary craft itself could grow. The resulting changes in his habitus, in his eyes and mind, delivered not only a new literary style and a new poetic perspective — but also permanent changes in his literary field (to the extent to which "mauditism" is often considered a cliché today).

Awareness of the arbitrariness of the social game, and related disobediences and political action, can also emerge when "awareness specialists," rather than social actors themselves, provide insight for them (Bourdieu 2000). The ideologue tries to bring arbitrary rules and ideas to life; the awareness specialist tries to extrude them from the domain of life. The Second Wave of feminism, for instance, created new sociological and political imaginations among women (and men). Betty Friedan's ideas helped fracture the organic harmony between women and their world, between habituses and fields, which ultimately fractured the social world itself, bringing forth new identities, new sexual standards, new ways of experiencing the body, as well as new norms and laws. Bourdieu's own sociological project — "the sociology that creates trouble," the sociology that "is a martial art" — aims to abet such awareness, to highlight the hidden bio-psycho-social mechanics that make us who we are, and that make the world what it is.[4]

Synthesis and Conclusion

On the one hand, Bourdieu managed to shine a blazing light into the domain of embodied subjectivity, illuminating the ways in which the arbitrariness of history encroaches upon the minds and bodies of social actors, helping us see how history often sediments a collective mythos, a seductive substance within us, which can mark the fate of individuals and groups. Bourdieu's position, grounded in quantitatively and qualitatively rigorous analyses, is defensible not only analytically but also politically, as it added needed reality checks on such purportedly meta-historical constructs as Will, Reason, and Agency; constructs that otherwise tend to appear as disembodied in the literature, as radically autonomous and disconnected from life as lived.

But on the other hand, his theory has limits, as I have suggested. Though Bourdieuan social actors are able to create new cultural spaces and new futures, particularly within limits imposed by the field, they are primarily created. Again, individual Will is in general limited by the conditions of possibility provided by the social world. And even the notion of "social games" suggests that *competition* among players actually tends to create harmony between the individual's will and the forces operant in the field. Competition, in this sense, is not an Adam-Smithian mechanism of continuous social renovation and creativity, but one that tends to sustain the social and economic forces that create the players' dispositions. Hence, as the configurations of the social game tend to be in-corporated by the player, changes generated by autonomous Bourdieuan social actors are rare, if and when they occur. Thus, Bourdieuan worlds tend toward stasis and reproduction, because players typically make their moves not as self-reflective, autonomous decision makers, but, almost as in Aristotle, in virtue of simply *being a player*. They typically play their arbitrary games "because that's just who I am," "because that's the way we do things around here." "*Hexis*," another Aristotelian moment in Bourdieu, describes this stage of investment in the field. "Bodily hexis is political mythology realized, em-bodied, turned into a permanent disposition, a durable way of standing, speaking, walking, and thereby of feeling and thinking" (Bourdieu 1990, 69-70).

This is why the Bourdieuan answer to the Hobbessian question is that social order is possible *not* primarily on a contractual-rational basis, where people come together to establish a consensus *sui juris*. Instead, the Bourdieuan social order is possible mostly on the basis of a collective *unawareness* of the hidden nature of the social game. It is possible on the basis of a collective "foolishness," he says after Pascal, which flows from history, sets in, and makes it irresistible for us to accept the nature of "nature," the processes whereby social forces become "organic," even if these processes go against us. Again, this approach is very useful, inasmuch as it helps us see important mechanisms of social ordering, but it becomes less useful when it is a question of understanding how social actors resist, recreate, and reconfigure the social world.

Temporally, Bourdieuan social actors are first and foremost the inheritors of the past. Their past is the main drive of their futures. Habitus is in fact mostly a preservative structure wherein inherited symbols and forces are sedimented. Indeed, his treatment of time, particularly of the future, brings to mind Heidegger's ideas about inauthenticity, which involve an inherited and inertial mode of being, where the person defends against new things, new possibilities, new futures. Similarly, Bourdieuan social actors often appear shackled by the past and thus thrown into futures that are not of their choosing. "Habitus," he says, "is that presence of the past in the present which makes possible the presence in the present of the forth-coming" (2000, 10). Again, I also have argued that the past can conscript the present and the future, but Bourdieu's theory tends to overemphasize not only the role of external social forces (spatially) but also the role of the past (temporally), the two spatio-temporal coordinates that provide the primary conditions of possibility for personhood. The question of social change, in other words, is the heel of Bourdieu's Achillean sociological project; and this is not only a question about change for good, but just about change, with good, bad and mixed consequences for individuals and groups.

At this point, we therefore need to interrogate his "social physics," and begin searching for any resistive and a-historical mechanisms within the social actor. Is the social actor endowed with any transactional and resistive mechanisms that, operating beyond historical structures, allow her to deflect the calls of history and thus open up new possibilities, new identities, new futures? What mechanisms, if any, can help the embodied subject emerge through the pressures of external social forces as a relatively autonomic construct? To answer these questions, we now turn to psychoanalytical theory, which — beyond its own deficits partly outlined in the appendix — can endow the Bourdieuan subject with these sorts of inner-directed mechanisms of self-formation and collective action.

NOTES

1. Kitchens, Friedan shows, became the center of women's lives; college attendance dropped; the number of women dropping out of college increased; marriage age dropped; birthrates increased; the size of women's bodies decreased. And the minds and affects of many women changed as well, as exemplified by the quote above.

2. Fussell's commentary on class, it has to be stated, is not accompanied by the sort of support that one finds, for example, in Bourdieu or other analysts of class (correspondence analysis, ethnographic descriptions, etc.). It is accompanied, instead, by tongue-in-cheek car-

toons, apparently intended to depict social types; cartoons that, going well beyond simple stereotyping, bring to mind The Great Lombroso and his now cultish socio-psycho-physiological typifications. Yet, Fussell's book is full of excellent vignettes and vivid examples that, the author's bilious wisdom notwithstanding, manage to sketch important aspects of social life in the U.S.

3.　Marx already thought that even the body of the worker would become a dehumanized aspect in the overall automation of the factory system. The germ of this Marxist idea may be seen in the memorable comedic images popularized by Charlie Chaplin in the movie *City Lights*. Our hero, a zany factory worker spending his days adjusting bolts that forever run on a conveyor belt, progressively assumes machine-like posturing, gesturing, and movements. The film is, of course, a mere caricature but it illustrates the Marxist notion that the logic of mass production is dehumanizing also in a somatic sense; such that the arm of a laborer working at a conveyor belt, for example, may only upon self-reflection feel as personal, as opposed to feeling like an integral part of the machinery. The smile of a cashier, as Hochschild has also argued (1979), may feel removed from any sense of emotion, while feeling attached, much as the arm of the laborer, to the logic of production. Marx argued that mechanical labor molds aspects the embodied existence. It gives the laborer a body that, in some ways, must adapt to the logic of mass production.

4.　Beyond the actions of individuals, beyond occasional misfirings, discordances, and "Don Quixote effects," instability occurs, naturally enough, when fields suffer violence from the outside, when the objective conditions sustaining the structure of the field are dislocated by larger forces: economic slumps, wars, etc. If this happens, *habituses* (you and I), accustomed as they were to their old harmony with the forces of their fields, no longer match up or harmonize with the new conditions. And thus people can either retreat or, depending on the degree of investment in the old game, they may act against the new objective conditions. Such individual misfirings and discordances can agglomerate to become more or less large-scale revolts. May 68, for Bourdieu, is an unromantic example of this sort of situation (1990a). Given these troubled scenarios, Bourdieuan actors can therefore fight against larger structures, and bring forth a number of changes. Social structures, for Bourdieu, do not simply stamp all social actors with pre-determined imperatives. He takes pains to point out the larger correspondences between the needs of social worlds and the needs and dispositions of social actors, but his model allows for these sorts of exceptions (and others explained in this chapter).

Chapter Five

Resistive Mechanisms (Phylogeny)

The "I" is the response of the organism to the attitudes of the others; the "me" is the organized set of attitudes of others which one himself assumes. The attitudes of the others constitute the organized "me," and then one reacts toward that as an "I."—George H. Mead

FROM BOURDIEU TO FREUD

It is odd that Bourdieu, so interested as he was in the ways in which culture encroaches upon human life, never said much about the Nietzschean Freud[1] who spoke, again, of originally pre-social and indeed impersonal psychosomatic mechanisms that constantly resist the calls of culture. Yet, this particular Freudian perspective can strengthen the Bourdieuan model. Much as all the French sociologists discussed above, Freud also helps us see that the subject adapts (superego is the agency that is in part responsible for adaptation) and that it can do so in ways that in fact compromise his/her ontological status. The Freudian subject may indeed yield to external demands to the point of forsaking the "true self," as Donald Winnicott says. But, as I argue in this chapter, Freud also suggests that in general adaptation is neither easy nor secure, because this subject carries the potential to deflect, and indeed erode, the claims of culture (which is primarily an effect of internal, id-related pressures). Hence, whereas Bourdieu illuminates the adaptive mechanisms of subjectivity, Freud sheds light on the limits of adaptation, helping us see how individuals and groups create new parameters of selfhood, new forms of social life, new futures — for better and for worse.

To be sure, Freud helps us see that the human subject and the social environment often co-adapt and co-arise; so that, as the body reflects cultural claims, culture also reflects biological claims, and indeed biology provides prototypes for important elements of culture (and prototypes for important elements of consciousness, as well).[2] Below I argue, first, that living organisms themselves, adaptive as they are, are not simply adaptive.[3] Organisms, Freud helps us see, are endowed with endogenous drives designed to defend the needs of the individual, internal mechanisms that often press against the claims of the environment. Freud also helps us see that organismic life is in fact intrinsically conflicted (precisely because it is characterized by an economy competing forces), and that this biological fact is not without consequences for human consciousness, and for the human experience, in general. Consciousness, which emerged phylogenetically from our biological form, reflects this archaic organismic conflict, and is largely structured, and defined by it. Thus, I finally argue, the Freudian subject is more complex than the "French" subject discussed above, which is primarily created by external forces, with limited internal input. (In subsequent chapters we see that this process also marks the development of ECMs, which, much as consciousness and much as life itself, are adaptive but not simply adaptive structures, resistive but not only resistive).

Before discussing these ideas and comparing and contrasting Freud and Bourdieu, I would like to provide two clarifications, as a way of transitioning from sociology and phenomenology to psychoanalytical theory. On the one hand, the specialist in Freud may see the discussion below as not Freudian enough and too tainted by external ideas. To such a cautious reader I can only suggest that the goal of this and the next chapters is not to amplify the psychoanalytical framework but merely to see Bourdieu and the French School through a Freudian filter, particularly through the notion that human beings, as suggested, are adaptive as well as resistive creatures. On the other hand, the non-specialist may wonder about the actual scientific status of psychoanalysis. After all, this discipline has been, from the very beginning, "scorned and despised," as Leo Lowenthal recalled (in Whitebook 1996, 2), and critics have argued that Freud provided a "fraudulent" "pseudo science" (Crews 1993) yoked to the vitalistic imagination (Peterfreund and Schwartz 1971) of a "petty generalissimo" (Crews 1993, 1994a, 1994b, 1995) who devised an infantile scheme (Peterfreund and Schwartz 1971), which stemmed from an "anthropomorphic" (ibid.) and "medieval" vision of the psychical apparatus (Crews 1993), a naïve vision which is not better than that of pseudo disciplines such as astrology (Popper 2003), a vast "confidence trick," as Peter Medawar says, which held the twentieth century under its sway (in Brunner 2001).

I discuss the scientific status of psychoanalysis in the appendix, but at this point I will suggest two initial ideas. Firstly, there are of course legitimate reasons for criticizing psychoanalytical theory, as Freud or any Freudian would agree. Louis Althusser said that Freud had no intellectual father, no shoulders of giants to stand upon, and therefore made many mistakes (such as the notion that girls and women are marked by a "penis envy" at the root of femininity). But secondly, there are also legitimate reasons that explain why psychoanalytical theory, rather than retreating to a corner to lick the wounds inflicted by critics, actually expanded across disciplines, languages, and generations in a Julianic fashion. There are reasons that explain why a pleiad of writers in the human sciences agree that Freud managed to touch the world because he was able to see new things within the domain of human nature.[4] The twentieth century, which in a certain sense was the Freudian century, was not simply conned by a petty generalissimo with an uncanny knack for selling fraudulent ideas, as some caustic critics suggest (see e.g., Crews 1993, 1994a, 1994b, 1995). And in fact, as we will see in this and the following chapters, psychoanalytical theory has provided useful theoretical constructs about the nature of the subject, and good clues that, in particular, can help us connect biology, psychology, and sociology, thus helping us amplify the "total" theory of subjectivity proposed by the French sociologists above.

LIFE TROUBLED (PHYLOGENY)

Freud's originally positivistic, decidedly modern ideas about the connection between the person and the world were, as suggested, adaptive but also transactional and resistive. He began his polemic as a biologist, indeed as a histologist,[5] thinking about life and about organisms in their environment, assuming that organisms respond to external environmental demands, adaptively, but also to internal claims, the needs and impulses of the organism itself. Freud thought that these endogenous impulses, which were designed to defend the claims of the individual organism, were fated to find restrictions and threats in the environment; for, though the environment is the source of survival, it is also a menace to life: "The living being . . . ," he says, "defends its own existence by destroying foreign bodies" (in Chatfield and Ilukhina 1994, 242).

Of course the environment is benefic; and, as satirist Mort Sahl says, every time an organism breathes, no matter how bloodthirsty it may be, it "makes a flower happy." But organic life is not, as Saint Paul argued, a haven invested with the goodness of God. Life, Freud says, is "hostile." Living organisms feed from dead organisms; the former need the latter to convert them into sap, blood, fat, and sperm. And struggle is thus a basic characteristic of life. (Note, indeed, that the very body of individual organisms, this community of cells that often feed from one another, recapitulates the larger drama that characterizes life-systems. In our case, as most of our cells are born to die within one year, the economy of life and death is the constant of our everyday bodily existence.) Life, as suggested, is an economy of forces that involves individual claims that constantly toil against supra-individual pressures designed to constrain them. (By contrast, inorganic life is inert and thus inertial. As it is not endowed with any sense of Will, in Schopenhauerian terms, it doesn't know about struggle or suffering, which result from limits imposed upon the Will.)

Freud argues, furthermore, that death is not only a fact of survival, but a paradoxical principle governing life. "[T]he most universal endeavor of all living substance," he says, is "to return to the quiescence of the inorganic world" (1961, 62). Organic life in fact has an "urge . . . to restore to an earlier state of things" to thus comply with its own catabolic laws (in Askay and Farquhar 2006, 198). "Everything living dies for internal reasons — becomes inorganic once again — [and thus] we shall be compelled to say that the aim of life is death" (Freud 1961, 32). To be sure, despite Freud's intention to establish a position entirely outside philosophy, psychoanalysis emerged interrogating old philosophical paradoxes: the idea that living is a form of dying, that life is a death sentence, that Eros, he says, is "always blended ['alloyed,' as we say] with a certain dosage of its opposite," Thanatos (in Nathan and Norden 1960, 186-203).[6] Freud thought, in other words, that organic matter as such is organized under a principle of conflict, precisely because life obeys opposing forces. It is not only that organisms are marked by internal and external pressures. They are also dynamized by a biological tendency that tries to fasten every organic particle to the organic world, a life principle; and, on the other hand, by an opposite biological tendency that tries to deliver everything organic into the inorganic world, a death principle inextricably glued to life.

Indeed, as Freud read Empedocles, he wondered whether this tension between Life and Death, Eros and Thanatos, might not be, perhaps, an extension from an even older and more elemental principle of attraction and repulsion at the root of all inorganic matter. Empedocles' "cosmic fantasy," as Freud says, aimed to describe a Divine Power that eternally and omnipresently manifests itself through Love (a principle of unity) and Strife (a principle of disunity) the two conflicting forces that govern matter, atomically and cosmically.[7] Does organic matter, Freud seems to have wondered, bear an archaic imprint left by these opposing principles governing particles and energies? (As we saw, living things, obeying a principle of unity, are always *allone*; and dead things, obeying a principle of disunity, are in essence alone.) "The analogy of our two basic instincts [Eros and Thanatos]," he says, "extends from the sphere of living things to the pair of opposite forces — attraction and repulsion — which rule in the inorganic world" (1940, 19).

Consciousness as an Economy of Biological and Social Forces

Freud's Empedoclean reflections are tentative, but what is clear for him is that human consciousness, as it extends evolutionarily from the troubled domain of organic matter, is also organized under a principle of conflict. As we will see below, this is not only an intrinsic but indeed a defining struggle, the very signature of the human experience. (And this is a struggle that, we will also see, provides a ground for the development of the embodied memories that vivify, enact, and express the human experience.)

Again, Freud had no intellectual parents and in particular he avoided philosophy so as to avoid biasing his originally Helmholtzian views on human nature. Yet, he provided a philosophical and indeed ontological account of our nature, which at this point may be useful to summarize: Freud began as a Schopenhauerian biologist, believing that life is troubled; an idea that set him in the pathway of a Darwinian psychologist who believed that the hostility of life marks the evolutionary development of consciousness; a pathway that, in turn, eventually led him in the direction of a Nietzschean social-psychologist, who believed that social life itself, bearing the hostile imprint of organic life, is also conflicted, the partial sublimation of biological processes and forces that press against the needs of gregariousness. [8]

Importantly, much as Schopenhauer, Darwin, and Nietzsche, Freud also eschewed the Paulinian and also romantic notion that life is inherently good; so that, as Rousseau had it, we are born "good" and goodness is our natural state. For Freud, organic life is not only hostile but, indeed, is a stranger to normative valences. It is an economy of internal and external forces *beyond good and evil*, as Nietzsche and Darwin may also agree. Saint Paul said that "Every creature of God is good" (1 Tim. 4:4), a position shared by Augustine, Aquinas and by the Christian tradition in general. By contrast, Freud would be comfortable with the idea that an amoral and benign indifference rests at the bottom and origin of life, in general, *and* of human life, in particular. Whereas mainstream Christianity speaks of good and evil as primordial forces, for Freud, good and evil (and heaven/hell, sacred/profane, etc.) are, so to speak, post-mordial. These dichotomies are the viewpoint of an already encultured creature that is one step removed from the older and more elemental logic of life. Primordial, for him, are the Empedoclean principles of Love and Strife: the disinterested and normatively blind conflict inherent to the cosmic order, a conflict inherited by life, and by human life in particular.

Another important difference between Freud and Christianity is that whereas a New-Testamentarian perspective would lead us to think that the conflict between Love and Strife has to be resolved in favor of Love (i.e., God), for Freud both of these forces, much as Eros and Thanatos, are indispensable aspects of human life. This conflict, for the Viennese doctor, cannot and indeed should not be resolved:

> Each of these instincts [Eros and Thanatos] is every whit as indispensable as its opposite, and all the phenomena of life derive from their activity, whether they work in concert or in opposition. It seems that an instinct of either category can operate but rarely in isolation . . . the instinct of self-preservation is certainly of an erotic nature, but to gain its end this very instinct necessitates aggressive action. In the same way the love instinct, when directed to a specific object, calls for an admixture of the acquisitive instinct if it is to enter into effective possession of that object. (Nathan and Norden 1960)

Again, Freud would agree with the idea that not only organic life, but also human life, the core of human nature, is not simply "good," either, in the Paulinian or romantic senses. But by the same token, and in contrast now to the French sociological tradition, he would also agree with the notion that the lower impulses at the core of life, though potentially dangerous, are not "bad" either. He thought that it is neither possible *nor desirable* to radically inhibit these lower, amoral agencies because they, as Nietzsche also thought, sustain the ownmost wants of the individual, our capacity for impulsiveness, and thus the potential for human spontaneity free from external constraints. Thus, the Freudian perspective lets us see that, just as Durkheimian morality and constraint make us human, these lower agencies underpin, as well, a fundamental aspect of the human experience.

Freud, it is important to clarify, was not an "inmoralist," as Nietzsche described himself. On this account, Freud was not a Nietzschean at all. On the contrary, a Jewish humanist, a man who died in 1939 and who experienced all the tragedies leading to WWII (four of his sisters eventually died in Nazi concentration camps), Freud wanted to strengthen the moral, that is, inhibitory and social, portion of human nature: the executive, self-reflective functions of the ego. And psychoanalysis in fact emerged as a tool to, in part, help us confront the normatively-blind and thus potentially dangerous demands of these amoral and natural impulses, a task inherited particularly by Freud's daughter, Anna, as well as by mainstream American analysts. But again, psychoanalysis never aimed to be a "disciplinary" discipline, in any Foucaultian sense: it never aimed to docilize, as Foucault would say, human nature. From the Greek *psyche* ("breath," "the soul") and *ana-lyein* ("to unchain, to release, to free from debt, to acquit") psychoanalysis literally aimed to unchain the human soul. It endeavored to acquit it from the excesses of instinct (related to the id, to the organism, and to the body) but also from the excesses of the law (related to superego and to sociality),[9] the two poles that come together in an agonistic encounter to nurse the sense of selfhood (related to the ego, an intermediary of id and of superego, as we will subsequently see). For Freud, I insist, the human subject is a social but also a biological animal formed at the intersection of the low and the high, biology and culture, a creature that emerges, onto- and phylogenetically, prodded by social and by biological forces, by adaptive as well as resistive mechanisms.

A longer phylogenic view may be helpful at this point, to extend and complete this important Freudian idea. Phylogenetically, the agonistic conflicts between the individual organism and the environment, as the Darwinian Freud assumed, were not without evolutionary consequences for the human subject. These exchanges resulted not only in satisfactions and tensions in the organism but also in related schemata of interpretation and understanding. The exchanges and eventual conflicts between the individual and the environment involve a learning process, positive and negative reinforcements that, marking the pace of evolution, also stamp the mental structures of organisms. Hence, when we move to the higher end of the phylogenetic scale, these exchanges and conflicts carry the germ of human consciousness. One may grant that, for Freud, consciousness is a fact "without parallel which defies all explanation and description" (1895, 311); but one can also argue that this "fact without parallel" is the result of evolution, and thus the result of ongoing conflict. Bear in mind that, as Darwin may agree, evolution patterns metaphorize, in various ways and through various life-forms and organismal shapes, the initial conflict inherent to life.

Hence, for this Darwinian Freud, consciousness is not a Cartesian and somehow autonomous entity, but a system of interpretation and understanding that largely distilled, onto- and phylogenetically, from the strained interactions that connect endogenous and exogenous forces. The neurobiologist Antonio Damasio, though not under the banner of psychoanalysis, sums up these ideas well. It is worth quoting his work at length.

> When we consider our own species . . . it is apparent that we must rely on highly evolved genetically based biological mechanisms, as well as on suprainstinctual survival strategies that have developed in society, are transmitted by culture, and require, for their application, consciousness, reasoned deliberation, and willpower. This is why human hunger, desire, and explosive anger do not proceed unchecked toward feeding frenzy, sexual assault, and murder, at least not always, assuming that a healthy human organism has developed in a society in which the suprainstinctual survival strategies are actively transmitted and respected.
>
> Western and eastern thinkers, religious and not, have been aware of this for millennia; closer to us the topic preoccupied both Descartes and Freud . . . .
> The control of animal inclination by thought, reason, and the will was what made us human, according to Descartes' *Passions of the Soul.* I agree with his formulation except that where he specified a control achieved by a nonphysical agent, I envision a biological operation structured within the human organism and not one bit less complex, admirable, or sublime. The creation of a superego which would accommodate instincts to social dictates was Freud's formulation . . . which was stripped of Cartesian dualism but was nowhere

explicit in neural terms. A task that faces neuroscientist today is to consider the
neurobiology supporting adaptive supraregulation, by which I mean the study
and understanding of the brain structures required to know about those regulations. I am not attempting to reduce social phenomenal to biological phenomena, but rather to discuss the powerful connection between them . . . . Culture
and civilization could not have arisen from a single individual and thus cannot
be reduced to biological mechanisms and, even less, can they be reduced to a
subset of genetic specifications. Their comprehension demands not just general biology and neurobiology but the methodologies of the social sciences as
well. (2005, 123-24)

Again, Damasio is offering a rather Freudian argument here, particularly
when he implies that hominids became human as their animal impulses and
reflexes progressively fell under the control of neurological mechanisms connected to the needs of gregariousness. Yet, to insist on a central ideal, Freud
would add that these suprainstinctual survival strategies and attendant neurological mechanisms never eliminated instinctual demands and never will.
"The fact that the reality principle has to be re-established continually in the
development of man," as Herbert Marcuse says, "indicates that its triumph
over the pleasure principle is never complete and never secure" (1962). Instinctual and suprainstinctual feedback have both carved the human subject.

Note also that, for Freud, human subjectivity, inherently conflicted such
as it is, is in fact marked by intrinsic elements of *morbidity*. The elemental
instincts at the root of our nature, which were phylogenetically designed to
fulfill the demands of life itself, are constantly beset by vicissitudes (*Schick-
sale*), as they come to partake from a social order that is based upon their
repression.[10] Hence, "the essence of the individual is repression," as Norman
Brown says (1985, 10); and indeed "Man's superiority over other animals is
his capacity for neurosis, and his capacity for neurosis is merely the obverse
of his capacity for cultural development" (ibid., my emphasis). Freud would
indeed agree with Nietzsche's formulation about the relationship between
biology and culture, nature and nurture. In combination, Nietzsche says, they
produce the "disease called man" (ibid.), which does not mean that human
nature is pathological *per se*, but that it is marked, precisely, by want and by
repression, and thus founded upon two expressive deficits: neither instincts
nor morality can be *exclusively and fully* articulated through the human experience. Freud would thus agree with Durkheim' characterization of the human soul, as a "theater of struggle," but whereas for the sociologist this
struggle tends to yield to the force of gregariousness, for the Schopenhauerian physician the struggle is and has always been the locus of human life.

It is worth noting, as well, that a similar deficit also characterizes culture,
a domain that, extending from human consciousness, also is also marked by
intrinsic elements of morbidity. And the idea, here, is that whereas life as
such is beyond good and evil, social life has to be predicated within the

coordinates of good and evil, the indispensable cultural tools that facilitate gregariousness. Thus, when human beings are concerned, organic life tends to clash against social life, precisely because the latter constantly attempts to regulate the former according to a (socio)logic that is foreign to the logic of organic matter itself. Bear in mind that the individual organism survives by trying to maximize pleasure and minimize unpleasure; and that, by contrast, and precisely because individualistic tendencies go against gregariousness, the social organism survives by restricting individualistic impulses, through norms and proscriptions that restrict, in particular, pleasure and aggressiveness. Indeed, the social organism survives through mechanisms that systematically dispense unpleasure: formal and informal sanctions that enforce the terms of the social contract. (As the late and increasingly pessimistic Freud suggested [2002], the civilizing process is thus fraught with discontent [*Unbehagen*, uneasiness], because civilization increasingly wants to exact a toll from the reserves of instinct, from Eros but also from Thanatos.) Yet, as individualistic impulses cannot be permanently suppressed, social life, much as human consciousness and much as life itself, is also dynamized by intrinsic tensions that involve higher and lower poles: sacred and profane domains; institutions designed to elicit conformity and stasis, and persistent patterns of deviance that sponsor social change. (And as we will see, these tensions can mark the nature of social structures. Just as the tensions intrinsic to consciousness can nudge certain life-courses for the individual, the tensions inherent to the social order can likewise sponsor certain historical directions for the group.)

Pleasure and Unpleasure and Good and Evil

To end this chapter, let me provide some examples that illustrate the foregoing discussion, particularly the idea that the conflict between instinct and gregariousness provides organic prototypes for the central motifs and patterns of consciousness, and for basic cultural-institutional structures. Let us consider basic organizational principles of consciousness and culture, the dichotomies of good/evil, heaven/hell, taboo/transgression, for example; and let us see how they come into being as biological demands related to pleasure-unpleasure meet the social mechanisms that govern over them.[11]

As Melanie Klein may agree, in a child, notions of good and evil (as well as the feelings of love and hate) are first understood bodily and pre-reflectively, particularly in terms of pleasure and unpleasure. "Good" begins to emerge as the baby's needs (e.g., hunger) meet positive environmental responses (e.g., the mother breastfeeds him); and in this initial sense, "good" means "good for survival." It is a (pre-social, pre-reflective) verdict of the species. Similarly, "evil" is originally nursed by negative environmental reinforcement (though Klein would argue that "evil" stems not exactly from the actions of external objects, such as the mother, but from intrapsychic representations of these objects). Good and evil, that is to say, begin to emerge through an initial economy of internal claims and external responses. Of course, in the adult these normative parameters are not primarily physiological, bodily, or pre-social. But such parameters, which largely organize consciousness *and* social systems, have to be understood initially by the body; and bodily claims have to provide organic prototypes for them. Good and evil, that is to say, are not substances in themselves, as the Manicheans believed. And the civilizing process neither creates them *ab ovo*, nor extracts them from a Platonic heaven of moral principles to then install them into consciousness. Instead, these moral parameters begin with the amoral claims of biology in interaction or in conflict with gregariousness.

Back to Damasio, "were it not for the possibility of sensing body states that are inherently ordained to be painful or pleasurable, there would be no suffering or bliss, no longing or mercy, no tragedy or glory in the human condition" (2005). Augustine can furnish an example of this idea (e.g., 1872). He says that if we control pleasure (*appetitus*) we invite eternal bliss, we prepare ourselves for "the treasure of heaven," the autonomous, platonic source of all goodness. By contrast, if we are controlled by pleasure (*cupiditas,* the "wretched" impulse to "enjoy oneself and one's neighbor"), we invite eternal pain, the "unlawfulness" of hell. Only a species that can experience bodily pleasure can construct such a notion of non-bodily, spiritual bliss (to characterize a form of non-bodily and therefore deathless, eternal life). On the other hand, only a species that can experience bodily pain can construct this Augustinian notion of hell, and the utilitarian ethics and the general ideological systems derived from it. Note, as well, that good and evil do not always correspond, respectively, to pleasure and unpleasure. Adam and Eve's sex, Augustine says, becomes lustful only after the fall, the birth of pleasure, the birth of evil. (Augustine's conversion to Christianity was a commitment to celibacy.) Pleasure has been historically associated with sense of transgression; it has been the harbinger of the fall, the post-lapsarian source of evil.

It is difficult to imagine, in other words, how an incorporeal and immortal being, God, could possibly formulate this type of Augustinian moral system. As Homer teaches us, the Gods, on account of their immortality, can hardly understand such human experiences as heroism, for example, a moral disposition reserved for beings that are finite, fragile, and fully able to experience pain. To be sure, Homeric gods, unlike other deities, are not all-good or all-evil, precisely because, as immortals, they can hardly understand moral parameters that befit the nature of finite and frail (human) beings. The consciousness of these Homeric mortals, as well as their ethics, values and norms, tell a story that begins with *their* bodies. The Augustinian heaven and hell, and the institutional order around them, seem to tell the story of these transient and nociceptive bodies as well.

And of course, it is not a question of dismissing the notions of good and evil, Christian or not, as "merely" having lowly bodily origins, as opposed to having "high," platonic, or divine origins. On the contrary, as we saw with Durkheim, moral parameters are important simply because they make us human. Yet, the point I want to underscore is that their genealogical roots go back not to an independent, platonic source of morality, but to the morally neutral logic of biology. And that, more generally, the human body, morally neutral such as it is, is nevertheless invested with the originally physical presences of morality — of heroism, mercy, tragedy, glory, good, as well as evil, sinfulness, cruelty and other such key motifs of human consciousness. These archetypical bodily presences become morality and consciousness as they become mediated by the needs of gregariousness.

William James can further clarify this idea. He says, "[O]ur mental life is knit up with our corporeal frame, in the strictest sense of the term. Rapture, love, ambition, indignation, and pride, considered as feelings, are fruits of the same soil with the grossest bodily sensations of pleasure and of pain" (1884). Consciousness, that is to say, is knit up not just with a Cartesian corporeal frame "made up of flesh and bones" — but with the claims that this frame encloses. Nietzsche similarly says that pain and pleasure are "teachers" (1978a) and that there is "wisdom" in them. These "best self-preservatives of a species," he adds, made us "take sail": they portended a certain domain of meaning for us, a domain that emerged as these teachers learned the language of a profoundly social species. Corporeal claims, as they have been critical for survival, have marked the evolution not only of consciousness, but also of the collective consciousness; and have thus marked culture and history, which also emerged as our biological horizon met, and clashed with, the social requirements of this exceptionally social species.

This Freudian perspective, in conclusion, helps us see that consciousness and personhood are more than the "French" terrains dominated by the external and rather autonomous forces of morality, culture — of sociality, in general. After Freud, this historicist, "sociologistic" model of consciousness seems useful and necessary but also incomplete. He helps us see that the human experience, in general, is an arena where biology and culture grapple for expression.[12] As we will subsequently see, this conflict intrinsic to our species also provides the ground for the embodied memories that, rooted in instinct as well as morality, vivify the contents and conflicts of consciousness. We saw that embodied collective memories can be colonized, rendered less resistive, but they nonetheless store resistive mechanisms that can deflect these cultural encroachments, and render these processes temporary and fluid.

NOTES

1. For the intersections between Nietzsche and Freud see Chapman and Chapman-Santana 1995.

2. It is worth noting that, for Nietzsche, the body is in fact a key factor in the development of history. And indeed, philosophy, he says, must be "medicine" for history: philosophy must help culture produce a healthy body, and by helping produce a healthy body, it should help produce a healthier culture and a worthwhile history. Incidentally, the term "Id" was claimed by Freud's student, Georg Groddeck, as his own. Freud acknowledged Groddeck's contribution in *The Ego and the Id* (Freud 1927), but Freud was likely thinking not of his student but of Nietzsche when he developed the notion of the id (see Freud 1923, 23). Nietzsche, in any case, used the term before Groddeck who published his *The Book of the It* 1923, 23 years after Nietzsche's death.

3. Organisms, as Richard Lewontin has shown (2000), not only respond to exogenous environmental pressures, passively, but can actively modify the environment.

4. If only to consider founding figures in sociology such as Jürgen Habermas and Talcott Parsons; or Hans Morgenthau in political science; Julia Kristeva in linguistics; René Spitz in pediatric medicine; Erik Erikson in developmental psychology; Gilles Deleuze, Jacques Derrida, Slavoj Žižek in philosophy; William Langer in history; Karl Pribram in neuroscience; Claude Levi-Strauss in anthropology; or more generally schools and movements, from Continental Feminism to Neuro-Psychoanalysis; from Psychoanalytic Anthropology to Queer Theory; from The Frankfurt School to Structuralism to Structural Functionalism; from Surrealism to German Expressionism. In the humanities and the arts, consider the work of André Breton and Georges Bataille in literature; Gustav Mahler in music; Salvador Dalí, Giorgio de Chirico, Hans Bellmer, Rene Magritte, Dorothea Tanning in painting (and every other surrealist); Luis Buñuel in filmmaking; Rainer Maria Rilke and Pier Paolo Pasolini in poetry; Man Ray in photography, etc. Einstein was also an admirer of Freud's "irresistible lucidity and "his "passion to ascertain the truth." "You see," Einstein tells Freud, "every Tuesday I read from your works [...] and cannot admire enough the beauty and truth of your presentation" (Nathan and Norden 1960, 186-203). No critic, however pugnacious, denies Freud's vast, global, and enduring influence.

5. "Starting in 1877," as Kaplan-Solms and Solms explain, "with the problem of the fine structure of spinal ganglion cells in a lowly animal [Freud moved] gradually through the animal series from crustacea and fish to the human being, up the nervous system via the spinal cord and brainstem to the cerebral cortex, and from the structure of the individual nerve cells to the functions of the brain" (Kaplan-Solms and Mark Solms 2002, 4).

6. Freud in fact urges us, in an almost Heideggerian fashion, to avow the fact of death: "If you want to endure life, prepare yourself for death." If you don't fully recognize the fact of death, your life would be merely like "an American flirtation, in which it is understood from the first that nothing is to happen," and such attitude has "a powerful effect on our lives. Live is impoverished, it loses interest [...] it becomes empty" (in Askay and Farquhar 2006, 200).

7. Consider the positive and negative valences of the atom, or the hypotheses about the expansive (Big Bang) and contractive (Big Crunch) tendencies of the universe.

8. Nietzsche asks, "What is life? Life — that is: continually shedding something that wants to die. Life — that is: being cruel and inexorable against everything about us that is growing old and weak — and not only about *us*. Life — that is, then: being without reverence for those who are dying, who are wretched, who are ancient? Constantly being a murderer? — And yet old Moses said 'Thou shalt not kill'" (1978a, 100). This Nietzschean statement provides a good, if partial, summary of Freud's own and evolving conception of life.

9. This latter idea took root particularly in France, becoming the battle cry of French surrealists, for example, whose work was influenced particularly by the Nietzschean Freud.

10. Animals are freer when it comes to expressing instinct, but they are of course trapped within it. Algerian artist Adel Abdessemed often deals with these ideas. At the 2011 Venice Biennale he presented a video of assorted animals penned together, scorpions, snakes, frogs, fighting cocks, pitbulls, and others. The denouement is predictable: animals are free from repression, but trapped precisely because they are free from it.

11.   It is worth noting that the phenomena of pleasure-unpleasure preoccupied Freud from the beginning to the end (from *The Project* in 1895 to the *Outline* in 1938), and that Freud's ideas about these phenomena and their connection to consciousness underwent many revisions. A detailed analysis of this process is beyond the scope of this book, and the discussion above provides only some pertinent ideas.

12.   And as Damasio (2006) says this is not a new idea. Indeed we have grappled with it for millennia. The Christian tradition already speaks of an original sin that, as suggested, constantly harries the soul. "Sin" and the flesh, is this sense, partake from a force that we, as encultured beings, have had to fight ever since humanity felled from Grace.

Chapter Six

Basic Instincts: Eros and Thanatos

EROS (LIFE)

In the previous chapter I suggested that our species-memory, conflicted such as it is, is the foundation of our being and the ground of consciousness and culture. In this chapter we see that the species-memory is also the ground of the embodied memories that bring consciousness to life. Here I focus on Eros and Thanatos, two elemental forces of our species-memory and two foundational psychoanalytical concepts.

I also suggested in the previous chapter that Eros, in the broadest sense, is the name for the biological principle that fastens organic elements to the organic world. (Thanatos, by contrast, delivers these elements into the inorganic world.) This idea needs to be specified, but it is important to first discuss the nature of life before discussing the nature of this life-principle, Eros. The origin of life is uncertain, perhaps it begun in a "primeval soup," over 3.8 billion years ago, as inert elements combined into self-reproducing molecules. What we do know, however, is that eventually these self-reproducing molecules combined to produce mechanisms of sentience — and of self-recognition. Of course early creatures were *not* self-conscious or introspective, but minimal mechanisms of self-recognition were nonetheless essential for life, if anything to prevent living creatures from eating their own bodies. Hence, unlike anything that existed before, these newly "interested" beings began to appropriate for themselves elements of the external world. Importantly, to do so they had to be endowed with *endogenous impulses*, which drove them to affirm their own needs, their self-recognized existence, their own element of difference.

Let me note as well that life doesn't follow a linear genesis, as in Descartes' clockwork model. And that it, instead, is a striving for complexity (e.g., Mazzocchi 2008). Life in fact aims to increase its diversity in order to increase the repertoire of responses to the environment, thus increasing the chances of survival (Gogarten 2000). Life, Nietzsche says, strives to improvise. And inasmuch as the larger life-system is driven by individual organisms that even if in the most elemental way sense their own element of difference, *life is a Nietzschean process that strives to multiply individual perspectives and differences*. Each living being, by virtue of partaking from life, is endowed with a singular perspective and is driven, for internal reasons, to affirm it and defend it, which is the key difference between organic and inorganic things.

Yet, if life affirms individual differences, individuals cannot exist independently from the supra-individual life-system, of course, as their needs can be satisfied only within this larger context. Organisms must be individuated to defend their own needs, but they can never be separate from the larger organization. And to be sure, as organisms are driven to satisfy their own needs, they are also driven, almost as in Adam Smith, to satisfy the needs of the larger organic system. Living things, that is to say, have to be individuated so as to defend their needs and their element of difference, but they cannot be separate. They must partake from a larger scale of being, and to an extent conform and adapt to it. As we saw, only death, Thanatos, severs ties to the system, and only dead things are separate in this sense.

With these considerations, let me suggest that Eros is the name for the life-principle whereby the endogenous claims of organisms push individuals to affirm their own needs — in the context of a supra-individual order. Eros is a principle, both biological and ontological, of individuation (affirmation of endogenous needs) but also of connectedness (needs satisfied in the larger order). As such, Eros also provides prototypes for consciousness. Indeed, as we will see, Eros provides prototypes for the embodied memories that enact consciousness, as well as for the social systems where these enactments take place. Bear in mind that, as we saw in previous chapters, consciousness itself is always individuated but cannot be separated from the world, and that the self as such is individuated but never separate. Much as memory, that is to say, selfhood recapitulates the operations of Eros. Cognitive and embodied memories are likewise individuated while never being separated from the world. They are always in-the-world, as Heidegger would probably agree. They are expressions of life and thus comply with life's demands. Cognitive and embodied memories are "erotic" in this literal sense. (By contrast, the progressive collapse of memory, we also saw, is a process whereby the individual retreats from the world, disconnects, and thus experiences a social death that precedes the death of the self. The person loses the faces and names of friends, his flag, his country: he dies socially, and the world disappears hand in hand with the self. Alzheimer is thus a thanatotic disease in that it aims to destroy the ties to the world, thus destroying identity and the self).

But beyond consciousness and memory, Eros also lends its nature to an array of specific human motifs and patterns: to psychological schemata, and thus to cultural schemata and to the embodied memories that bring them to life.

Eros and Plato

Freud's notion of a life instinct, Eros, was informed not only by biology but also by the philosophy of "the Divine Plato," as he says, particularly by Plato's dialogical character, Socrates, who suggests that Eros is the daemon of the between, the spirit of relation (and thus, again, a principle of connectedness but also of individuation). According to the Platonic schema, when mortals contemplatively open their minds to the domain of ideas, of Platonic Forms, they (erotically) reach unto the domain of immortality. Bear in mind that, for Plato, Idea is immortal. (So that, for example, whereas a material triangle is destructible and finite, its *ideal* expression, $A^2+B^2=C^2$, is indestructible and thus eternal.) And that in contemplation of Ideas, mortals reach unto eternity. Mortals thus bridge (their) finitude and eternity, they connect becoming to Being, a literally erotic excursion. And because mortality can be fully understood only against the backdrop of eternity, mortals thus come to understand an essential aspect of their nature: that they are finite and bodily creatures, but creatures that nonetheless are able to reach unto eternity. In an almost Augustinian manner, they see that their lowly, worldly, and finite life can (erotically) stretch towards a higher and otherworldly domain. Thus arising, their lives and souls acquire the qualities of fire. Hence, mortals come to see what fundamentally *differentiates* them from other creatures: they are finite beings that, carrying a spark of the eternal, are *connected* to the larger order of Being (a notion that Plato bequeathed to Christianity). [1]

Importantly, Eros was not only daemonic in this positive sense. It was also demonic in the contemporary negative sense. Eros was a demon whose anger or mischievousness sowed misfortune, one who targeted his own mother and even Zeus. Again, "Eros is always [alloyed] with its opposite," Thanatos. Eros can be dangerous in two ways. It can elevate the sense of *connection* that he oversees — to the point that it can dissolve individuality, in a thanatotic manner. For example, altruistic suicides involve a mode of connection — to the (thanatotic) point of self-destruction. On the other hand, the sense of *individuation* that Eros also oversees can likewise be dangerously elevated to the point that the person's connections and ties to the world are also destroyed. Narcissus, for example, is condemned to have no real connections to anyone but himself, and tragically dies alone on the bank of the Meniscus. [2] Yet, as suggested above, Eros can also provide a sense of atonement in the literal sense of at-one-ment: it can strengthen the truer and ownmost aspects of the self to then connect this truer self to a larger scale of being.

Eros and Sexuality

Soon we will see how Freud uses these ideas, and how they relate to the theme of embodied memory. But before doing that, we need to see why Eros is associated with sexuality and sexual pleasure. Eros, Octavio Paz says, "is the child of Poverty and Abundance and this explains his nature as an intermediary: he links light with darkness, the world of the senses with the world of ideas" (1993, 45). Perhaps because his "mission . . . is to communicate and to unite living beings," Paz adds, "we confuse him with the wind and represent him with wings" (ibid., 46). Eros is thus opposed to unfettered aggressiveness, to Thanatos, to the death instinct. Bear in mind that though aggressiveness may establish strong links between interactors, its aim is to destroy one of the terms of the relation, thereby destroying *"the spirit of relation,"* in the phrase by Paz, and thus the *spirit of difference*, because difference involves individuals that relate. As the spirit of relation, Eros is associated with love, pleasure, and sexuality, without being love, pleasure, or sexuality, strictly speaking. As Paz says, "The act in which the erotic experience culminates, orgasm . . . is a sensation that goes from extreme tension to the most complete self-surrender and from *single-minded concentration to the forgetfulness of the self*. The reuniting of opposites in the space of a second: *the affirmation of the ego and its dissolution*, ascent and fall, there and here, time and timelessness" (Paz 1993, 134, my emphases).

Again, Eros is a principle whereby organisms affirm their individual organic needs to thus partake from the larger organic system. Sexual pleasure, as Paz argues, intensifies internal, elemental, *ownmost* claims but to elevate them to a liminal point after which the individual falls into the embrace of the other, as these claims can be enacted only with the other. As an individual in her own right, the Other is also driven by egotistic demands and as such invites owmost expressions while also containing them. The Other limits the element of excess in these expressions and thus preserves the spirit of relation.[3] (Pathologically, sexuality can be a pathway whereby the Other not only limits the self, but actually penetrates the self to colonize elemental wants, so that the self loses its capacity to avow these internal drives and needs, thereby losing its capacity to relate *as an individual:* again, Eros devolving into Thanatos.) Sexuality, that is to say, recapitulates the life-principle of individuation and connectedness. It involves individualistic, ownmost expressions and their external limits; it involves the individual and the larger order; an order that therefore encroaches upon the structures of desire, impinging upon elemental aspects of individuality, but generally not to the point of colonizing the structures that sustain subjectivity. Sexuality in this sense is a channel whereby Eros (as individuation-connectedness) penetrates into consciousness and thus into the collective consciousness, one individual at a time. Indeed, sexuality is a channel whereby this life-principle modifies patterns of psychological as well as social organization, as we will presently see.

Herbert Marcuse (1962) argues that Eros, including sexuality and pleasure, is an important factor of social life. In the sphere of culture, Eros is a mechanism that affirms and disseminates individual wants and differences within the social order, while also tying individuals together. In an almost Nietzschean manner, Marcuse implies that, in the first sense, Eros can multiply individual differences and perspectives over and against equalizing, undifferentiating (thanatotic) demands of the social code; for example, against the demands of the heterosexual matrix. And the idea is that cultures that tend to foster and defend individuality and difference, while also bringing different elements together, are "erotic" in this specific sense. By contrast, cultures that foster and defend "the spirit of the Herd," as Nietzsche would say, cultures that aim to destroy individuality and difference, are thanatotic. George Orwell's *1984*, as we will see later on, provided an extreme and dystopic view into this idea. Durkheim's notion of altruistic suicide also provides an extreme example of this thanatotic type of social order. Such thanatotic cultures privilege the *status quo ante*: they privilege the given over the new, the past over the future, and actuality over possibility. By contrast Eros privileges the new, difference, the future, and possibility. On the other hand, thanatotic cultures may also aim to destroy the sense of organic *connection* between individuals and their social order, and here we may use the Durkhemian notion of anomy. Anomic suicides provide examples of this literally thanatotic sense of disconnection. Such societies destroy any sense of *status quo*, and the sense of organic connectedness between the individual and the group.

Note also that, because Eros and eroticism can be channels for individuality and for difference, they therefore carry the potential for instability. Not coincidentally, sexuality has historically been a critical aspect of social instability and thus of social control. Because of this potential for instability, Eros is targeted by social mechanisms of repression in various ways and degrees, which, if effective, dilute the activity of this life-principle and strengthen the activity of Thanatos. The individual may thus lose a sense of the ownmost, become much more attuned to the social code, and may relinquish her capacity for individuation. Consider, for example, the institutional mechanisms that Christianity has deployed to control "the flesh," often aiming to eliminate precisely the ownmost element of desire and individuality, to therefore render the believer utterly open to the will of the Church, to the Lord — to the will of the Other, as I will further discuss in a subsequent chapter. (On the other hand, if societies have weak repressive mechanisms, and thus cannot contain the individuating capacities of Eros, anomy may result.)

Eros and Capitalism

Back to capitalism, this system has also devised mechanisms to channel the differentiating and individualizing activity of sexuality and eroticism, as Marcuse also implies. He says that this system has deployed a "surplus repression," which has altered various aspects of eroticism and sexuality. In capitalistic societies we find "eroticism" everywhere, because desire, including sexual desire, is of course always promoted by the market. But desire here is mixed with thanatotic — that is, undifferentiating, equalizing, de-individualizing — characteristics. Inasmuch as desire is, so to speak, standardized, "focus-grouped," readymade, the individualizing potential of Eros is effectively repressed. Bear in mind that desire in general and sexual desire in particular, are key targets of, and vehicles for, the market (e.g., Reichert 2002); and that desire in fact tends to be mass-mediated in the double sense of the word: broadcasted and elicited by the media, but also, back to Hegel, mediated: invested by external interests, which are not necessarily concordant with those of the individual. It is not only that the preferences and emotional responses of the consumer are often influenced by the stream of images and the interests behind them. Rather, the larger point is that the actual experience of desire may itself become mediated and transformed into a functional element of the market. Aspects of eroticism and sexuality may be manufactured by the cultural industry, as anyone familiar with marketing techniques may agree, so as to fulfill not personal but systemic needs and goals.

Taking a clue from *Civilization and its Discontents*, Marcuse implies, in summary, that such systematic and indeed sophisticated repression and exploitation of Eros has been an important requisite for the formation of the subject under capitalism. A subject whose desires had to be abetted, but whose actual ownmost wants had to be inhibited, at least to the point of rendering him open to external economic needs. I argue that, inasmuch as capitalism thus modifies aspects of desire, it modifies aspects of embodied collective memories, as desire, including sexual desire, provides important dynamics for the constitution of these bio-psycho-social structures.

It is also worth noting Slavoj Žižek's perspective at this point: civilization today, we may infer from him, rather than striving to repress Eros, attempts to seduce it. In contrast to Marcuse, Žižek says that capitalism today is not a repressive system in any classical sense. On the contrary, it purports to speak on behalf of Eros itself, constantly pushing us to "enjoy" (i.e., to consume). And yet, this economic system tells consumers not simply to enjoy but it tells them how to enjoy. It doesn't tell them what to desire or what to buy, but how to desire, how to expend and invest their libidinal resources. The market, in this sense, "clarifies" the very nature of desire for us. Žižek seems to imply, that is to say, that civilization today is the bearer of discontent not because it represses desire, but because it encourages heteronomic forms of desire. So that it becomes even more difficult for us to know not only the actual nature of our own wants — but the nature of desire as such. Of course consciousness is already a veil that hides the deeper aspects of desire (which, again, is already encultured and partly molded by social norms). But capitalism, we infer from Žižek, purporting to unveil Eros, to "show" us our desires — thereby hides them in a much more recondite manner. In a sense, here we are back with a theory of symbolic violence, and with the idea that heteronomic wants, rooted primarily in external needs, can dynamize the key aspects of subjectivity: the identity and the wants of the subject, in particular.

But if Eros and sexuality can be colonized via various forms of repression or, as Žižek may agree, via the seduction of desire itself, such processes are never permanent or secure, as Marcuse also implied. Eros, Norman Brown says, is "an indestructible demand of human nature" (1985, 40). Back to Marcuse, he wrote *Eros and Civilization* in 1955, a time that hadn't seen the full impact of the sexual revolutions of the 1960s (which were partly aided by his ideas). In retrospect, however, we see that, through these sexual and countercultural revolutions, Eros returned; and that its return encouraged new individualities and new differences (e.g., feminist and gay), locally and eventually globally, which were not merely the effects of this economic system. Indeed, these new collective processes emerged to transform at least some aspects of this system. Such processes still emerge, and are still transforming dominant discourses about (hetero)sexuality, laws about marriage, prevalent definitions of family, etc. They emerge to transform social, legal, ideological parameters.

Sexuality and eroticism, in summary, also involve a merging of biological and cultural horizons. In capitalism, the latter, reinforced by the market and the cultural industry, may change important aspects of the former. But drives return with life itself. As argued, life feeds from instinctual, endogenous, ownmost impulses that, though easily suppressed, are difficult to colonize securely and permanently. Eros may therefore return to demarcate new parameters and possibilities, new social dynamics, new public spheres (e.g., gay, feminist).

THANATOS (DEATH)

But just as these colonizing processes are never permanent or secure, the expressions of Eros, immortal as they are, are not permanent or secure either. Eros always confronts a thanatotic principle of equalization and indifferentiation that, as indicated, is also at the core of life itself. Again, as culture is confronted with the individualizing activity of Eros, it is also confronted with potential instability, and therefore the social order tends to deploy defenses against Eros, in different ways and degrees. Bear in mind that, to twist the famous phrase from Nietzsche, Eros is constructive destruction, emphasis on "destruction." Feminism, gayness, the sexual revolutions mentioned above, for example, sponsored new desires, perspectives, identities, and social struc-tures — while thereby destabilizing the given order of things and the iden-tities rooted in it. And thus, such destabilizing ideas and movements were confronted, indeed attacked by the institutions in charge of maintaining the systemic order: those of the church, the family, the law (again, under sodomy laws, oral sex was a felony punishable with jail, up to 2003).

Again, Thanatos is the biological principle that, limiting individuality and individual perspectives, also limits complexity. As we saw, it is paradoxical-ly vital that living things die to provide energy for life; so that, as it is vital for life to be limited, life's striving for complexity always has limits as well. But importantly, Thanatos thus limits the destabilizing potential of Eros. And just as this principle applies to the life system, it also applies to social sys-tems. Thanatos is also necessary for social systems, as it can provide a measure of stability for them. Indeed, as such Thanatos can be appealing to the individual and to the group. As it inhibits individualistic demands, Tha-natos relieves the individual from the anxieties that often result from pursu-ing new and different existential avenues, and the conflicts that likely result when the person makes choices that go against the collective order. And the social actor may therefore embrace a thanatotic, inertial (inert) disposition, precisely to avoid the expenditures of energy required by Eros. As it helps us avoid the unhomeliness of difference, Thanatos can make our life easier in this limited and closeted sense, lulling the individual and the collective into a sort of dogmatic slumber.

Temporally, if Eros fosters new things and therefore new futures, Thana-tos fosters given things and the past, as previously implied. As we may infer from Alan Bass (2000), Thanatos involves unconscious defenses that target not the traumas of the past, but the idea of the new, the future, which can also have traumatic qualities. From a sociological point of view, Thanatos may, as suggested, manifest itself as a cultural tendency to diminish difference, to sponsor an evenness of vision, dogmatic ideas, related institutions, inert-ial traditions. Fundamentalist and dogmatic orders are thanatotic. (And to be sure, radical fundamentalisms aim not only to eliminate differences in an abstract sense, but also in a concrete sense — for example, infidels, gays, Jewish people, Palestinians. Thanatos has been, in a literal sense, a death-principle that provides punctuation marks for history.)

Thanatos, in summary, is a principle of destruction of differential ele-ments and, if limited by Eros, may therefore work as a principle of stability.

When subjectivity collapses — for instance, via symbolic violence or altruistic suicide — the connection between the person and the world acquires a thanatotic, *non-relational* character (again, catastrophic loss of memory is also thanatotic as it eliminates relational ties). Here, internal-external tensions are lessened, and related expenditures of endogenous energy are also lessened. If Eros spends energy affirming individuality, Thanatos saves energy to contain it, and thus provides rest, a break from being "condemned to be an individual," as Nietzsche mockingly says. (And death involves no expenditure of energy at all, a final sense of "rest," as we colloquially say.) When such thanatotic mode of being is activated, the ownmost demands of the individual are lessened; and the internal world therefore becomes vulnerable to external demands, even to the point where the individual, having disavowed his ownmost claims, takes the next logical step and aims to destroy himself. Again, symbolic violence is possible insofar human nature carries a thanatotic drive that limits ownmost aspects of individuality, thus eliciting a sense of passive and inertial acceptance of external things. Yet, symbolic violence is not secure and complete either, because human nature as such also carries an erotic drive that returns to affirm ownmost claims. This is also an important aspect in the development of habitus and of embodied memory in general.

NOTES

1. Apuleius and others have noted that a mortal woman named Soul (Psyche) felt in love with this agent of the between, Eros, thereby herself becoming immortal, daemonic. A spark of immortality, however, was left in the human body from which she was released. This is why Immortality always comes to meet us after we die, to claim a portion of its own lineage, our soul, which is thus released from the mortal body. The human soul is thus erotic in nature, the point of connection between becoming and being, mortality and immortality.

2. But even Narcissus, awaiting on the Meniscus "for the stranger who could make [him] happy," addresses the boy in the water in the second person: "you laugh when I laugh, I have watched your tears through my tears." When he discovers his curse and asks for death and death is given, he still addresses the Other vanishing under the surface of the water: "farewell, you incomparable boy, I have loved you in vain."

3. Though, again, this does not mean that Eros is a principle of democratic dialogue between the internal world and the world, as this encounter can have, in the end, good or bad or mixed consequences for the individual.

Chapter Seven

The Subject (Ontogeny)

OCEANIC BEGINNINGS

The previous two chapters provided a phylogenic view of the development of consciousness and how it emerges as the species-memory goes out to meet the world. These chapters also suggest that thus embodied memory also emerges. In this and the next chapters, I provide an ontogenetic view. Below I argue that the individual also surfaces from the impersonal domain of the species-memory, that culture pries us away from this domain, and that thus we grow a personal and yet collectivized embodied memory.

As I suggested, all creatures in the zoological spectrum, the human infant included, have to have some degree of self-awareness; and even amoebas need mechanisms of self-recognition, if only to avoid eating their own bodies. But the self-awareness of these lower animals is empty of epistemic content, in the sense that they are unable to take an inward turn to reflect about their sensations, perceptions, and their existence. Some animals on the higher end of the philogenetic scale are endowed with higher levels of self-awareness.[1] But, in contrast to all other living things, we are not only aware, but are *aware of our awareness*. We possess a "meta-awareness," as Ramachandran says (in Blackmore 2000, 188-189). We have thoughts about our thoughts, the ability to represent representations, a sense of distance from ourselves, as though "another parasitic brain," Ramachandran says, were using "the input of the 'first' brain as its input" (ibid.). We are thus the only beings, to paraphrase Heidegger, through which the question of being can come into question, an ability that involved, as Ramachandran says, a "quantum jump in the mind of an ape" (ibid.). Surely, our capacity for self-awareness is limited and limiting, as we will see soon. But we are the only known beings able to turn the apparatus of sensation and cognition inwardly to hence question its origins, its presence and its possibilities. According to Kant, this capacity to say "I," the ability of the self to name itself, is what fundamentally makes us human. For only as the self becomes its own object of understanding, Kant says, can the road to self-knowledge open up along with the possibility of self-mastery and that of (moral) self-judgment.

But back to the human infant, she is not born with this sense of meta-awareness and, in this sense, does not have a clear sense of self. Bear in mind that we are not only born in a state of dependence but, as Freud has argued (1926), we are born prematurely (also, Lacan 1977), unfit for life, bearing premature senses and motor mechanisms, profound insufficiencies that we overcome only because we have the help of others. (Again, a member of a profoundly social species, the infant may not survive without human contact — even if all her physical needs, warmth, food, etc., are met.[2]) As Margaret Mahler suggests, we are indeed thrown into the world at a point in life that does not coincide with the birth of the self (Mahler 2000).[3] This helpless infant, as we will see, cannot experience a clear sense of individuation and separateness with respect to the external world (ibid.). The baby, the late Freud argued, is marked by an "oceanic feeling," which precludes her from experiencing the distinct Cartesian divide between subject and object, between self and other — between baby and breast, for example. (Overcoming his original Cartesianism, the late Freud says that the baby cannot *have* the breast. The baby, he says, "*is* the breast" [1941f, 1938, my emphasis].) Unable to re-present objects via symbols, the baby is also unable to take either a conceptual or an ontological leap away from objects. And, as Piaget has shown (1977), she is indeed unable to see objects as objects: as distinct and permanent things. A bearer of primitive cognitive and memorial capacities, she thus gazes at an alien world that, invested with the sense of impermanence, appears to be in constant flight from itself. And this impermanent world, to borrow a phrase from Heidegger, returns her gaze "with the inexorability of an enigma." At this primary-narcissistic stage, the baby thus lacks a Cartesian sense of subjectivity, which emerges developmentally, as certain conditions become aligned. [4]

A clear and distinct sense of ownership over the first person perspective emerges, firstly, as the baby develops a bodily schema. This neural map of the body, which provides implicit knowledge of the position of hands, legs, posture and movement within space, is undeveloped at birth (or perhaps absent as Simmel argues [1958]). It appears to develop only in-the-world, as the baby begins to explore objects and to mirror people (Iacoboni 2009). As this body schema develops in contact with the world, beyond the uterine relation between body and space, it provides a sense of bodily integration and unity that allows the baby to feel, as we say, like "some-body" — like a Dasein, in the Heideggerian sense. As the brain maps the relation body-world via sensory-motor information, the Heideggerian sense of "being-there" (Dasein) begins to be constituted (though as we will see, symbols, and the capacity of the self to name itself, will add another dimension to the feeling of being-there).

The body schema — wherein embodied memory will develop in connection to the world — gives the infant an objective awareness of her own body, which helps ground, psychologically, the sense of self-awareness. Otherwise, much as the external objects around her, her body is also invested with rather Piagetan, apparitional qualities; so that arms and legs, for example, may flutter and flail without much control or self-awareness and thus enter within a primitive perceptual-conceptual field to then fade out, as though phenomenologically adrift, as if the body were *ex-static*, outside the primitive sense of self. By contrast, this neural-corporeal map will provide the feeling of bodily unity and separateness, the organic prototype for the psychological sense of unity and self-integration. Bear in mind that, as Antonio Damasio (2005) and Marco Iacoboni (2009) would argue, the mind indeed arises only through mutual brain-body interactions. Ego-formation, Freud also argues, is in fact always linked to the somatic experience: "The ego is first and foremost a bodily ego," he says, "it is not a surface entity, but is itself the projection of a surface" (1927). The ego, this "mass of neurons" with good facilitations connecting them, "is ultimately derived from bodily sensations, chiefly from those springing from the surface of the body. It may thus be regarded as a mental projection of the surface of the body, besides . . . representing the superficies of the mental apparatus" (1923).

Secondly, this sense of ego-integration and differentiation also emerges hand in hand with symbolic capacities, particularly with our capacity to represent this newfound bodily unity, our ability to say "I." Symbols pry the external world apart from the internal world; so that when the child is finally able to say "you," for example, she thus establishes a distance between "you" and "me."[5] As she re-presents external objects, she emerges, almost as in Martin Buber, as an "I." Naming external things, that is to say, also helps her emerge as the bearer of an egoic, first-person perspective.

Note, as well, that this embodied and symbolically mediated ego arises only as the infant mirrors others (Iacoboni 2009). As we saw, Iacoboni asks, "How can we even think of the 'self' except in terms of the 'other' that the self is not? Without self, it makes little sense to define an other, and without that other, it does not make a lot of sense to define the self" (ibid., 133). These symbolic and embodied boundaries that provide a sense of separation and integration for the ego are always othered. As suggested in a previous chapter, they are always co-constituted (and thus any sense of proto-self that may exist *in utero* or at birth will be merely embryonic). Hence, these symbolic and embodied boundaries provide a sense of separation but also of connectedness, so that the person is never radically individuated in the Cartesian sense. The sense of a unitary self involves embodied and symbolic dimensions that are always othered. Only thus we begin to construct, back to Heidegger, the ontic illusion of ontological separateness.

Importantly, as we climb beyond the nebulous domain of the species-memory and thus grasp this sense of ownership over the first person perspective, a bodily memory also begins to develop, set in motion by the body schema. This schema maps the ongoing relation between body and physical space, and the embodied memory records the ongoing relation between body and social space. The schema provides organic unity and individuality but also the sense of connectness with physical space. Bodily memory provides organic unity but also the sense of connectedness to a shared social space and to a common past.

The person, in summary, emerges as the species-wide embodied memory receives external input (cultural, institutional) that modifies species-wide demands. This input separates us from, and attaches us to, the external world. As we build a bodily memory that grows hand in hand with the cognitive and encultured aspects of memory, we become invested with our familiar and specific sense of singularity. We develop this familiar sense of embodied self-ownership, and the sense of wholeness and of ontological permanence. The self thus emerges as its own object among other external objects that populate the world. (Though of course this embodied self emerges as a very unique object, as the only "lived-object," as Merleau-Ponty says.)

Objects, Needs, and Desires

It is important to clarify that almost as soon as they can see, human infants react to objects, for example to faces (with a "goony grin," Karl Sagan says; see e.g., Meltzoff and Moore 1977), and that even shortly after birth this baby may reflexively react to the mother's smell and voice, as Daniel Stern has shown (1984). But these faces and these objects, even the mother, are not objective Cartesian entities. Again, things acquire their Cartesian objectivity only as the self emerges as an object unto itself. Bear in mind that, back to Piaget, the things that confront the infant are marked by impermanence and thus imbued with apparitional qualities. They drift in from nowhere, enter into a fledging perceptual-conceptual field, and then drift out, as if devoid, precisely, of ontological stability (Piaget 1977). The world of this infant, in general, may be described as an apparitional world, and even the mother may be described as an apparitional mother. (Initially, she is a known but unthought entity, a scent that elicits reflexive responses, a known sound that fades into the world to amend the qualities of existence, to then fade out.) Only by month five or so, as Margaret Mahler argues (2000), this formerly "oceanic" baby begins to see primary objects, such as the mother, as distinct objects. From month five to ten, Mahler also shows, the infant identifies primary and secondary objects (e.g., mother and toys, respectively) as distinct objects. And again, as he develops basic motor abilities that allow him to explore the world, and as he thus progresses in terms of body integration and in terms of the bodily and symbolic aspects of memory, he also emerges as an object unto himself. (According to Lacan [2005], the discovery of the self occurs from the sixth to the eighteenth month of life, particularly when the baby recognizes himself in a mirror, though, Lacan says, all kinds of things in the world "behave like mirrors.")

Importantly, the pre-objective, oceanic world of the infant was often at rest, but, to insist on an important point, it was also cyclically filled with sensations and wants that were not moored to symbols or to representation. Pains and rages erupted within this early existential domain, spread, omnipotently transformed the quality of existence, and then disappeared, as meaninglessly as they arose. On the other hand, the infant was also cradled by unthought and, to borrow from Winnicott, "all-holding" pleasures (1986, 1989); pleasures that, not moored to an individuated ego, also had all-encompassing and fluid characteristics. This baby was cyclically encircled by sensations, smells, tonalities of sound — by gratifications and pains that arose, spread, and vanished in a rather benighted manner. Eventually, however, these sensations also acquired objective, rather Cartesian qualities, as we will see. Eventually, the unconscious and the conscious become clearly separated. And thus, the differentiated, "objective" and conscious ego acquired a degree of control and input over them. Hence the ego comes to have some control over the aspects of personhood — and of the embodied memory attached to it — which are dynamized by want.

To put it differently, the early, oceanic sensations and needs were not owned by an embodied, objective, self-referential ego. Only needs drove this elemental world — not desires, as desire involves a differentiated subject (who desires) an object (of desire) and the capacity of representation mediating in between. This infant experienced not desires but impulses detached from both an embodied ego and a symbolic register. These impulses were fundamentally physiological, known but unthought, meaningful primarily at the level of the body, existentially. The baby who cannot say "I," and who is therefore beyond the embodied Cartesian ego, cannot experience want in a proprietary, ego-mediated manner. (So that the hunger of the baby, for example, involves a throng of sensations devoid of egoic categories of representation, devoid of objectivity, and devoid of a clear sense of ownership over the sensation. This means that only from the point of view of a detached observer we may say that "the baby is hungry," but from the point of view of the baby we may first say that he "is hunger.") From the point of view of the infant, needs may be described as rather autonomous forces that emanate from a benighted domain, the domain of species memory, which defines his primary mode of existence.

But as the baby climbs past the domain of the species memory, and thus develops a clear and objective sense of self, desire appears. Now want is linked not only to the species, but to three ("total") sources that, in various ways and degrees, contribute to its nature, the nature of want itself. These are: the body (the original source of want), culture, and the subject herself (who, often caught between bodily and cultural/social demands, attempts to manage and negotiate resulting conflicts). Bear in mind that, in contrast to the baby, the autonomous Cartesian self will not only experience desire, but will also be able to observe it, objectively, and will thus be able to have input and some control over it (by contrast, the baby is mostly controlled by need). As I will argue below, the development of naturalized dispositions, habit-us — and embodied memory — will be responsive to this total motivic structure, involving the body, the self, and culture, which in turn are related, respectively, to the id, the ego, and the superego.

A Summary: The Ego and its Embodied Memory

Once it emerges, the differentiated ego will be in charge of channeling inter-nal, id-related energies and finding external objects that may alleviate endog-enous homeostatic pressures. But it will also filter these energies to prevent their automatic, reflexive expression (otherwise gregariousness, the domain of ego, is jeopardized). The ego may also try to disavow these internal wants, but in general it tries to disguise them, to make them socially acceptable, before accepting them itself, before integrating them into its existential do-main. As an agency in charge of adaptive operations, the ego, as suggested, is constantly swayed by the attempts of the outside world to establish its "em-pire over consciousness," as Durkheim may agree. The reality principle, as it speaks on behalf of gregariousness, carries the power of the community and can therefore mark the desires, thoughts, behaviors, and dispositions attached to the ego. But the ego is also swayed by constant internal pressures to seek pleasure and to avoid unpleasure, even at the expense of gregariousness. Back to Marcuse, the fact that the reality principle has to constantly reassert itself, "indicates that its triumph over the pleasure principle is never complete and never secure" (1962, 15). If the reality principle feeds from the social order, the pleasure principle feeds from the largest container of psychical energy, the id, and thus the ego is often "overtaken," as we colloquially say, by "the wild, strange tyranny of [the] body," to use D.H. Lawrence's image, by id-related subverting tendencies.

Note also that, as the ego often fails as an agency of containment, a higher censor emerges, developmentally, to further inhibit pre-social claims.[6] This internal lawgiver, superego, is more effective in suppressing these at times tyrannical claims, mainly by converting them via mechanisms of sublimation or through compromise formations. But this super-adaptive part of the self is not free of failures either; and even under its rule, the id continues to exert pressures over the ego, such that we may also slip, and want and behave outside the norm, for better and for worse. The ego, the holder of the first person perspective, is therefore often caught between this idealized version of itself, superego, and the material and bodily pressures that often limit its idealized goals from being fulfilled. Indeed, this seemingly unitary and Cartesian portion of the self is sometimes split between these poles. On the one hand, the most elemental claims of the person encounter superegoic obstacles against fulfillment; and, on the other, altruistic, superegoic, social impulses are burdened by lower pressures that compete for fulfillment.[7] These higher and lower demands provide motives, the dynamics for the development of ego and for the development of habits and habitus. Thus, aspects of embodied memory emerge via a tripartite economy involving the demands of the id, those of superego, and the conciliatory activity of ego mediating in between.

To conclude this chapter, it is worth noting that, at best, superego may usher in ethical capacities and a heightened ability to engage in a social contract. But at worst, it can inhibit ownmost, authentic desires, and can thus usher in symbolic violence. Under the influence of superego, the ego may primarily speak on behalf of the Other. And on behalf of the Other the ego may become its own censor.[8] The id, on the other hand, at best resembles Mead's "I," which represents not the conscious ego but "the response of the organism" itself, Mead says, "to the attitudes of the others" (1934, 175). And much as the Meadean "I," the id is also an agency that *resists* the demands of the social order, and can therefore give us the sense of spontaneity and freedom. Under the influence of the id, the conscious ego may primarily speak on behalf of the self, defend ownmost claims, and deflect the claims of the Other. But the id is also the source of wants and drives that can be unsettling and dangerous for the encultured ego. At worst, the unpredictable Id can result in anomic and self-defeating impulses and behaviors. These superegoic and id-related demands, good, bad and mixed, form a structure of possibilities for embodied memory.

NOTES

1. Chimpanzees , for instance, seem to recognize their own image in the mirror (Gallup 1970) and probably have a primitive first-person ontology and a minimum of self-reflective capacities.

2. Discovered by Rene Spitz (1897), these deficits were initially known as "hospitalism" and subsequently categorized as "pediatric failure to thrive." Psychosomatic deficits resulting from lack of contact include mental and *physical* retardation and, in severe cases, death.

3. When referencing Mahler one must note that her initial ideas about the "normal autistic phase," with which Mahler attempted to describe the first five weeks of life as a state of almost complete self-absorption, were discredited, particularly by the work of Daniel Stern (1984), and subsequently abandoned by Mahler. Nonetheless, her suggestion that the self, and the sense of

ownership over a first person perspective, are achieved at a stage of development which does not coincide with birth — are still helpful as I will presently show.

4. Daniel Stern provided a competing theory (1984). He experimentally tested memorial and cognitive abilities in the infant and provided groundbreaking data. In one of these experiments, the infant suckles on an artificial nipple thus activating, in an almost behaviorist fashion, an apparatus that plays the recorded voice of the mother. The infant, Stern concludes, seeks out this voice because he "recognizes" the voice of the mother (ibid., 2-3). The quality of the data notwithstanding, this interpretation is excessive. The notion of re-cognition (emphasis on the prefix) suggests a meta-awareness, a cognition of the cognition, a re-cognition of the mother's voice. Stern's conclusion implies that subject-object abilities are present in an infant that bears a first-person ontology. But the baby *cognizes* a familiar sound marked with positive valences, reflexively reacting to its presence. Re-cognition is absent in this pre-symbolic infant.

5. The pre-symbolic infant is yet to emerge as a self-reflective "I." Insofar as she cannot represent herself, she in fact has an impersonal existence largely dominated by the id, the IT, the German "Es": an individual and internal and yet not personal agency. The id sometimes overrides the conscious ego (we are "overtaken," we colloquially say). At some level the demands of the id are known to the infant (at an "existential" level, as Winnicott may say), but they are unknown to her at the level of cognition, thought, or representation.

6. This higher agency, Freud says, is born the moment in which incestual demands are repressed by the symbolic presence of the father (the Oedipus Complex). The father figure enters into a domain formerly dominated by primal libidinal demands as the initial enforcer of the reality principle. The child gives up his oedipal demands and transforms them into a mechanism of identification. Thus the prohibition is internalized, and superego emerges as the psychical representative of the law.

7. Of course id and superego provide degrees of satisfaction. The former can fulfill elemental and private wants, and the latter can fulfill desires associated with gregariousness. But much as the satisfactions provided by the id, the satisfactions provided by superego also tend to leap back to want, and thus back to lack, because they are in constant tension against lower needs competing, at times successfully, for resolution. As in Plato's Symposium (1953), where Aristophanes explains that we are constantly seeking a missing part of ourselves. The ego is constantly seeking out objects to fulfill its existential lack (objects related to friendship, love, ideology, religion, etc.); objects that, however, often stand as mere metaphors for elemental, oceanic satisfactions that the adult experiences to the extent to which they fulfill the requirements of the social contract and its representative, superego. This existential lack is an important aspect of our motivic structure. Lack is therefore part of the dynamics that generate dispositions, habituses, aspects of embodied memory.

8. Superego is an agency that at its worst involves internalized demands that are indeed pathogenic and pathological in nature. At worst, superego can be a Kafkian creature in the business of enforcing injunctions that issue from the remote, largely unknown, and yet all-present Castle of trauma. A maternal superego drives Norman Bates, the leading character in Hitchcock's psychological thriller Psycho, to commit the atrocities famously depicted by the film.

Chapter Eight

Biology and Meaning (Phylogeny)

THE SPEAKING SUBJECT (PHYLOGENY)

As suggested, the reality of ego largely stems from perception-consciousness, a system that, involving the sensory periphery and the central nervous system, is designed to discern "external and internal perceptions from psychical phenomena as a whole" (Laplanche-Pontalis 1973, 84). As the point of connection between the internal and the external world, this system processes sense data so that quantities (e.g., electrochemical), exogenous and endogenous, are transduced as qualities (e.g., meanings), as "indications of reality," Freud says.[1] Consider "redness," for example. It stems from objective factors in the world, but these factors become "redness" only through perception-consciousness; only as quanta enter into this system to take a "mysterious leap," Freud says, into the domain of qualia.[2] Think of an apple. Redness and sweetness are not, in Kantian terms, in the apple itself. Instead, they are processes through which we model the combinations of carbon, hydrogen, oxygen in the apple, according to our perceptual and conceptual capacities and limitations. Sweetness is the meeting of external and internal factors. It involves these combinations of carbon, hydrogen, oxygen, plus gustative papillae, nerve firing, synaptic interactions — and then the Freudian mysterious leap into the subjective experience.[3] And of course not only the apple but the world is devoid of sweetness. Indeed, in itself the world is devoid of "beauty," "mystery," "luminosity," etc, which also point toward the nature of perception-consciousness, and toward the vicissitudes of our species-memory (as we will see, the world does not disclose itself as beautiful to a lion, for example). Naturally, aspects of the world are "beautiful" for us. But the idea is that their beauty is in the eye of the beholder: that beauty emerges from the point of view of human consciousness.

Again, the reality that the ego experiences is not reality as such; and indeed egoic reality implies a flight from reality in itself, a leap into a standardized domain of meanings and symbols that purport to represent reality. These meanings and symbols in fact arrest reality-processes. They aim to catch reality within relatively stable and standardized parameters of meaning; and thus words, to borrow the image from Lacan, are like "gravestones," as they point toward a reality that they cannot quite reach, and as they are therefore like dead pieces of reality. To borrow now from Nietzsche, words and concepts are like "dissected birds."

Note also that, if words are removed from the external reality as such, they are also removed from strictly private, internal sensations. My toothache is, in itself, incommunicable, because it is confined to my consciousness. Yet, the word "pain" provides the illusion that we all can understand it. Similarly, "sweetness" also stems from a strictly private experience, which remains inaccessible to all but the experiencing subject himself. Yet, as this word provides a seemingly fixed and shared category of reality, reality seems accessible to everyone who shares this meaning. It is because speakers partake from the same "bastard logic" of words, as Plato would say, that we can experience the illusion of a common external reality. Hence, if words are "gravestones," if they are weak versions of reality, they are also the foundations of the human experience. They bring speakers together. It is precisely because words are removed from the thing itself — and thus re-present reality in ways that are accessible to all who share the same words — that they can provide a shared domain of meaning for all speaking subjects.

Let me discuss a story from *El Quixote*, to provide an example. One of Sancho's kinsmen takes a sip of wine from a barrel and "gives . . . his verdict in favour of the wine; but with the reserve of a taste of iron." He was "ridiculed for this judgment. But who laughed in the end? On emptying the hogshead, there was found at the bottom, an old key" (in Hume 1757). I cannot detect any nuances in wine; my palate is not that of Sancho's kinsman; his world of flavors and sensations is not mine; his experience of reality is not mine, and I can only inferentially and analogically imagine it. But because both of us share such words as "sweet," we also share a degree of epistemic symmetry, and have the impression that we partake from a reality that simply emanates from the external world. Naturally, all human beings have a degree of phenomenological and epistemic symmetry: as we saw, we can understand others from body to body, as Bourdieu says; we can model in our brains the suffering of others; our mirror cells can model their emotions, embarrassment, movements (Iacoboni 2009). But as I cannot button up their nervous system around mine, their experience of reality remains private, and I can understand it only inferentially and analogically, as the example provided by Sancho suggests. (And sometimes these inferences are deceiving. For example, some people may have a much higher tolerance of pain, so that my understanding of their pain will be biased by my own and relatively hypersensitive experiences with pain. As Wall and Melzack report, in

> East Africa, men and women undergo an operation entirely without anaesthetics or pain reliving drugs . . . as the man or woman sits calmly, without flinching or grimacing, holding a pan under their chin to catch the dripping blood. Films of this procedure are extraordinary to watch because of the discomfort they induce in the observers, which is *in striking contrast* to the apparent lack of discomfort in the people undergoing the operation. [1996, 17]

I understand that these men and women undergo "pain," but I don't have an isomorphic sense of their pain).

Note also that, much as symbols themselves, the memory traces that these symbols invoke are typically one step removed, as well, from the reality that they purport to store and re-present. Perception-consciousness facilitates the storage of quantities, via neuromodulatory facilitations, and their recall as qualities, particularly via symbols and words. But when thus re-called, called anew, the original events at the root of memory traces are often distorted (particularly if the connection between images and their traces involve limited reinforcement). As Halbwach may agree, total recall is not typical at all, and recall typically involves re-creations, re-constructions of the past. Much as words, memories also tend to filter reality. And in this sense, as well, the conscious subject inhabits not reality as such, but a certain domain of meaning that seems to be reality itself.

Embodiment and Meaning: "If a Lion Could Talk"

This domain of symbols and meanings seems to remove the speaking subject from the oceanic obscurities of biology, transporting him into a higher and indeed more real domain, as Plato would say, the domain of ideas (which for Plato is more real, as we saw in the previous chapter). Ideas, conceptual abstractions, as Plato also argued, seem removed from the body. They do not seem biologically rooted or mediated. Instead they appear to belong to an altogether different dimension of subjectivity with an ontological status of its own.[4] Yet, as we will presently see, symbols do not release the speaking subject "above" the body, to a higher reality. Instead, they remain largely attached to, and even dependent on, bodily processes, which often mark abstractions with the stamp of their "lower" nature.

Indeed, abstractions are phylogenetically rooted in the species memory (again, the ground of embodied memory; in subsequent chapters we will see that abstractions are also rooted in culturally mediated aspects of embodiment, in embodied collective memories). Consider, for example, Wittgenstein's famous remark that "if a lion could talk, we could not understand him" (1958). Suggested by this widely debated phrase is that we would not be able to understand the speaking lion because its mind and meanings would necessarily partake from its own life form, from the nature of its nature — not from ours. What Wittgenstein seems to imply is that words and meanings are linked to the shape of our muscles, to our teeth and nails (as opposed to claws), to our musculoskeletal frame, and to the biological needs that these bodily things satisfy. The speaking lion and I share the same symbolic parameters (English), but the animal speaks through its own semiotic parameters: through its own needs, drives, through its own body. Because these needs are foreign to my life-form, related meanings escape my understanding. I can only understand this animal inferentially, through my own embodied perspective. A dialogue with the lion would resemble, back to Lacan, an exchange of gravestones, an exchange of symbols that would point to different experiences.

But what if, as Jenny Teichman has quipped (in Burns 1994), the lion said, "Ludwig, I'm going to eat you all up"? Wouldn't that be understandable? In this sense, we would of course understand the lion, crisply and urgently. But insofar as it is not in *my* nature to say, "Ludwig, I'm going to eat you all up" — while sensing the predatory drive suggested by this phrase — the sentence is still incomprehensible to me. As I cannot button up the animal's musculoskeletal frame around mine to then look through its hungry eyes, Teichman's sentence is beyond my phenomenological horizon. The illusion that I understand the lion, hinges on the symbolic isomorphism between the lion's words and my words. But beyond that, there is no pre-linguistic isomorphism, and thus no epistemic or phenomenological symmetry between us. All speaking lions, from Aesop to Disney, provide a mirror of our minds, of our own species-memory. And of course the speaking lion doesn't understand me, either. When I tell him that lions are "ferocious," "predatorial," etc., I am invoking an evolutionary need of my own species, the need to communicate clawless distress to peers. "Ferocious" indicates that the predatory capacities of my species were long ago detached from the sheer mechanics of our bodies, attached to our brains, and then extended, via hands and opposable thumbs, to tools, stones, spears, guns — to the domain of culture. Having no thumbs, the speaking lion cannot fully grasp the meanings underpinning "ferocity," as this word is a miniaturized version of our own species-memory, and is invested by, and limited to, the attributes of our life-form.

Meaning, in other words, and related symbols and words, are rooted in our life-form, in our phylogenetic past. Our consciousness is not only alloyed with sensations such as pleasure and pain, as suggested previously, but also with fingernails, teeth — with the embodied experience in general. Our sphere of meaning does not issue from a brain in a vat, but from a brain connected to the world through an upright posture, certain parameters of vision, speed and smell, through non-seasonal sexuality. Only through these things does our brain invoke certain meanings, and addresses certain dimensions of reality. Back to Freud, biology is destiny because it has taken us, phylogenetically, to a certain sphere of meaning. Importantly, Freud is not making the obvious and already redundant claim that one needs a body to think. He is making the less obvious claim that human meanings are very much invested by the human body, and enabled and limited by it. Furthermore, the idea is that, as Lakoff and Johnson explain, "the very structure of reason itself comes from the details of our embodiment ... Thus, to understand reason we must understand the details of our visual system, our motor system, and the general mechanism of neural binding" (1999, 4). Let me quote Antonio Damasio,

> [T]he mind arises from activity in neural circuits, to be sure, but many of those circuits were shaped in evolution by functional requisites of the organism, and . . . a normal mind will happen only if those circuits contain basic representations of the organism, and if they continue monitoring the states of the organism in action. In brief, neural circuits represent the organism continuously, as it is perturbed by stimuli from the physical and sociocultural environments, and as it acts on those environments. If the basic topic of those representations were not an organism anchored in the body, we might have some form of mind, but I doubt that it would be the mind we do have . . . I am not saying that the mind is the body. I am saying that the body contributes more than life support and modulatory effects to the brain. It contributes a content that is part and parcel of the workings of the normal mind. (2005, 226)

Wittengstein's aphorism, in summary, has a Protagorean ring that suggests that "man" is the measure of his meanings, just as the lion is the measure of its own meanings. "Man," Protagoras said, "is the measure of all things, of things which are . . . and of things which are not." Our body as a whole is the measure of meanings which are and which are not. As Ernst Mach argued, meaning is largely attached to our sensorial capacities and limitations; so that, the Kantian Mach said, we do not measure the thing in itself, *das Ding an sich*, but the possibilities of our nature. Schopenhauer said that the world "hangs on the thread of consciousness." The world, more precisely, hangs on the thread of an embodied consciousness, a consciousness that in fact is not possible but as embodied.

To conclude this chapter, let me discuss the concept of time once again, and how this purportedly a-priori idea is also rooted in the body. Back to Kant, he is arguably the most important proponent of the notion that time is a "pure intuition" unrelated to the embodied experience, proof of a very important and disembodied dimension of consciousness. To state his position very crudely, we may say that, for him, the concept of time is a non-experiential category of understanding because time cannot be seen, smelled, heard, touched, or tasted, and therefore cannot hinge on sensory experience. (This is why empiricism, for Kant, is a limited and limiting analytical strategy, particularly weak when it comes to the most elemental categories of meaning such as time.) As the intuition of time is in fact prior to the senses, we thus infer that it is entirely outside embodiment (and outside history).[5]

Logical as this seems, we can nonetheless still defend the idea that time is necessarily an embodied category of intuition and understanding rooted, indeed, in the species memory. Ontogenetically, time begins to tick only as we emerge from the oceanic experience described above. This allows us to grasp discreteness and separateness, which are necessary for any sense of succession or simultaneity. Naturally, the infant has successions of perceptions, but, as Piaget says (1971), she may not have the perception of succession: the sense of a time-sequence involving discrete ordinal units. It is only as the self emerges as an embodied *object among objects* — objects that are now imbued with a sense of permanence and discreteness — that trains of succession may be set in motion before the eyes of the percipient. Otherwise, during this sensorimotor stage, when objects are invested with the quality of impermanence (Piaget 1977), when things are constantly in flight from themselves, their presence is precarious; and therefore the world can hardly sponsor a clear sense of the present. Bear in mind as well that when these impermanent objects take their leave from the primitive perceptual field of the infant, they thus vanish, as though ontologically on and off, and that, as these impermanent objects cannot promise to return, they cannot sponsor a clear sense of the forthcoming either. Furthermore, having limited memorial and symbolic capacities, this baby has a limited grasp of the past as well, and cannot quite re-*present* past events. Of course, as Piaget also argues (ibid.), even the early sensorimotor baby experiences a primitive sense of time — before understanding object permanence, when, for example, she is hungry and is waiting to be fed (time as duration). But as an arithmetical construct that involves a sense that discrete things are present, have a past, or are forthcoming, time hinges on a clearer sense of objectivity, including self-objectivity. It is only as differentiated — that is to say: as embodied — and self-reflective individuals that we can begin to grasp, however precariously at first, the discreteness of time, in the clock and the calendar, for example. The sense of bodily unity and separation provides not only the organic prototype for ego-unity, as I discussed, but also for time.[6]

Philogenetically, time is related to the age-old spectacle of day and night, to the sensations of winter and summer, to the regular rhythms of nature. Rather than being an a-priori category of intuition and understanding, time is a concept that emerges through bodies that experience natural but also, back to Durkheim (1965), social rhythms. So that, as suggested, time can in fact vary with time (and place), and different cultures have stumbled upon different referents and metaphors to make sense of temporality (Lackoff and Johnson 1999; Eliade 1967, 1961).[7] Recall, finally, that, as Einstein noted, a watch doesn't provide a transcendent temporal perspective. Rather, it only caters to our "habit of thought," Einstein says, and mirrors the capacities and limitations of consciousness, which, back to Wittgenstein, mirror the capacities and limitations of our biological form. A watch caters to the vicissitudes in the history of our species. In this phylogenic sense, time is an effect of the species' embodied memory.

NOTES

1. "It is to be expected from the structure of the nervous system," Freud says, "that it consists of contrivances for transforming external quantity into quality" (in Pribram and Gill 1976, 20). Indeed the central nervous system constantly works to exclude internal and external quantities, such that qualities may emerge in their stead: "It would seem as though the characteristic of quality (that is, conscious sensation) comes about only where quantities are as far as possible excluded" (Freud 1950, 309).

2. For this, Freud has been accused of vitalism, as though he is suggesting that a spectral force is thus added to biological processes to account for subjectivity (Peterfreund and Schwartz 1971). But Freud simply suggests that we don't know the processes wherefore quanta become qualia, whereby stimuli becomes subjectivity and consciousness. Indeed, even at our own stage in the history of science — when we have hypotheses about limits of the known universe and of what lays outside it — we still do not know how, or why, nerve firing results in the experience of subjectivity. The problem is as mysterious for us as it was for Freud. As Kevin O'Reagan says, nobody seems to have found "any reasonable physic-chemical mechanism that could make that link [between the experience and the brain process]" (in Blackmore 2006, 161). The notion of qualia, incidentally, has been the subject of a well known debate (ibid.), with contenders affirming and denying their reality. But, even if at the expense of philosophical nuance, we can define qualia simply as physical sensations that can lead to a level of meaning, even to the point that they may be translated into words: sweetness, redness, etc.

3. The term "synapse" is not Freud's. He speaks of "contact barriers." As the appendix indicates, Freud's neurobiology is outdated in many ways. But the model nonetheless describes a "garden variety neurophysiology," as Pribram and Gill say (1976). It indeed anticipates, as these authors show, current advances in neuroscience, particularly concerning processes whereby stimuli enter into the psychosomatic apparatus to give way to subjective meaning and memory.

4. As suggested in a previous chapter, the history of thought in the West shows how persistent and widespread this idea has been, the idea that this subject finally moves away from all "philosophical grossness," in the phrase by Spencer; and that he therefore enters into a "higher" and "purer" domain, the archetype of which is the platonic heaven, a society of ideas that coexist in a state of purity (the archetype of the Christian heaven: a society of pure souls).

5. Bergson (1990) also argued that time is an individualistic construct, so that, as we may argue following his logic, the infant who hypothetically manages to survive and grow within a black chamber without contact and without culture, will still have a sense that time is passing. Hence, the argument goes, time is pure intuition. But this Bergsonian notion of "time" is not time in the sense that we actually sense it. For us, "time" is an arithmetical construct ontologically attached to symbols, units, seconds, seasons, winter, summer, thaw, harvest, night and day, obligations, deadlines, to notions such as youth and old age, to impending death, to expectations and regrets. Time for us is attached to culture. Back to Durkheim, it is connected, in particular, to the "rhythm of social life."

6. It is worth noting that, as Piaget also shows, the adult sense of time — the notion that independent successions or time-events are all part of a general time-system — is not present until age of eight or so. So that a child of six or seven may think that the time of an event, such as him running from point A to point B, is not really a part of the larger flow of time, but an

isolated and independent time-event. This child often conflates time and space, so that, much as there are different spaces, there are also, correspondingly, different times. For example, two children begin running at the same time from point A to point C. Child One runs faster and gets there sooner. Child Two runs slower and stops at point B — at the exact time as child One stopped at point C. Both children agree that they began the race at the same time, and stopped at the same time, but they typically do not see that they ran for the same amount of time. They may argue that the child who ran the longest space, from point A to point C, also ran the longest time (Piaget 1977).

7.   Again, Durkheim showed that time is in fact related to the regular rhythms of social life, which often follow the temporality of nature (winter, spring; sowing, harvesting); and thus, different cultures can have different intuitions and metaphors related to time (Lackoff and Johnson 1999), and different historical periods can likewise revolve around different conceptions of time (Eliade 1967, 1961). Before the invention of the mechanical clock, for example, time was more fluid. And after the clock became popularized, a sense of temporal discreteness began to appear within the collective mind. A temporal revolution was thus released. Or bear in mind the following examples: whereas Westerners point forward to indicate the future, the Peruvian Aymaras sense that the past is actually forward (Lackoff and Johnson 1999). An Aymara acquaintance told me that "things that happen in the past, such as having a child, are the ones you can see"; they are therefore "ahead," "before one's eyes." Both the Aymara and the Westerner take for granted the linearity of time. But such linearity can be disentangled from the web of history. Linearity in the West stems from the Hebrew tradition, from the messianic Jewish prophets and their ideas about the end of time, about the *eskaton* awaiting at the end of history (Eliade 1967, 1961). By contrast, pagan time was often circular. Note also that whereas pre-capitalist notions and habits related to time were often dilatory, in capitalism time became associated to economic metaphors (and behaviors) that speak of "wasting," "saving," or "investing" time. "Time," in the famous phrase by Benjamin Franklin, "is money." Time, for all these reasons, is historically variable.

Chapter Nine

Biology and Meaning (Ontogeny)

THE SPEAKING SUBJECT (ONTOGENY)

Wittengstein's aphorism helps us understand the origins of the speaking subject and how we stumbled upon a range of meanings relevant to, and circumscribed by our "life-form," he says. This long philogenetic view provides an introduction to the ways in which biology in general, and the body in particular, also frame the meanings of everyday life. In this chapter I draw primarily from Julia Kristeva who has provided a leading perspective on the embodied and the socially embedded aspects of meaning. Kristeva can add sociological detail to the discussion on Wittgenstein, and can also show that the pre-social body, the lower Durkheimian pole, contributes in its own right to the creation of collective meanings. This lower pole, we will see, at times competes effectively, in the domain of meaning, against the (higher) symbolic mechanisms of culture.

Words and Bodies

Let me discuss the connection between meaning and embodiment by focusing first on spoken words. Words are attached to all sorts of embodied mechanisms and events: to the pulse of the speaker, to his cardiac output (relaxed, exited), which often mark words, their tone, volume, emphasis, timbre, modulation. Words are attached to the cadences of respiration, signals from the eyes, facial muscles, hands, and bearing. At times these bodily things only provide the material backdrop for words to convey abstract images and meanings. But sometimes, words express meanings only as synchronized with bodily signals that, as Michael Argyle notes, "leak" important elements of information (Argyle 2007, 74-80). Yet at other times, bodily signals, rather than standing as accessories to the meaning of words, transmit meaning in their own right, consciously or unconsciously. "We speak with our vocal organs," Abercrombie reminds us, "but we converse with our whole body" (1968). As Bourdieu shows, words can in fact cease to be the main agents of meaning. Indeed, "we have seen," Argyle and colleagues report, "that NV [non-verbal] signals for interpersonal attitudes are far more powerful than initially similar verbal ones" (2007, 305). (These researchers asked subjects to rate interpersonal friendliness, neutrality, or hostility in an experimental setting; and they found that NV cues "had about five times the effect of the verbal ones on final ratings. When the two were in conflict the verbal message was largely ignored" [ibid., 92]). Interactions indeed may become significant primarily as interactors decode and feel, viscerally and benightedly, the embodied aspects of the exchange, which include voluntary signals governed by the motor cortex — and involuntary signals governed primarily by older, "reptilian" brain structures, such as the limbic system.

A paleomammalian perspective should be useful here. Every social animal is designed to be keenly attuned to the corporeal language of members of the group, as bodily signals not only help maintain social equilibrium but are in fact critical for survival. "Animals," Argyle notes, "conduct their entire social life by means of non-verbal communication: they make friends, find mates, rear children, co-operate in groups, establish leadership hierarchies, and get rid of enemies entirely by the use of NV [non-verbal] signals" (2007, 27). The body has always been a beacon and an alarm system for territoriality, danger, and sexuality, trigging life-saving and species-saving flight, fight, or freeze responses. And it is therefore not surprising that our own gestures, as innate vestiges of a zoogenic past or learned in a cultural context, may also become primary aspects of meaning. As an exquisitely social species, learning to decode even minute bodily events (e.g., movements of the lips and brows) has been very important for us, and of course it still is.

Much as with other social animals, our own interactions also involve social norms that are codified by display rules; rules that govern quasi-ethological reactions: an underlying stream of feelings, impulses, biological automaticity — *the reactions of the organism itself to the interaction*, which may or may not leak beyond superegoic rule-display. [1] Interactors that decode these gestural events also emit their own gestural feedback, consciously or unconsciously as well; so that interactions may indeed resemble "gestural dances" that metaphorize social codes, or such things as desire, dominance, or status. (Interestingly, Argyle notes that "boxing," and not "dancing," may be a better metaphor for interactions, as interactors often respond to the other, "apparently at speeds greater than normal [i.e., intentional] reaction time" [Argyle 2007, 118].)

Magnetic resonance imaging studies (Hariri and Whalen 2011) have shown that photographs of angry faces can trigger strong brain activity, associated in particular to the amygdale, an older brain structure linked to emotion and aggression (even if, at the conscious level, participants feel safe facing, after all, only an innocuous photograph). These physiological and neurological responses triggered by bodily signals (i.e., by faces) are meaningful, again, primarily at the level of the organism, not at the level of consciousness. Not the mind, but the organism is here the sender (e.g., the face) and the decoder of meaning — meaning that, decoded at the level of the amygdale, is in turn expressed by limbic activity and related physiological responses such as sweating, arterial pressure, flushing, faster cardiac output.

Consider also John Donne (1991), the celebrated metaphysical poet. He speaks of the "eloquence" of blood and cheeks, and says that he can understand a woman (whose body contains nothing else than "The Westerne treasure [and] the Easterne spiceree") fundamentally "by her sight." "Her pure and eloquent blood," he says, "Spoke in her cheekes, and so distinctly wrought// That one might almost say, her bodie thought" (ibid., 361). Her body speaks eloquently about its "bodily thoughts," and Donne decodes these "thoughts" also at the level of his body. Clinical psychoanalysts have perfected this form of bodily communication, and often serve as transducers for embodied signals from the patient, feeling and then connecting these signals to words, to metaphors, to thus open up encysted, perhaps painful, and yet hidden meanings to the cognitive awareness of the analysand. [2]

Kristeva and the Eloquence of Blood

The examples above show that the cognitive subject can extract meanings from the interlocutor's words, but that bodies can also extract meanings from other bodies, from sensations and feelings themselves. Again, Bourdieu has helped us understand that the body is a critical factor of communication, and that this is not without consequences for individuals and groups. Thanks to him and others we better see that embodied collective memories are crucibles of meanings that are cognitive and embodied at once. But beyond Bourdieu, embodied meanings also stem, precisely, from "the eloquence of blood." Julia Kristeva, in particular, has shown that everyday embodied meanings stem not only from gestures, movements, and hesitations — but from the organismic forces that often underpin these things: forces at the root of the Freudian "drives," the "lower" vectors of meaning. She helps us see that presocial elements and pre-social claims often intrude within the sphere of meaning, within the sphere of discourse, and within the general domain of cognitive and symbolic exchange. [3]

Let us enlist Kelly Oliver to begin discussing these ideas, an important commentator who has provided an excellent summary of Kristeva's theory, as it pertains to the crisscrossing of meaning, embodiment, and culture. It is worth quoting at length. For Kristeva,

[A]ll signification [has] two elements, the symbolic and the semiotic. The symbolic element is what philosophers might think of as referential meaning . . . the structures by which symbols operate. The symbolic is the structure or grammar that governs the ways in which symbols can refer. The semiotic element, on the other hand, is the organization of drives in language. It is associated with rhythms and tones that are meaningful parts of language and yet do not represent or signify something. . . . [R]hythms and tones do not represent bodily drives; rather bodily drives are discharged through rhythms and tones. ...[T]he meaning of the semiotic element of language is "translinguistic" or "nonlinguistic" [and] irreducible to language [or] its "grammatical and logical structures." This is to say that they are irreducible to the symbolic element of language.

The dialectical oscillation between the semiotic and the symbolic is what makes signification possible. Without the symbolic element of signification, we have only sounds or delirious babble. But without the semiotic element of signification, signification would be empty and we would not speak; for the semiotic provides the motivation for engaging in signifying processes. We have a bodily need to communicate. The symbolic provides the structure necessary to communicate. Both elements are essential to signification. And it is the *tension* between them that makes signification dynamic. The semiotic both motivates signification and threatens the symbolic element. The semiotic provides the movement or negativity and the symbolic provides the stasis or stability that keeps signification both dynamic and structured.

While the symbolic element gives signification its meaning in the strict sense of reference, the semiotic element gives signification meaning in a broader sense. That is, the semiotic element makes symbols matter; by discharging drive force in symbols, it makes them significant. Even though the semiotic challenges meaning in the strict [symbolic] sense . . . it gives symbols their meaning for our lives. Signification makes our lives meaningful, in both senses of meaning — signifying something and having significance — through its symbolic and semiotic elements. The interdependence of the symbolic and semiotic elements of signification guarantees a relationship between language and life, signification and experience; the interdependence between the symbolic and semiotic guarantees a relationship between body (*soma*) and soul (*psyche*).

By insisting that the language expresses bodily drives through its semiotic element, Kristeva's articulation of the relationship between language and the body circumvents the traditional problems of representation. The tones and rhythms of language, the materiality of language, is bodily. Kristeva's theory addresses the problem of the relationship between language and bodily experience by postulating that, through the semiotic element, bodily drives manifest themselves in language. . . . The force of language is living drive force transferred into language. Signification is like a transfusion of the living body into language . . . . Language is not cut off from the body. And, while, for Kristeva, bodily drives involve a type of violence, negation, or force, this process does not merely necessitate sacrifice and loss. The drives are not sacrificed to signification; rather bodily drives are an essential semiotic element of signification. (Oliver 2005, 344)

We can now amplify Bourdieu's ideas and say that communication occurs not only from body to body, from gesture to gesture, but also from unconscious to unconscious, and from drive to drive. Meaning hinges not merely on the surface of the body — gesture, movement — but also on deeper structures, on mostly unconscious pushes (*Trieben*) that have their origins in the demands of biology discussed previously. Importantly, these "pre-meanings," as Kristeva names them, are different from the signals emitted by habitus, which tend to recapitulate social requirements. Recall that, for Bourdieu, the body is often in the business of quoting the social code. By contrast, these Kristevan pre-meanings quote social forces *as well as* biological forces that are contrary to the social order and often contrary to the norms that sustain it. The signaling capacities of habitus, as Mauss also argued, speak of tradition and have a function within a tradition. By contrast, Kristevan pre-meanings, which antecede words but contribute to meaning, can be dysfunctional, and can erode tradition. During the exchange between interlocutors, pre-meanings can effectively dismantle the tradition that interactors typically invoke to govern the exchange.

Kristeva also says that when recurring, when habitual, when sedimented in speech, such embodied pre-meanings give shape to our "semiotic disposition." Let me provide the example of gender; and let us discuss, first, the ways in which the semiotic disposition of the genders recapitulates the social code. As suggested, there is a sense in which gender *is* a sedimented repertoire of gestures, collectively significant eye expressions, tonal colors, inflections and rhythms, phonetic, gestural, affective habituses — an embodied collective memory profoundly marked by the social order. Engendered bodies are often gravid with collective meanings, with social injunctions and social hierarchies, with the "imaginations of the dead," in the phrase by Rorty. Women sometimes inhabit a body attuned to social hierarchies. Their bodies often tend to take up less space than those of men; women smile more (though female and male infants smile the same), use intonation more frequently, laugh more, look more, approach others more and more closely, walk less expansively, etc. (Argyle 2007, 99 and 283-85). Women often display subordinate gestures that enact related social meanings and legitimize and solidify the hierarchies of gender and the larger symbolic order, one exchange at a time, one gesture at a time. As Bourdieu argues, these bodily dispositions carry meanings that help maintain the boundaries and hierarchies of the social order, silently and naturally, as though the motor mechanisms of these bodies developed to analogize social mechanisms.

To be sure, much as Bourdieu, a Marxist Kristeva also helps us see that the speaker's semiotic disposition can be colonized by social demands, so that words — and their embodied scaffolding — can convey his socioeconomic history and his subordinate position within the socioeconomic grid. As Bourdieu, she also helps us see that, as these culturally-framed semiotic dispositions privilege the claims of the social order, they can limit the meanings, the claims, the ontological status of the individual. And that, particularly when these dispositions become naturalized and fraught with automatisms, they are important instruments of social control, which keep self-regulated social actors in line, and the socioeconomic apparatus marching in a particular historical direction. (At the beginning of the twentieth century, for example, homosexuals typically sought to uproot their wants and identities, thus actively contributing to the heteronormative order that oppressed them [Krafft-Ebing 1998]. [4])

But Kristeva also shows that these gestures and movements can press against these structures. When gestures and movements convey pre-social meanings rooted in our zoogenic past, they can be disruptive. Donne's lady, whose body contains all the spices of the Orient, is a vehicle for the eloquence of blood itself, as though her autonomous body, despite her better judgment, were taking the initiative of addressing the other in its own way. Her body in fact seems to take on the role of a confederate in the midst of internalized social expectations; so that beyond inherited standards of gender (and class), her body seems to encloses the germ of autonomy, even if it paradoxically goes against her own will, against her superegoic sense of propriety. The larger (psychoanalytical and Kristevan) point to be made is that drives often intervene in the area of interpersonal communication, and that this is an important aspect of embodied memory, which is not captured by the notion of habitus. Embodied memory involves these destabilizing organismic operations that sometimes determine the dynamic of the interaction.

This Freudian Kristeva lets us see that even internalized and embodied parameters of meaning (i.e., related to habitus) are unstable, and that they can be modified when and if the speaking subject is pushed beyond the social code precisely by internal drives. (In part, this is why the order of things depicted by Krafft-Ebing eventually collapsed, and Queer politics emerged: Queer discourses, that is to say, stem not only from ideologies, but also from bodily wants and drives at the root of signifying capacities, dispositions, and habituses, individual and collective. Back to Bourdieu, no amount of symbolic violence was able to permanently control these pre-social impulses or the meanings and dispositions that, emerging from them, eventually sedimented as new habituses and as collectively relevant semiotic dispositions.)

Note also that, as Kristeva says, "Identifying the semiotic disposition means in fact identifying the shift in the speaking subject, *his capacity for renewing the order in which he is [otherwise] inescapably caught up*; and this capacity is, for the *subject,* the capacity for enjoyment" (1986, 29, first italics mine, second italics hers). Such innate "capacity for enjoyment" and renewal, that is to say, involves inherited human drives that tend to reappropriate social signals, as these signals tend to represent the reality principle and thus tend to be in conflict with egotistic gratifications. Drives, in the Freudian sense of "pushes," even if unconscious, often press individuals and groups against dominant systems of meaning. Back to Donne, blood and cheeks often press against cultural pressures. Back to Queerness, these sorts of wants and drives signaled new (Queer) meanings, which underpinned not only new "natures" — for example, new ways of living masculinity and femininity — but also new ideas, and eventually new laws and new social structures. [5]

It is important to clarify that this "capacity for enjoyment" may erroneously bring to mind romantic ideas, which suggest that the core of nature, as discussed above, is good. Or it may erroneously remind us, back to Breton, of surrealist ideas about desire as the "generally spontaneous tendency that drives all beings to 'appropriate' for themselves in some way or other an element of the exterior world" (in Mundy 2001, 11).[6] This "capacity for enjoyment" may certainly have this Bretonian function, but the speaker who slips outside the normative and logical borders that are guarded by speech — is not necessarily freer or better off. As Kristeva remind us, infantile or psychotic babble are entirely "free" of these social constraints. Unintended transgressions, unconscious desires and motives, in their socially disruptive form, can help, but can also diminish the individual, socially, psychologically, existentially.[7] Again, the mixture of desire and transgression holds the potential for liberation, but also for anomy in the Durkhemian sense. The sexual scandals associated with the Catholic Church, for instance, which involve the figure of the Pope himself, have diminished the church's institutional capacity to generate collective meanings, to facilitate and demarcate existential domains. The anomic and sordid quality of these scenarios arguably originates at the point where Eros, as I have also suggested, acquires Thanatotic qualities and becomes a principle of disintegration. They originate in the disruptive elements of the drive. Eros, again, is always alloyed with Thanatos, and the line that separates them can be thin, so that the transgressions that stem from these pre-social portions of desire can become harmful, individually and collectively, as the victims of these sexual scandals and violations unmistakably attest. On the other hand, Queerness and feminism provide many positive examples of the ways in which desires that are pre-social in origin can give way to transformative individual and collective dispositions, to new habituses, and new aspects of the embodied collective memory.

In any case, this "capacity for enjoyment" can become, for better or for worse, an important mechanism of action and of transformation, individually or collectively.

A Summary

Like mushrooms from mycelia, meanings stem from a tangle of cognitive, affective, bodily, and social roots. Meaning, Kristeva says, is not "the act of a *transcendental ego*, cut off from the body, its unconscious, and also its history." It is, instead, related to "bio-physiological processes (themselves already inescapably part of signifying processes, what Freud labeled 'drives'); and, on the other hand, to social constraints (family structures, modes of production, etc.)" (1986, original emphasis). If words are invested with history, and carry and convey the logic of the social order, they are not reducible to logical or normative structures, as they are also invested with pre-social pushes. I will finish this chapter with two examples that illustrate this idea, the words "man" and "woman." They are miniaturized versions of history and contain entire social cosmologies. Indeed, they carry the social cosmology that, precisely through these words, encroaches upon the minds, wants, and bodies of people designated by them. From the moment a sono-gram announces a "girl," people congregate to construct the living girl, the semiotic support for discourses about gender; so that her gestures, bodily rhythms, aspects of her motives and desires, may eventually become mediat-ed by ideology. For this to happen, pre-social motives have to be repressed and sublimated to the extent to which they no longer pose a significant threat to these cultural codes. *The Feminine Mystique*, for example, thus seduced many women, so that their ideas, wants, and embodied memories became espoused to narrow ideological and existential parameters. The dominant embodied collective memories were vehicles for these words and these ideol-ogies. These ideologies came to life through these bodies.

But when Friedan and colleagues said "woman" and "man," they not only articulated new ideas, but also invoked old, inhibited, to some extent uncon-scious wants. Soon, a new stream of ideas, desires, gestures surfaced to transform local and eventually global social ecologies. Of course, the causes underpinning these historical changes were complex and cannot be captured by this idea alone. But the Second Wave had roots in Kristevan pre-meanings and wants that were expressed through the new discourses, and the changes portended by this social movement cannot be understood without them. Bear in mind that their concept of freedom was often predicated in embodied terms: as sexual freedom, freedom to desire, freedom of experience, which many Second Wavers saw as prerequisites for other modalities of freedom: political, economic, existential. The Second Wave articulated drives thereto outside the reach of words ("the problem that has no name") thus unlocking, in an almost psychoanalytical manner, new visions and motives that sus-tained new dispositions and habituses. New bodies began to appear, bearing new styles, gestures, desires. Dominant embodied collective memories were transformed. New realities were called in, as well as new futures.

NOTES

1. Gergen and Barton placed groups of seven and eight strangers in small rooms, some of which were illuminated and some that were in total darkness. Eighty percent of participants in the rooms with no lights felt sexual excitement; no participants reported this emotion in the illuminated rooms. This suggests that light provides a cue for young men and women to inhibit sexual feelings and/or to manage them via rule-display (1973).

2. The "talking cure" involves, precisely, the ability of the patient to transfer these bodily meanings to the level of language. When "bodily memories," as Christopher Bollas (1997) says, become attached to language, a sense of self-realization, literally and figuratively, takes place. The person can thus turn the apparatus of cognition inwardly, in an almost Kantian fashion, to see meanings that are hidden to the outward directed gaze. This shortens the gap between the self and the unknown self, and provides a more integrated self-system.

3. But to insist: collective meaning is — never just a question of bodily and unthought meanings, of course. As Kristeva argues, if communication were limited to this level of bodily signification only, it would resemble the world of the psychotic or the babbling of the young infant.

4. Many men, Krafft-Ebing shows, actively sought out medical advice and treatment for their "condition" (homosexuality was the newly coined term of diagnosis). Threatened not only by external norms, but also by internalized norms, these men insisted on undergoing the many indignities prescribed by Krafft-Ebing: small electrical shocks (faradizations); going to brothels; receiving such medical recommendations as "coitus," masturbation, "society of ladies," etc. (ibid.).

5. Queer politics in fact has been a crucible for Eros and Thanatos: for Queer desires and for anti-Queer aggressiveness, the two principles that, governing organic life, have left their imprint on aspects of social life, as suggested above. Just as Queerness is rooted in desires and drives, anti-queerness and related collective agreements, rational as they purport to be, are often spurred by drives, as well, which speak through related habituses, related semiotic dispositions, and related pre-meanings, pre-reflectively to an extent.

6. For this very Freudian Breton such manifestation of desire is in fact "the medium through which nature generally makes itself known to man [*sic*], affecting him in relation to what is [and at the same time, to what is not], and through which it [nature] expresses itself spontaneously to him as a fully formed imperative" (ibid., 16, first and third brackets are mine).

7. This idea was analyzed by Freud in his *The Psychopathology of Everyday Life* (2003), which shows that desire leads not necessarily to creativity or freedom but sometimes to embarrassment, to social and psychological diminution.

Chapter Ten

Embodying the Past and Embodying the Future

EMBODYING THE PAST AND THE FUTURE

In the often quoted passage below, Bourdieu speaks of the ways in which embodied social actors learn to comply with social requirements:

> Adapting a phrase of Proust's, one might say that arms and legs are full of numb imperatives. One could endlessly enumerate the values given body, made body, by the hidden persuasion of an implicit pedagogy which can instill a whole cosmology, through injunctions as insignificant as "sit up straight" or "don't hold your knife in your left hand" and inscribe the most fundamental principles of the arbitrary content of a culture . . . so putting them beyond the reach of consciousness and explicit statement. (1990, 69)

A very useful and important statement, to be sure, but as we saw in the previous chapter, social actors are not always "full of numb imperatives." And again, "cultural cosmologies" expressed by habituses may be contested through likewise "insignificant" and accumulative embodied signals that rest in the subject's own "capacity for renewing the order in which he is [other-wise] inescapably caught up," as Kristeva says (1986, 29). "Sitting up straight" bolsters a certain social order, but if a person and then a community sit up "gay," then the "fundamental principles" of a culture are put within "the reach of consciousness." When two men hold hands at a church gathering something might be set in motion, as it happened in places such as New York (Chauncey 1994). When a person and then a group of people thus begin to "live in truth," as Vaclav Havel says (in Goldfarb 2006, 29), a new collective order may emerge. In general, this human capacity for renewing the given social order may bring about new semiotic dispositions, new features of the embodied collective memory, new traditions, new laws, indeed new social structures, as the previous chapter suggests.

These are the ideas that I have tried to emphasize thus far, but it is important to note, as well, that if disentangling oneself from the past can have advantages, embodying the past can also have advantages, as Aristotle may agree. To see these advantages, we need to turn, in this brief chapter, to a very different but related theoretical source, Aristotle's theory of virtue, which arguably set in motion this important (conservative) idea.[1] To begin this discussion, let me provide a contrasting backdrop for this Aristotelian theory: the Kantian theory of virtue, which largely informs the way we understand morality today. Kant said that moral agents may choose the good according to two forms of moral judgment. They may make imperative choices, which involve doing the right thing for the sake of virtue itself. And they may make hypothetical choices, which involve considerations about utilitarian advantages. Examples of "hypothetical imperatives" are given by the Old Testament, where the virtuous person does the right thing *because of* his fear of God, and by the New Testament, where the person is virtuous because of his love of God, both of which involve hypotheses about one's behavior and its consequences: if I do X, then Y should follow.

By contrast, Aristotle wants us to consider the idea that virtue can be a naturalized and more or less automatic and, we may say, embodied disposition that actually does not hinge on self-conscious (categorical or imperative) choices. Arguably, this Aristotelian theory revolves around the notion of "*hexis*" (variously translated as "disposition" or "active condition"), which carries connotations akin to the English "*virtuosity.*" Much as virtuosity, *hexis* also involves a very ingrained disposition in the person, in the virtuoso. As virtuosity, *hexis* is also the product of a life-long training that, to paraphrase Bourdieu, instills a whole cosmology of values, through everyday, normalized moral injunctions. Importantly, *hexis* is deeply rooted in one's traditions. It flows from a collective past that has refined a *nomos*, and that has built certain institutional and ideological apparatuses that inject virtue into everyday life. Of course, a tradition may inculcate the wrong *hexis*, ignoble, base, heteronomic and yet also naturalized and embodied dispositions. But, as Aristotle would argue, if underpinned by the correct *nomos* and the correct social order, tradition may also inscribe virtue deep in the embodied collective memory. Such virtuous persons, whose everyday lives have been guided by this *nomos*, are virtuous simply because they ARE virtuous, and no tautology should be read here from the man who invented logic. This Aristotelian virtuous person doesn't lie simply because he is not a liar, ontologically, simply because he carries virtue in his being in the same way in which the virtuoso piano player, for instance, carries artistry (*techne*) and virtuosity (*hexis*) in his hands. Indeed, much as the virtuoso piano-player, the Aristotelian virtuous person does not and cannot quite stop to think about each one of his actions (as in Rational Choice Theory, for example), lest the performance fail, lest he fail to be virtuosic. He does not, and cannot, stop to make ratiocinated, Kantian choices about his performance. Aristotle, in other words, in a sense reverses the Bourdieuan model (or perhaps Bourdieu reversed Aristotle); the model suggested by the quote at the beginning of this chapter: whereas Bourdieu reminds us that traditions and the values of the past may come to conscript the future, and to perpetuate various forms of symbolic violence, Aristotle helps us see that traditions can provide the ground for positive and indeed self-affirming *and self-mastered* aspects of embodied collective memory.

Anticipating Merleau-Ponty's notion of "phenomenological fields," which speaks of the enmeshing of the subject and the object of her action, Aristotle also speaks of an ontological entanglement between "the haver and what is had." (The French phenomenologist provides the example of a soccer player to illustrate the notion of phenomenological fields: the player, Merleau-Ponty says, is a sensuous being whose performance is never primarily cognitive. The player's body, primarily, and not merely his mind, brings the structure, the norms, and the stakes of the game to life. His/her moves express, enact, and synthesize the history, the "culture," and the stakes attached to the game.) Aristotle's notion of virtuosity also suggests a *synthesis in action* that connects the doer, the doing and the deed. He also says that these three terms can be ontologically connected. And to insist on a key point, such synthesis in action is possible only as a naturalized expression of the past, as it involves a life-long training in the folkways and mores given by a certain tradition. The past, Aristotle helps us see, may provide vital support for embodied collective memories, ideally sponsoring a well-tempered and naturalized will, an effortless taste that organically emerges in the citizens' thoughts and actions, as though the will of *Virtue itself* precedes their conscious willing. In general, the social actor does not invent virtue by himself. One generally inherits it, one grows with it, and it grows with us, organically. Embodiment, according to this Aristotelian model, is functional from the point of view of the social order, almost as in Mauss. To be sure, one may infer here that these aspects of embodied memory that are attached to tradition are not only functional but indeed indispensable for a good polis.

This Aristotelian theory is utopian, to an extent. It provides an ideal, but, as we saw, human beings are constantly prodded by pre-social impulses that press against tradition. Yet, to the extent to which we are also pressed, and indeed created by tradition, to the extent to which human beings are not only biological but also social animals, tradition may contribute to the process of naturalization in useful ways. The past can be very useful. The dead can come to assist the living.

Let me note as well that, if this Aristotelian perspective helps us see that the past, thus embodied and naturalized, may provide good bases for the future, it also helps us infer that the goal of unfair, dogmatic, fundamentalist traditions would be to merge with nature, to become incarnate, to thus colonize the future. As George Orwell may agree, the goal of such ideologies would be to encroach upon embodied collective memories, to acquire "total" dimensions, in the Maussian sense, to thus become invested with the air of the normal. An approximation to this may be inferred from Bourdieu's study of the Kabyle.

Embodying the Future

Extrapolating from Aristotle's ideas, we could also infer that individuals and groups may embody aspects not of the past, but of the future, a process that can also carry advantages and disadvantages. Heidegger's notion of "authenticity" suggests that the authentic person can detach himself, in mind and body, from the imperatives of the past and incarnate "unhomely," unfamiliar visions and dispositions. Back to Baudelaire, his life and craft provide examples that illustrate this idea. But beyond such unusual occurrences, which only eventually surface to disturb everyday life, we may also consider more everyday examples. In the closet, for instance, the temporal modality that dominates is the past, tradition, but as the person steps outside the closet, the temporal modality that switches on is the future: life is stamped with new potential (as well as with new obstacles and anxieties). Similarly, the Second Wave removed large portions of social life from the organic grip of the past, thus invoking elements of the future, new ideas and symbols that became incorporated, alive, and eventually enacted as a matter of course (in the next chapter we will see that race can also be an aspect of embodied memory that quotes the past but also the possible).

If the person and the group detach the past from the domain of embodied memory, possibilities become actualities. Life as lived begins to flow from the "Nocturnal river of hours [of tomorrow]," to borrow the phrase by Unamuno. Through small and everyday acts of embodied autonomy — which bring to mind Jeffrey Goldfarb's (2006) theory of the "politics of small things" — gay people and feminists disentangled themselves from certain requisites from the past and, as suggested, thus invoked new social, mental, legal, symbolic structures. That a gay man today may feel at home in erstwhile unhomely manners and corporeal rhythms suggests that aspects of tradition are no longer attached to his body. That new aspects of embodied memory may be seen in gay communities across the world suggest that new branches of history have been set in motion. Bodies may become detached from the past and transition into new and unknown futures.

In summary, time can be rendered continuous or discontinuous, and history can become, by degrees, rigid or pliable. When ECMs largely and inertially flow from the past, history thus "organically" flows into the present. By contrast, when embodied social actors deflect the claims of tradition, disrupt the flow of the past, they may open windows into new futures. As suggested, embodied collective memories are structures of possibilities for individuals and for groups. Embodying features of the past or features of the new can involve advantages and/or disadvantages for individuals and groups, and situations of conflict and struggle between opposing social forces. Jacques Le Goff (1992) says that collective memories are key aspects "in the struggle for 'power' among social forces." Likewise with embodied collective memories: they are also important elements in the struggle for power. Again, ECMs are not dichotomous structures involving either passive acceptances or active transgressions. And features of ECMs may bring to mind the Nietzschean idea of a "midnight of forces": liminal temporal points where social actors incorporate the past and the forthcoming, adaptively and not.[2] But schematically, we may nonetheless say that embodied memories sometimes are driven particularly by elements of the past (tradition) or pulled by new and conflicting visions of the future (collective aspirations, goals), for better or for worse.

NOTES

1. Aristotle also anticipates Bourdieu's concept of "habitus." For the Greek habitus is a mode or state of being. It involves "[A]n active habit or 'having,' a kind of action or motion on the part of the 'haver' to what is 'had'; for, between a doer and his deed there is the doing. So, too, between him who has a garment and the garment he has, there is a having […] The same term also means a state or disposition, being well or ill disposed, and that either with regard to itself or in relation to something else; for example, health is a state of being, since it is such as disposition" (Aristotle 2003, 113-114). Against radical rationalism, Aristotle's theory has no concept of freewill in opposition to necessity (or agency vs. structure, etc.). Although Aristotle makes a distinction between *intended* and *unintended* actions (*hekousios* and *akousios*), he posits no radical separation between these terms or between freedom and constraint. These pairs coexist and co-arise in the Aristotelian notion of habitus, which subsumes individuality and supra-individuality, and thus choice and constraint, freedom and necessity. From this perspective — which subsumes the doer, the deed, and the doing — theories positing a radical sense of Will may emerge only if the doer and the deed, the haver and what is had, are ontologically separated, as radically autonomous entities on their own right.

2. Here it is worth recalling Foucault's distinction between his theory of the carceral system and the actual jails: the theory provided a clear analytical outline, but the jails themselves were a "witches' brew," he said, in itself antithetical to schematization. Similarly, my goal is to capture ECMs within simple analytical parameters (illustrated by simple examples) but they are *in themselves* antithetical to schematization.

Chapter Eleven

An Example of
Embodied Collective Memory: Race

RACE AND THE PAST

In this chapter, I provide an example to illustrate the idea that embodied collective memory may be either an expression of the past, or, by contrast, a stage for new things, for unhomely historical possibilities, and thus a platform for the future. The example is race. On the one hand, I will argue that race is not an aspect of nature but a process whereby inherited collective ideas become internalized, naturalized and sedimented within the domain of embodied collective memory. But on the other hand, I also argue that, as an embodied dimension of social life, race sometimes resists the flow of tradition, so that the organic grip that dominant ideas may have on social life is weakened. The example of "race," that is to say, will illustrate a central idea from the previous chapter: that ECMs can become channels for the past or, by contrast, may deflect the past, for better or worse, and may thus render history discontinuous, even if by small degrees.

Let me begin by defining race first. Arguably, most people in the world today take for granted the purported biological reality of race. Race seems to be a biologically valid construct. As the biological anthropologist Michael Blakey notes, race is as obvious for us as the fact that the sun rises every morning at an appointed hour. Yet, as Blakey also implies, just as the sunrise is merely a Ptolemaic illusion, race is a biological illusion. The sun, we saw with Copernicus, has never risen in the morning. Races, we will see in this chapter, never dawned from the horizon of human history, except, of course, as illusions (see also, Marks 2002; Goodman 2012); illusions that, encroaching upon identities and upon embodied collective memories, have marked the lives and the "natures" of individuals, and the histories and fates of countries and continents.

The idea that race is a biologically invalid category is not new. This well-known theory, which we may very well call "Copernican," has been the near-consensus among anthropologists, particularly among biological anthropologists and paleo- and molecular-anthropologists, at least since the late 1990's. After centuries of errors, these disciplines have helped us see that there is greater genetic variation *within* than across racial groups. (By contrast, these centennial errors, arguably set in motion in the eighteenth century, particularly by Carolus Linnaeus's Eurocentric taxonomy of the human races and by Johann F. Blumenbach's moral-anatomical classification of "the five human races," suggested that races were biologically specific.) The racial categories that we generally have in mind, as the American Anthropological Association's official statement on race states, differ in more or less six percent of their genes, which means that ninety four percent of variation occurs *within* these conventional racial categories.[1] More precisely, Richard Lewontin has shown that eighty five percent of human genetic variation occurs "between any two individuals from the same ethnic group." Eight percent of variation occurs "between ethnic groups within a race" (e.g., Britons, Spaniards, Irish); and only seven percent of variation occurs across major racial categories (Lewontin 1993). Hence, though often seen as a genetic construct, race is a construct without genetic basis (also Gould 2002; Fullilove 1998; Goodman 2000; Lee et al. 2001; Braun 2002; Duster 2003, 2005; Stevens 2003; Kahn 2004; Sankar et al. 2002). Race, as the American Anthropological Association also states, is not a biological fact.

About 40,000 years ago there were various human subspecies, various "races," as we may say. Of course, anthropologists would not speak of "races" in this particular context. They speak of "parallel species" that, under the genus "*homo,*" coexisted and indeed inhabited the same areas of Western Europe and the Middle East, as the bones seem to suggest. At least in Europe, these "races" sometimes fought for scarce resources, sometimes cooperated, and perhaps even mated. We, *Homo sapiens* (or "*Homo sapiens sapiens*" according to the competing classification) were one of them. We were genetically similar to other sapiens of the same subspecies and relatively different from our competitors, *Homo neandertalensis* (or *Homo sapiens neanderta-lensis* in the competing view). This was a separate "race" that, in turn, also shared genetic and biological traits, a robust musculoskeletal frame, shorter stature, bigger teeth, prominent brow ridges and sloping foreheads, longer arms, possibly bigger brains, etc. But about 30,000 years ago Neandertals disappeared. (How would the world be today, geo-politically, culturally, if they had managed to survive?) We are not sure why they became extinct. Perhaps we outcompeted them and eventually replaced them, as the "replacement hypothesis" suggests. Perhaps Neandertals had an apocalyptic end, killed off by volcanic activity in Europe and attendant climatic changes. (Or perhaps both of these leading hypotheses are correct so that these two factors, and others, partially contributed to their extinction.) But whatever the reasons for their disappearance, we were the only ones who managed to survive. And, for better or for worse, we happened to be the ones who eventually conquered the world (which some environmental biologists see as a negative event in the history of life, inasmuch as the rise of *Homo sapiens* has brought forth unparalleled environmental pressures and indeed important threats to organic life).

We came from Africa, according to the most widely accepted theory, and within a span of about 125,000 years, we walked across the earth.[2] As we moved north, the sun lessened in intensity, and we therefore adapted. Depending on the latitude at which we eventually settled, our skin became lighter, probably to absorb enough vitamin D, which synthesizes as the sun strikes the skin (Jablonski 2004).[3] Those who remained in areas with more sun, and more ultraviolet radiation, retained darker pigmentations to prevent skin cancer, damage to sweat glands, ultraviolet photolysis of folate, etc. (Sturm et al. 2001; Rees 2003). Beyond skin color, bodies also responded to other geographical pressures. The differential height of "races," for instance, resulted, in part, from such pressures as those related to heat intensity. Longer and slender bodies (e.g., sub-Saharan) are optimal for heat reduction, and shorter bodies (which one may associate with Eskimos, for example) are optimal for heat retention. Other geographical factors, such as availability of specific nutrients, humidity, and altitude, also contributed to other "racial" features. High altitudes, for instance, anthropologically defined as 10,000 feet and above, tended to mold shorter and stockier bodies, an adaptive trait that is partly explained by the typical cold weather in these regions, as well as by the lower availability of breathable oxygen, which results in larger lungs and hearts and thus in larger thoraxes (hence, the typical "racial" features of Andean "Indians," for example).

Geography, in any case, installed the racial physical differences that we see today. But when these adaptive traits occurred, our genetic code was nearly complete, such that these genetic alterations added only an insignificantly small portion to it, not enough to separate us into latitude-based, color-coded subspecies. Our species is simply too recent in origin, and has been too driven by gene flow, for speciation to have occurred. Yet, we eventually did become divided into color-coded "races," a notion that, the American Anthropological Association says, was set in motion as a "social mechanism invented during the 18th century," and used primarily to justify the European colonial expansion. The notion that there are human subspecies, implicit in today's mainstream discourses, stems from colonial interests and myths, from a colonial form of bio-power, as we may say borrowing the term from Foucault. It stems particularly from the Linnaeusian idea that nature, and thus God, ordained a hierarchy of races, a belief that justified race-based slavery, and underpinned the laws and the logic that governed the colonial economies.

Consider, for example, the notion that there is a "White race," which is generally defined in the U.S. as "descent from any of the original peoples of Europe," as recent censuses claim. The idea that a White race naturally stems from *any* European roots is very recent. Bear in mind that the ancient Romans, for example, or the Greeks, the Gauls, the Franks, etc., never thought of themselves as "White," as sharing the same racial boat by virtue of being "Europeans." Julius Caesar could not possibly think of himself as White. A direct descendant from Aphrodite, he was, instead, of the race of the gods. The idea is that, though some ancient cultures had color-coded ethnic categories (Egyptians, for example, saw themselves as "red" and saw others as "white" or "black" or "yellow"), our definition of whiteness is very recent. To find people who believe, as we do today, that European ancestry, broadly conceived, endows them with a race, we have to go all the way to the twentieth century. We have to picture a time when the children and grandchildren of European immigrants to the U.S. melted into a common culture, in a common "pot," and eventually into a common "White race" (Haney Lopez 2006; Jacobson 1998).

This was a time when the descendants of new "ethnic" European immigrants acquired a common racial identity as they left the old culture behind (clothes, language, food, music), a time when shared aspects of an embodied collective memory also emerged. These features of embodied memory strengthened the illusion that they partook from a common nature, from a common "race" that indeed made them (naturally) different from others. Yet, whiteness is a "falsely homogenizing term," Ian Haney Lopez explains. "'White' is capitalized to indicate its reference to a specific social group, but this group is recognized to possess fluid borders and heterogeneous members. . . . 'White' does not denote a rigidly defined, congeneric grouping of indistinguishable individuals. It refers to an unstable category which gains its meaning only through social relations and that encompasses a profoundly diverse set of persons" (Haney Lopez 2006, xxi-xxii). By the middle of the twentieth century, however, "Whites" melted into a "singular" and "congeneric" race; the "race" that we perceive and experience today as a matter of course.

The following example illustrates the idea that our sense of whiteness is recent: in 1922, Jim Rollings, a black man from Alabama, was taken to a court accused of the crime of miscegenation, of having had consensual sex with a White woman, one Edith Labue. Luckily for the defendant, Labue was Italian. And as soon as the judge discovered that important piece of information, he swiftly dismissed the case, reasoning that the fact that she was Sicilian "can in no sense be taken as conclusive that she was therefore a

White woman" (Jacobson 1998, 4 and 62). The judge is here bespeaking notions of whiteness that were typical of the time. Bear in mind that, at the beginning of the twentieth century, the definitions of whiteness were under scrutiny and were in fact undergoing changes that eventually resulted in the legal (not necessarily cultural) inclusion of Italians into the category of whiteness.

Importantly, this court "did not find that a Sicilian was *necessarily* non-white," Matthew Jacobson says (ibid. my emphasis). But the point is that "its finding that a Sicilian was *inconclusively* white does speak volumes about whiteness in 1920s Alabama" (ibid. my emphasis). Edith might be, perhaps, White, but not the kind of White that may be protected by the law, as Jacobson notes. Note also that, during this time period, many people thought that Italians were "Mediterraneans," not exactly White. Bear in mind, as well, that Italians themselves did not come to the U.S. bearing a "White" identity. Rather, only eventually they came to assume, in various ways and degrees, the latter and Americanized sense of self. This also happened with Slavs, Irish, "Alpines," "Hebrews" and other "darker European races," as they were often called at the beginning of the twentieth century.[4] Their "whiteness" also came into being in this American context. (A cultural, historical, and legal context which dictated, up until 1952, that to become an American citizen, applicants had to be White; a context that therefore encouraged immigrants with more or less lighter skin pigmentation, including East Indians, in the direction of a "White" identity.) To be sure, at the beginning of the twentieth century, the facts of whiteness were so confused and confusing that U.S. courts also ruled that, as suggested, East Indians, Arabs and Syrians were White (Haney Lopez 2006). At the end of the nineteenth century, the same courts determined that Mexicans were likewise White, "White by law," Haney Lopez says (ibid.). Then and today, that is to say, "whiteness" involved a series of fluid notions and myths attached to a certain range of skin colors (Jacobson 1998; Haney Lopez 2006), notions that, to reiterate, eventually became attached not only to the identities of social actors but also to aspects of the dominant embodied collective memories that brought these identities and related meanings to life.

In this context, it might be sacrilegious to borrow from Heidegger, who died with an unexpired membership card in the Nazi Party, but the idea is that one is White only *in-the-world*, when thrown into a (contemporary) world that is not of one's choosing. Similarly with the "Black race": consider the simple fact that no Black woman in the U.S. can have a White child, and that, conversely, any White woman can have a Black child. Barack Obama is considered the first Black U.S. president, regardless of his ancestry. What better demonstration can we have of the idea that race, and blackness in this case, is a social construct? But furthermore, bear in mind that, also at the beginning of the twentieth century, the "Negro race" was differentially defined from state to state: Florida defined it as 1/8 of African descent; Virginia defined it as 1/16; Alabama defined it as any "African blood." A person may be "Negro" in one state and White in the next. One could change races by moving from place to place. Blackness was, and is today, a cultural and political construct. Blackness in the U.S. today is not what blackness was in the past. Blackness in the U.S. is not what it is in Brazil or Africa. One is Black, once again, only in-the-world.

Much as whiteness — much as race, in general — blackness is also an idea attached to tones of skin, cultural conventions, legal and bureaucratic categories ascribed to phenotypes. Blackness is a crucible of constantly changing ideas. It is in fact a figure of speech, as Mathew Jacobson would probably agree. And it is also an aspect of our modern perceptual collective memory (which is an aspect of the dominant embodied collective memory). "The American eye," Jacobson says, "sees a certain person as black, for instance, whom Haitian or Brazilian eyes might see as white. Similarly, an earlier generation of Americans *saw* Celtic, Hebrew, Anglo-Saxon, or Mediterranean physiognomies where today we see only subtly varying shades of a mostly undifferentiated whiteness" (Jacobson 1998, 10 original emphasis). "Race," in summary, involves collective ideas vivified and enacted by racialized social actors; ideas that thus become organically tied to the social order. "Race" provides an example of the ways in which traditions, ideologies, and even fictions and myths, become collective memories that become embodied collective memories.

RACE AND THE FUTURE

Note also that merely because race is a myth, it is not somehow less real. Human life, in general, has been a haven for errors that have often reorganized aspects of life, our self-regard, our "natures." And race is thus one of the most palpable and stark realities of modernity; one that has become attached not only to the lives of individuals but, as suggested, also to countries and continents. The ideologies of race have become a key aspect of reality because they have managed, again, to enter into the texture of life itself, locally and globally. Hand in hand with larger cultural and socioeconomic structures, racial discourses have become glued not only to ideas and identities, but also to corporeal rhythms, gestures, linguistic schemata, phonetic habituses, to minds, and hearts — to many of the embodied and cognitive dispositions that make us who we are. Argyle provides the following examples:

> West Indians in Britain seem rude because they do not indicate sentence endings by a rising tone, and they use sudden increases of pitch and loudness for emphasis, sounding [to English ears] like outbursts of bad temper. Black

Americans give their utterances a rhythmic structure, and use a wide range of voice quality. . . . The Japanese are restrained in this channel, as in others. They modify their vocal style according to the gender and status of the other. (2007, 64)

Similarly with other dimensions of embodiment, from facial gestures to patterns of walking, from sartorial standards to expression of emotion, from use of space to touching (self and others), from comfort with peripersonal space to comfort with smells: these dimensions also vary along "racial" lines (ibid.). Back to Argyle, his Oxfordian eye, his Oxfordian and "White" corporeal rhythm encourage him to say that, "[B]lack Americans walk and move with energy and style [they] swing and swagger in a rhythmic manner, exhibiting their bodily competence and creativity" (ibid., 62). To quote Cornel West again,

White-supremacist assaults on black intelligence, ability, beauty and character required persistent black efforts to hold self-doubt, self-contempt and even self-hatred at bay. Selective appropriations, incorporation and rearticulation of European ideologies, cultures and institutions alongside an African heritage — a heritage more or less confined to linguistic innovation in rhetorical practices, stylizations of the body in forms of occupying an alien social space (hairstyles, ways of walking, standing, hand expressions, talking) and means of constituting and sustaining camaraderie and community (e.g., antiphonal, call-and-response styles, rhythmic repetition, risk-ridden syncopation in spectacular modes in musical and rhetorical expressions) — were some of the strategies employed [by African Americans]. (1999, 129)

Race, West seems to suggest, is rooted in specific historical circumstances. It tends to flow from the past, from history, to become embodied memory. But importantly, it also involves the present (thought, action) and indeed the forthcoming: creation of new styles, new ideas and ideologies, new aspects of embodiment. "Blackness" involves not only "appropriations" and "incorporation," but also "rearticulations" and "strategies," a constant interaction between the individual and the collective, the individual and history, whereby history may become, as I suggested at the beginning of the chapter, sedimented or rearticulated. The "race" of an individual often intersects with the *longue duree*.[5] The *longue duree* is often expressed in (racialized) bodily and mental schemata, in ways of walking, speaking, in ways of thinking and feeling, in the personal but also in the social dynamics of groups, churches, neighborhoods, and even countries. As I suggested in the previous chapter, aspects of ECMs can be thus determined by the past. And in this sense, "blackness," often involves the enactment and the performance of history, and indeed the embodiment of historical time. Yet, the history of blackness also involves transgressive signals, as West suggests, new embodied signals that, portending new aspects of embodied memory, also portended new futures. Intellectuals such as West, artists such as Spike Lee, and an army of "awareness specialists," as Bourdieu may call them, provide alternative ideas that may agglomerate to form alternative symbolic universes. This is an aspect in the dynamics of social change. It is an aspect of the politics of small things, as Jeffrey Goldfarb may agree. But if such symbols and ideas become incarnate, consigned to embodied collective memory, related changes become more durable, in the Aristotelian sense above, as they come to partake from the organic texture of history.

Note, as well, that of course other "races" have similarly inherited a set of particular social dynamics that have exerted their influence on (racialized) social actors within range. These dynamics have also influenced the reactions of individuals who adapt to them, or who resist them in various ways and degrees. Recall, for instance, the doctrines of temperance, asceticism and social control that racialized the descendants of Winthrop and of the New England Puritans. This milieu — this matrix of ideas, radical innovations, and conservative fervors; these sets of anxieties and economic and legislative systems — also provided a framework that, back to West, influenced people's "ways of walking, standing, hand expressions, talking" — features of embodied memory that were collectively experienced and articulated. This Puritan milieu, so concerned with things that "fermented in the depths of the souls," as Tocqueville says (2000), was also concerned with things that fermented on the surfaces of bodies. For how can a society penetrate the soul of the citizen without touching her body first, without first addressing her clothes, her appearance, her tone of voice, her manners, and her appetites? Hence, these temperate bodies, moved, felt, looked, talked, and appeared in ways that largely reflected their own history. And thus they came to see themselves, particularly during colonial times, as naturally different from Others. These bodies subsumed and thus exuded a different "nature," a different race, a different embodied collective memory, "innate," inherited, and, as many people still believe today, "genetically" distinct.

Conclusion

Again, "race" does not always involve reflective or even conscious "strategies," in West's terms. These "ways of walking, standing, hand expressions, talking" are largely automatic, part of an inherited and embodied spatio-temporal idiom, and social actors do not usually stop to conjure up and strategically deploy this racialized gesture and that rhythm. Back to Aristotle, racialized social actors are doers who are not always prior to their deeds. Yet aspects of race, and aspects of embodied collective memory, in general, can be more or less conscious, performative, autonomic and indeed "strategic," part of "a very rich culture of resistance," as West says. As Hazel Markus and Paula Moya argue, race is "done" but also undone (2010). It is enacted and enacted anew. The performer may automatically quote racial scripts, or, as Harry Elam also argues, "[reconfigure] established gestures, behaviors, linguistic patterns, cultural attitudes, and social expectations associated with race" (2010).

The history of race reminds us that collective discourses, and even collective fictions can become incarnate, and that embodied collective memories, in general, can, as implied above, mark individuals as well as continents. Race also reminds us that, when collective ideas are vivified by social actors, when ideas become organically tied to the social order, the body becomes a key channel of social control. Certain "Negro" identities were necessary to construct and sustain the colonial order. Likewise, certain minority (and majority) identities are today needed to sustain social structures, boundaries, and hierarchies. But "race" also lets us see that embodiment holds the potential for renewal, resistance, and creativity. The supersession of Negro identities, and the construction and embodiment of Black and African American identities, devitalized the colonial logic, and the social structures rooted in it. A theory of embodied memory cannot fully explain the emergence of these new social structures, but the idea is that, as these new racial identities became embodied, as the embodied collective memory therefore creaked and groaned with new internal dynamics, different *social* dynamics were sponsored by these processes. The history of race, characterized by movement and flux, suggests, in summary, that discourses, even if embodied, are fluid. Race today is not race yesterday. Whiteness is different today. Today people are no longer "Hittites," "Alpines," "Iberics." Much as the history of gender, the history of race also underscores that ECMs can open the way to new "natures": for example, to new ways of living blackness or whiteness; to new natures that can also release new configurations of power underlying the social order.

NOTES

1. http://www.aaanet.org/stmts/racepp.htm. Last visited: 11/12/2011.

2. This was a second migration, as the earlier ancestor of the modern human lineage, *Homo erectus*, appears to have emigrated out of Africa about 1.9 million years ago, shortly after evolving from *Homo habilis*. *Erectus* probably reached Asia 1.8 million years ago or so. Back to the replacement hypothesis, its descendants seem to have been, precisely, replaced, in the wake of the second immigration, by the more advanced African descendants of *Homo erectus*, us, *Homo sapiens*.

3. Such adaptive change, incidentally, would be critical because lack of vitamin D is related to bone deformity, including pelvic deformity, which would have had reproductive consequences for the species.

4. Note also that these European groups were targets of racism by, we may say, "officially white" people. H.F.K Gunther, in his The Racial Elements of European History (1927) says that the Nordic is naturally driven to "truth and justice, prudence, reserve, and steadfastness." Alpines "are petty criminals, small-time swindlers, sneak thieves, and sexual perverts." Mediterraneans are "strongly swayed by sexual life" (in Haney Lopez 2006, 75).

5. Coined by historian Ferdinand Braudel, and belonging to French Annales School, the term *longue duree* refers primarily to the historical analysis of social structures that evolve very slowly and, precisely, through long extensions of time. The *longue duree* designates deep structures that, often entrenched within cultures, resist transformation, even if they thus resist logical or ethical reforms as well. "Race" involves precisely these sorts of long-term and deeply seated historical as well as mental structures, which, I argue, are inseparable from embodied collective memories that bring these structures to life.

Chapter Twelve

Layers of ECMs

LAYERS OF ECMS

Embodied collective memories are not univocal and monolithic but multilayered and, as the previous chapter suggests, pliable and fluid, as I further discuss in this and the next chapters. A large empirical and theoretical corpus has already considered many of the layers of embodiment, though without providing an integrated theory of embodied collective memory. This corpus involves, for example, the history of sexuality and pleasure (Foucault 1976, 1984a, and 1984b), the sociology of gender and engenderment (Butler 1993; Bourdieu 2001), the fragments that we have from the history of sentiments (Camille 1998; Paz 1993), of laughter (Bakhtin 1984; Provine 2000), and of gestures (Schmitt 1990). This corpus also touches on the ethics and aesthetics of gesture (Elias 1978; Bakhtin 1984; Goffman 1971). It deals with sensations such as physical pain and how internalized norms contribute to these experiences (Wall 2002). It has provided a sociological perspective on phonetics (Bourdieu 1991), a historical perspective on bodily embarrassment, revulsion, and disgust (Elias 1978). Writers have provided fragments from the history of scatology (Paster 1993; Narvaez 2003) and anthropological theories to understand changing norms pertaining to hygiene, bodily purity and profanity (Durkheim 1965; Douglas 2000; Goffman 1971; Hoy 1995, Ashenburg 2007). This corpus deals, as well, with schemata of perception, and suggests that vision, hearing, tasting, and smelling are invested with culture and in this sense change with time and place (Ashenburg 2007; Merleau-Ponty 1964; Debord 2010; Berger 1980; Hoy 1995). The literature has helped us understand the history and the evolution of manners (Elias 1978), the social psychology of touch and interpersonal space (Argyle 2007), the cultural history of food, which is also the history of taste and nutrition (Mintz

1984; Elias 1978). It has also provided insight on how bodily height, weight, strength, exertion, health, disease, pain, longevity, and death have changed with history, particularly over the past 300 years (Boas 2001; Floud et al. 2011; Hobsbawn 1996, 8), etc. Paul Valery has asked:

> Don't you see that you are just so many simple objects of extravagant experiments, that thousands of unknown actions and substances are being tested upon you? They want to know how your organs will react to high speeds and low pressures; if your blood can adapt to strongly carburated air if your retinas can withstand increasingly energetic light and radiation . . . and that is without mentioning the odors and noises that you tolerate, the vibrations and currents of every frequency, the synthetic foods and lots more! . . . your senses are obliged to absorb, without a single day's pause, so much music, art, drugs, strange drinks, spectacles, movement, sudden changes in elevation and temperature, political and economic anxiety, as all the rest of humanity put together was once able to absorb over the course of three centuries . . . You are so many guinea pigs, my dear humans, and guinea pigs treated particularly badly, since the tests to which you are subjected are inflicted, varied and repeated constantly and solely at random chance. There is no scientist, there is not even a laboratory assistant who regulates, adjusts, monitors, or interprets certain experiments, certain artificial vicissitudes, of which no one can foresee the effects, of greater or lesser profundity, upon your precious persons. (in Alfano 2004, 249)

The literature suggests, in any case, that embodiment, broadly conceived, indeed changes with time and place, and that collectively significant symbols become incarnated in a large array of bodily elements that underpin the embodied experience. Drawing from this theoretical and empirical corpus, in this chapter I provide a range of examples that illustrate the idea that these bodily elements, biologically grounded as they are, nonetheless become linked to culture in various ways and degrees. And here I also provide examples that illustrate a notion often under-theorized by these writers: that the various layers of ECM, as I have been suggesting, also resist the encroachments of culture. In this chapter, that is to say, I illustrate the idea that embodied memory binds seemingly separate things: muscle and mind, culture and muscle, concept and percept, concept and affect, internal and external worlds, consciousness and unconsciousness, the drives of the organism and the institutions that regulate them, the individual and her history. The examples below also show that changes in any layer of embodiment often carry consequences, as these layers are gravid with possibilities that can affect the lives and the futures of individuals and groups.

Food, Nutrition, and Embodiment

Let us begin by briefly considering the history of food — sugar, salt, and fat, in particular — and how it has affected some of the most visible and obvious aspects of the embodied experience and of embodied memory, in general. Let us think of sugar, first, one of our dietary necessities today. About 20,000 years ago, a cave painting already depicted "a human figure stealing honey from a hive" (Mintz 1999, 85) and we have been chasing after this taste ever since. But of course the "paleo-diet" was extremely low in sugars, if compared, particularly, to the modern diet. And to be sure, any diet other than the modern one was also extremely low in these kinds of carbohydrates. When invented on the Indian subcontinent, around 350 AD, sugar (sucrose), was rare; and during the Renaissance it was in fact a symbol of power (royal feasts boasted sugary "renditions . . . of the works of Bernini and Michelangelo [and] embodied kingly and ecclesiastical power because they were costly consumables" [Mintz 1999, 93]). Today, by contrast, sugar is massively consumed and our world is infinitely "sweeter" than ever before. "In 1800, the world sugar output stood at about 250,000 tons; in 1900, about eight million tons; in 1950, about thirty million tons; in 1993 about 110 million tons" (ibid., 95). "For five centuries, no other food has so successfully captured the interest of Everyman [in the U.S]. Sugar's zenith seems to be the fin de siècle America" (ibid.). Similarly with salt: before modernity salt was also comparatively rare (and if we consider paleo-nutrition, it was extremely rare). Ancient wars were fought over salt; Roman soldiers sometimes got paid with salt (they were worth their salt); ancient cultures had salt deities, salt collecting and distributing rituals (Kurlansky 2002). By contrast, our world today is infinitely saltier.

Sugar and salt consumption has thus changed. Diet in general has dramatically changed. And as a consequence, bodies, palates included, have also changed, as we will see below. Particularly after the European colonial expansion, diets the world over indeed took a dramatic turn, as pre-Columbian foods were added to postcolonial diets. The newfound potato, a rare aphrodisiac according to the Elizabethans, this "devil luxury," as Shakespeare's Falstaff says, eventually spread and "changed the history of the world," as William McNeill has shown (1999). Foods such as American corn, legumes, tropical fruits, and Indian and Asian spices changed gustative habituses. Colonists discovered a new world and also a new world of flavors and nutrients that nudged new palates and new aspects of embodied memory, in general. (Gonzalo Fernandez de Oviedo, a sixteenth century Spaniard, is in awe of the new flavors, textures, and aromas. The guanabana is much superior to the apple, he thinks. The *mamey* is finger-licking and indeed "nothing better exists." "But he bites into a medlar and an aroma unequaled even by musk invades his head. *The medlar is the best fruit*, he corrects himself, *and nothing comparable can be found*" [Galeano 1985, original emphasis]. Eventually, however, he discovers that the pineapple, a delicacy that "outdoes [all fruits], as the feathers of the peacock outshine those of any other bird" [ibid].)

Today, not only available foods, but also patterns of food consumption and production, foodlore, rituals, and ideas about food are radically different than those of any other historical period. We produce much more food, for example, and consume less fiber, and of course eat much more processed, artificial, and engineered foods. Unlike other historical periods, food products such as meat and fat are today massively produced and consumed (animals, to be sure, are produced via a factory model that has largely replaced the farming model). And, again, bodies have responded to these trends (Floud et al. 2011). The average weight for an adult American male was 146 lbs in 1850 and today he weighs 191 lbs, as the New York Times reports [1] (see also Odgen et al. 2004). Whereas famine and malnutrition were constant throughout pre-modernity, today one in three adults in the U.S. is obese,[2] with all of what that implies from the point of view of the embodied experience: embodied identity, movement, rhythm, health, affects — these central aspects of embodied collective memory. And indeed, as Floud, Fogel, Harris, et al. report (2011), post-industrial bodies have changed in ways that have no parallel in the history of the 7,000 or so generations of humans that have inhabited the earth.[3] Today, food consumption, particularly in the West, has changed important aspects of embodiment, key aspects of modern embodied collective memories.

Pain and Tears, Affects, Sexual Pleasure, and Laughter

But beyond such broad and immediately understandable aspects of embodiment as diet and bodily sizes, the deeper, most "universal" and seemingly unchanging aspects of the embodied experience — sensations and affects, for example — have also changed. As I will presently show, these aspects of embodiment have also been invested by culture, and have also changed over time. Sensations and affects, I will argue, are thus ingredients of embodied collective memories and, as such, are also ingredients of the social order vivified by these memories.

Let us begin with one of the most private sensations: pain. There is, of course, a raw dimension of pain that is biological, universal, not related to culture; and indeed, a species-survival rule says that infants must be able to express pain outside their little bit of consciousness, independently of even conscious self-awareness. But precisely because pain begs to be expressed, the cultural order always confers meanings to it; meanings that, as we will see below, can modify aspects of the sensation (Wall 2002, 62-70; Wall and Melzack 1996). Culture can become a component of the sensation itself.

The work of Lanzetta and colleagues, one of the first studies to show that pain can be mediated by the attitudes of the sufferer, showed that subjects instructed to inhibit their reactions to electrical shocks experienced less pain, as self-reported and as measured by skin conductance, than subjects instructed to exaggerate their expressions (Lanzetta et al. 1976). As Argyle also reports, the conscious control of facial expression can have modulatory effects on autonomic states related to "anger, happiness, sadness, pain, fear, and humor" (2007, 74).[4] And the inference to be made after these studies is that, insofar as these levels of pain can be modified by social circumstances that govern expression of emotion (Lanzetta et al. 1976), the experience of pain may respond to cultural rules and expectations. This is in fact a well-accepted idea today. As Madelon Peters explains, "Processes at an organic (spinal sensitization, cortical reorganization), individual psychological (pain cognition and beliefs, hypervigilance), and social level (learned behavior) may contribute to pain perception and pain behavior and ultimately to maintenance of pain" (in Lautenbacher and Fillingim 2004, 71; see also Melzack and Casey 1968). To be sure, as Patrick Wall has argued (2002), cultural factors, such as those related to gender, enormously contribute to the experience of pain, exerting stronger influences on the individual experience than, for example, genetic factors. Wall suggests, for example, that "women [have] a higher threshold for heat pain whereas men [have] a higher threshold for painful electric shocks. In our society," he says, "women have far more experience handling hot plates . . . while men, with their enthusiastic fiddling with car engines and electrical gadgets, are usually familiar with tingling or stabbing electric shocks" (ibid., 65).

One may consider also the case of the Wild Child of Aveyron (Benzaquén 2006),[5] the boy who, in 1800, was found in the woods of France, at the age of twelve or so, where he had managed to survive alone for most of his life. Naked, this boy-minus-culture played blithely in the snow. "[E]xtreme cold did not affect him. Even in winter he went barefoot and covered himself with a single sheet to sleep" (ibid., 158). "There was no way to make him wait until [very hot potatoes] had cooled off a bit," his caretaker reports, "he burned himself, and expressed his pain with loud inarticulate sounds, which were however not plaintive" (ibid., 150). He seemed to tolerate extreme cold and extreme heat particularly well, as though lacking culture — and thus lacking the meanings, images, associations related to these sensations — had a protective effect for him. But beyond these examples concerning low levels of tissue damage, there are also examples concerning high levels of damage, which also show that pain, even at this level, can be affected by culture. As Wall and Melzack report:

> One of the most striking examples of the impact of cultural values on pain is the hook swinging ritual in practice in part of India [Kosambi 1976]. The

ceremony derives from an ancient practice in which a member of a social group is chosen to represent the power of the gods. The role of the chosen man (or 'celebrant') is to bless . . . children and crops. . . . What is remarkable about the ritual is that the steel hooks . . . are shoved under his skin and muscles on both sides of the back . . . . [A]t the climax of the ceremony . . . he swings free, hanging only from those hooks embedded in his back, to bless the children and crops. Astonishingly, there is no evidence that the man is in pain during the ritual; rather, he appears to be in a 'state of exaltation.' (Wall and Melzack 1996, 16-17)

Let me amplify a quote I provided previously: the authors add that,

There are many examples of comparable procedures in other cultures. In East Africa, men and women undergo an operation entirely without anaesthetics or pain reliving drugs — called "trepanation," in which the scalp and underlying muscles are cut in order to expose a large area of the skull. The skull is then scraped by the doktari as the man or woman sits calmly, without flinching or grimacing, holding a pan under their chin to catch the dripping blood. Films of this procedure are extraordinary to watch because of the discomfort they in-duce in the observers, which is in striking contrast to the apparent lack of discomfort in the people undergoing the operation. There is no reason to believe that these people are physiologically different in any way. Rather, the operation is accepted by their culture as a procedure that brings relief of chronic pain. (ibid., 17)

Combined, the examples above suggests that we experience such sensations biologically and reflexively, as any other animal, but also reflectively, through cultural meanings, associations, and symbols that seem to be impor-tant not only for the management of pain, but also for the experience of pain, and for sensation, in general (e.g., extreme cold). Such meanings, it seems, are often inserted between the stimulus and the response. Again, some forms of pain, particularly extreme pain, may escape cultural factors, and thus we may speak of a *primordium* of pain, as John Watson may agree. A scream of pain may in fact feel foreign to the bearer of pain, as though some unfamiliar voice had momentarily leased the self. But the idea that pain is always a "pure" sensation involves, as Wall argues (2002), age-old Cartesian biases, which still insist today on the radical separation between mind and body, and subject and object. As Wall observes, we don't detect pain like machines. Instead, we often undergo these experiences like the encultured creatures that we are. Inasmuch as time and place contribute to the phenomenology of pain, we may speak of nociceptive collective memories attached to various times and places.

Tears, Funerals

Likewise, universal experiences related to psychological pain may also be altered, by degrees, by culture. Let us consider tears, for instance (which are quintessentially human: no other animal expresses emotion through tears). As Heidegger would agree (2001), tears contain not only traces of biology, traces of phylogeny, proteins and salts, but also traces of experience. Tears are not only attached to evolution but are also attached to the social world.[6] They are, in this Heideggerian sense, in-the-world, so that the tears of Madame Bovary, for instance, contained private elements, but also elements of romanticism, the prevalent affective discourse that provided a sentimental education for this Flaubertian character. "Would [Madame Bovary's] sentimental sufferings have been so dreadful," Milan Kundera asks, "if she had not been guided by [historically specific] models of romantic love?" (in Cervantes 1999, viii). Would Werther's tears have been so Wertherian if not attached to romantic models as well? Would the tears of Saint Therese or Saint John of the Cross have been so "avid" and "voluptuous," as Cioran says (2004), if not guided by Christian ideas about suffering? (Bear in mind that branches of the Christian tradition, from Benedict to John Paul II, have exalted the experience of pain, and suffering, in general, as bringing the believer closer to the passion of Christ; and that some groups have indeed lavished suffering with libido, regarded it as a gift, "the "Gift of Tears," the "gift of a laceration," which "tenderly wounded" Saint John of the Cross, and made Margaret-Mary Alacoque say that "None of my sufferings has been equal to that of not having suffered enough" [ibid.]).

These sorts of tears, romantic, "voluptuous," "avid," "mystic," "Wertherian," stem, at least in part, from certain systems of meaning. (And thus they would certainly be beyond the affective and nociceptive horizon of the wild boy above.) As Mauss observes, "Not only weeping but all kinds of oral expressions of emotions are essentially, not exclusively psychological or physiological phenomena, but social phenomena eminently stamped by non-spontaneity and by the most complete obligation" (1921). (To be sure, not only why, but *how* we invoke and perform shared sentiments can be culturally mediated. The abstract images in the memory of the weeper and the concrete ways in which he sheds his tears are points of intersection between the individual and the collective, between nature and culture, the present and the past.[7])

It is also instructive to think of funerals, and how social actors from different social locations may weep with different intensities, rhythms, at different times, with different senses of privacy, of self-control, of decorum, which may indeed vary with class, ethnicity, religion. Many Indian women feverishly jumped into the funerary pyres burning their dead husbands, pushed, of course, by custom (Galeano 2008, 31). The codes that govern expression of grief among Egyptian Bedouins prescribe a sense of indifference, or blame or anger, which often governs the public behavior of the bereaved; a code that, however, also prescribes extreme private grief (Abu-Lughod 1985). The Ifaluk, in the South Pacific, think that grieving for the dead should be very intense and very brief (Lutz 1988). As Catherine Lutz reports, the bereaved should "scream and wail for the twenty four hours of the funeral and then stop thinking about the deceased." This, Lutz also notes, was very different from her own "surreptitious tears," and her "stifled," "stiff," American emotional style (ibid., 100). In the northern Peruvian Sierras, where I spent my childhood, surreptitious funerary tears were not the norm. On the contrary, professional wailers (*lloronas*) were often hired to deploy their stentorian and overly melodramatic wailing during wakes and funerals. Victorians, in their turn, encouraged open expressions of grief at funerals, while diverting emotional expression away from death itself, from the decay of the flesh (introducing, for such purposes, procedures such as embalming or the application of makeup to the deceased [Stearns 1994]). They saw funerals as occasions to conquer the fear of death (ibid.). Their grief was thus framed.

One may also think about the dimension of time, and how it affects the meanings and experiences pertaining to grief. Contemporary funerary rites are, in general, invested with different meanings if compared to those of previous historical periods. Bear in mind that our lives are much longer than ever before (Lancaster 1990), that we are less often visited by death, that before modernity death had a strong presence in the collective imagination (and in the perceptual register: eyes, ears, noses), and that death, today, has therefore become invested with new significations.[8] As Rainer Maria Rilke says,

> Everyone [before modernity] has had a death of their own. Those men who bore it within their armour, enclosed like a prisoner, those women who became exceedingly old and minute and then passed away on a huge bed as if on a giant stage, before their entire family, the servants and the dogs, with discretion and control. Even the children, even the very smallest children, did not have just any infant death, they gathered themselves and they died in what they had already become and in which they would someday turn into. It was that which gave those women a melancholy beauty, when they were heavy with a child and they stood there, their bodies huge, their small hands resting on those bodies involuntarily concealing two fruits: a child and a death. (in Alfano 2004, 74)

"Dying," Walter Benjamin adds, "was once a public process in the life of the individual and a most exemplary one; think of the medieval pictures in which the death bed has turned into a throne toward which the people press through the wide-open doors of the death house … there used to be no house, hardly a room, in which someone had not once died" (1968, 94). By contrast, dying today "has been pushed further and further out of the perceptual world of the living" (ibid.). We "live in rooms that have never been touched by death" (ibid.). Thus, to the extent to which death has thus retreated from the sphere of life, not only funerals but also the experience of grieving for the dead has become, as suggested, invested with new meanings.

In summary, different times and places provide explicit or tacit rules for the management and expression of emotions, even of intimate emotions such as grief (Hochschild 1979). And, inasmuch as these sentimental educations are learned and naturalized, we may speak of affective collective memories. Tears also contain *primordia* of emotion and a sense of impulsiveness that is biological in origin and independent from culture, but they contain, as well, cultural meanings. These can be more or less conscious, but can in either case affect the experience of these emotions (ibid.), the phenomenology of grief, the ways in which the person signals the experience, the emotional style of the person, and the emotional memory of the group. It is not surprising that the boy of Aveyron initially did not weep to express displeasure or grief. Only after being contacted he learnt to express emotion in such a way.

Sexuality and Sexual Pleasure

From tears and pain we can now visit affects at the other end of the spectrum: connubial affects and sexual pleasure, which are also primordial while also changing with time and place. Human sexuality includes, of course, homeostatic pressures that have nothing to do with culture, but, as Freud argues, it is not merely a question of homeostatic imbalance and discharge, as that of lower animals. Beyond homeodynamics, human sexuality always includes elements of fantasy, such that sex is always narrativized and pleasure is always othered. These elements of fantasy involve "imagoes," in the Freidan idiom, such as those related to the oedipal triangle, which can arise regardless of culture. But sexual fantasy also involves the images, prescriptions, taboos of specific cultures and historical periods.

Octavio Paz (1993) has provided examples pertaining, precisely, to the *Ars Amatoria* of various eras and places: Japanese lovers, Paz says, often saw their loving "from the point of view of a melancholy philosophy steeped in Buddhism, and the sense of the impermanence of the things in this world" (ibid., 36-37). Chinese lovers, by contrast, saw it as a reaction to the "stern" and "tedious" Confucian "set of prohibitions and precepts with which adults attempt to thwart youth" (ibid.). In turn, ancient Greek lovers saw love and sexuality from the point of view of ancient Greece, of course. Males, for example, often pined for boys (Foucault 1979, 1984b), an affect that has disappeared today, along with ancient Greece, and along with the Greek aura of normality that surrounded related ideas, rituals and sentiments. Penelope listened with delight to the tales recounting her husband's sexual adventures, the hero Odysseus, who navigated his homecoming by means of wit, valor, *and* sexual tactics (seducing indeed two goddess, Calypso and Circe, to enlist their help). Odysseus' and Penelope's connubial sentiments seem exempt from the romantic imperatives that largely underpin connubial sentiments today, particularly those that, having their longer roots in the Chivalric Age, prescribe strict secrecy to "protect" women from emotional injury.

Let us stay with this idea for a moment. The example of chivalric romanticism is very instructive in this context, as it lets us see the ways in which sentiments, including those associated with sexuality, can be affected, even framed, by historical circumstances. Chivalric romanticism, romanticism in general, and related affects, did not emerge *ab ovo,* but as only as a set of objective social conditions aligned to frame the affective economies and the affective collective memories of the time (Paz 1993; Camille 1998). These objective conditions included, for example, the decrease of famine and increase of available tilling labor, which made romantic sentiments more affordable, and allowed pertinent aspects of the affective experience. By contrast, famine and other harsh conditions of life encouraged more callused sentiments. Secondly, the chivalric affective economy was also encouraged by the rebirth of the ancients, Ovid in particular, and of the Ovidian notion of an "art of love," a new discourse that emerged to provide new symbols, new affective goals, and a new affective language for noble men. (Ovid, recall, gave his male readers tactical and strategic advice on how to get their way with women, by means of rhetoric, poesis, deception, etc.). Thirdly, Chivalric romanticism was also made possible by the rise of the status of medieval women, which rose hand in hand with a renewed theological and popular valuation of the Virgin Mary, which, in the eyes of many men, redeemed women from the notion that they were guilty for the downfall of men, of Adam; a circumstance that also made their romantic sentiments more affordable, emotionally. Fourthly, this affective discourse was possible on account of customs regarding inheritance, which proscribed younger male siblings from inheriting substantive portions of the land — as well as from working, which created a situation where the socioeconomic standing of these men depended either on rapine, battle — or on finding a consort with a good dowry. This economic and social scenario, in summary, framed chivalric affects, and the dominant affective collective memory.

These conditions that marked chivalric patterns of courtship and marriage provided, again, a vocabulary, gestures, images, and values for men and women (encapsulated in the saccharine songs of the troubadours), which informed and framed their affective economies. In contrast to previous periods, these connubial affects became invested with such notions as attraction, as opposed to election, and the sense of emotional fidelity and betrayal, as opposed to breaking contractual agreements (see Paz 1993). Hence, sometimes chivalric courting, literally "the affective tactics of courtiers," was invested with intense affects, such as those related to the binaries purity/impurity and fidelity/infidelity.[9] But sometimes, it was primarily a utilitarian strategy where men deployed gentle Ovidian weaponry that helped them home in on affective, sexual, and economic resources.

Note as well that other cultures never developed any such "culture of love." For example, the very notion was sinful among puritan Americans. Hence, aspects of the Puritan's sexual and affective experiences were invested by yet another set of discourses. In the seventeenth century, a New England woman, charged with the sin of fornication, believed that she had brought the wrath of God "not on my selve but allso apon the place where I live," as she confessed to her County Court (in Morgan 1966). In the nineteenth century, another New England woman was punished with a fine for allowing herself to be given a kiss (Tocqueville 2000, 38). Guilt, a sense of transgression, and related images and symbols, had a strong presence in the sexual and affective experiences of these early American communities.

By contrast, many American men and women today experience sexual affects in very different ways, having detached not only this puritan ethos but also many elements of romanticism from these experiences. Today, a "hookup culture," for example, is reportedly emerging among youth, particularly on American college campuses (England and Thomas 2006). This seems to be a new sexual and affective discourse that exempts sex from affective involvement. Indeed, in contrast to the romantic affective schema, this new type of sexual involvement is not the culminating point of emotional involvement, but rather it seems that it often precedes it (ibid.). The inference to be made, in any case, is that the phenomenology of sexuality, which involves ideas, pleasures, and affects, was different in the groups mentioned above: the knights and ladies of the twelfth century, the Chinese, Greek, and Japanese lovers, the puritans, and the men and women on college campuses today. In his *La Vita Nova*, Dante says that "love does not exist in and for itself as a substance: it is the accident of a substance." "Love" involves primordial but also "accidental" aspects.

Likewise with a range of other human affects, which are also accidents of substances. Let us also consider, for example, the expressions of affect in the following missive: "Now that great distance separates us, my desire to be with you has grown. I know not what wretched stream of thought inclines us toward things we cannot have and make us want them even more than things which are permitted. Today, in a burst of affection, my heart leapt to you across barriers of countries and, soaring high above the peaks, went to visit my loved one, but with a fresh tenderness" (in Schama 1999, 96). Petrarch to Laura? Heloise to Abelard? This paragraph was taken from a letter by Philip Rubens to his brother Peter Paul, paragons of seventeenth century brotherly love. Perhaps the brotherly nature of this letter was not apparent. If so, this would show that expressions of sentiment have changed in the intervening years. I argue, furthermore, that it is not only the epistolary style that has changed, but the affective style, and indeed the affective collective memory. Of course brothers everywhere know brotherly love, but the meaning of brotherliness, the degrees of respect allotted to, and expected from, older or younger brothers, the way in which brothers relate, all change with time and place, and thus related affects also change. Rubens' affective register, as anyone else's, included of course raw, unmediated elements,[10] but also elements of culture.

Let me refer to another and very elucidative example of affective memory: laughter. Much as other emotions, such as grief, laughter is also a universal, evolutionary, phylogenic outcome that, however, varies with culture and indeed with specific social categories such as class, race, and gender. Eduardo Galeano (1991) tells us of a man who spent his life, "tape recorder in hand," collecting different kinds of laughter, which he sold to the radio studios and to movies and television. This peculiar salesman, Galeano says, recorded the *natural* "joy of children at play and the weary mirth of the aged . . . the giggles of lovers . . . the whooping gales and roars of lunatics, sincere laughter" — but he also recorded "black, mulatto, and white laughter, poor, rich, and in between" (Galeano 1991, 221). He recorded natural and sociological dimensions of laughter. Brym and Lie (2009) say that "People with higher status get more laughs. People with lower status laugh more." Women tend to laugh more than men (Provine 2000). Laughter, as an aspect of gender expression, indeed helps sustain gender dynamics and hierarchies. A Kayapó myth, Galeano also says, forbids warriors from laughing, as laughing is appropriate for women and children (1991).

Bear in mind, as well, that laughter often has little to do with laughing and more to do with a cultural rhetoric that facilitates interpersonal exchanges and affirms the codes that govern interactions (Goffman 1971a). Of course, this type of laugher is particularly dependent on cultural scripts.

It is also worth noting that smiling patterns are likewise dependent on cultural scripts (Argyle 2007). Smiling is timeless but also affected by time, place, and social location. Even the muscular event that we call "smile," As Dacher Keltner has argued, may vary according to cultural parameters (in Max 2005). Henry Seaford, for instance, found that Americans from southern states, in contrast to Americans from northern states, often deployed "pursed smiles": tighter lips that could be closed or open and accompanied by tongue display (1978). People from different nationalities may also smile for different reasons and more or less often (Poyatos 1996), and these patterns often change over time. Countries whose economies increasingly rely on the service sector, for example, often create and extend new display rules that encourage smiling (and that govern emotions, in general) (Hochschild 1979 and 2003). McDonald's managers had trouble training unaccustomed Greenlander cashiers to smile right and left throughout their eight hour shift, American style. But, as Anthony Giddens and colleagues report, in many supermarkets in Greenland the staff are now increasingly "shown training videos of friendly service techniques [including smiling training sessions, and] some have been even sent abroad on training classes" (2010). As I have suggested elsewhere, a glance at the official portraits of the U.S. presidents in chronological order reveals that the smiling curve begins to peak only by the middle of the twentieth century. Just as one may speak of an economy and a sociology of smiles, one may also speak of a history to the meaning of smiling (Narvaez, 2009).

To summarize, different histories involve different sentimental educations, and overlapping and universal, but also specific affective features that characterize various affective collective memories. "We no longer have 'melancholy,'" Argyle notes, "an Elizabethan emotion more positive than depression and a valued aesthetic state. We do not have the Japanese 'amae,' a relation of childish dependence on another adult" (2007, 302). "The Utku, an Inuit band, are so strict about hiding their anger after infancy," Peter Stearns explains, "that some do not even have a separate word for the emotion" (1999).

> In some societies, including the Ifaluk as described by [Catherine] Lutz and the Inuit group described by [Jean] Briggs..., people are suspicious of anger. For an adult to display anger in such societies would be equivalent in a Western society to being introduced to a stranger and dissolving in embarrassment, staring at the floor, and remaining silent. [This] would be enough to label the person as unable to take part in ordinary interactions. By contrast, in the West anger is seen as sometimes necessary to protect one's rights, and to maintain a respect for the self. So — surprisingly perhaps — anger in Western societies is not primarily the emotion of rejection. It is the emotion of conflict, but of also of negotiation, as [James] Averill [1982] found. (Jenkins et al 1998, 90)

The constellation of affects is private but also othered, unique and also tied to a variety of social memories. (Hence our affective memory is different than that of the wild child.)

Laughter and Desire: Affective Control Betrayed

Let me finally discuss the ways in which affects resist cultural inscription. If affects can be modulated, and affective memories conditioned or even colonized by the social order, the affective order is never a mere reflection of culture. And if the social conditioning of affective memories is not without consequences for individuals and for groups, the resistances of the affective order are not without consequences either. To conclude this chapter, let me go back in time and briefly consider one last example, related to Saint Bernard de Clairvaux; an example that provides a stark reminder of the ways in which, precisely, the affective order, and the organism itself, resist inscription.[11] Let us focus on this central, powerful, orthodox medieval figure, a man whose type of monastic spirit, Schmitt says, was the sort where "tears of compunction should reign and laughter be banished" (1990, 137). Having roots in Benedict's doctrines,[12] Clairvaux's program condensed about five centuries of monastic ideology; and, to borrow the term from Michel Foucault, it indeed condensed a veritable "technology of ascetic practices," inclusive of elaborate techniques of bodily disciplining and mortification. In the obsessive and highly efficient religious fortresses under his rule, every hour of the day was regimented and monitored. Their compulsory rhythm of existence aimed first and foremost to control the appetitive body of the monk who, save exceptions, was an Olympic athlete of asceticism and self-mortification, a man whose affective, sensorial and nociceptive experiences seem responsive to the monastic code. Such Orwellian life in fact aimed, to borrow the notion from Foucault again, to *create* the body of the monk, as if "out of formless clay"; for, thus vanquishing the obstacles placed by the monk's body, it could fully penetrate his soul (Coakley 1997).

Saint Bernard de Clairvaux tells us that any "strange movement of the body reveals a new disease in the soul." "A wicked man," he says, "winketh with his eyes, speaketh with his feet, teacheth with his fingers" (in Schmitt 1990, 137). Such gestures had to be surveilled and also mastered. Sensations had to be mastered as well. The very perceptual act had to be controlled: "We who have withdrawn from the people," Clairvaux writes, "we who have left behind all that is precious and beautiful in this world for the sake of Christ . . . regard as dung all things shining in beauty, soothing in sound, agreeable in fragrance, sweet in taste, pleasant in touch" (in Janson and Janson 2003, 389). Yet, such firm disciplinary technologies notwithstanding, the system had breakdowns (of course). Below, for example, the saint speaks about the monks' blunders and vanities, and their lack of virtue and piety.

> Facetiousness [Clairvaux's complains] appears in [the monk's] gestures, merriment in his face, vanity in his stride. He likes to make jokes; he is easily and quickly moved to laughter...For just as a windbag with a small vent, if compressed when it is distended with air, will whistle as it deflates, and the escaping air, not leaking out but shot out, keeps making a noise, so the monk who has filled his heart with silly and ludicrous thoughts, finding no outlet for the blasphemous blast because of the rule of silence, lets it escape from his throat in snorts. He keeps covering his face from shame, he compresses his lips, he grinds his teeth; he laughs without wanting to, he guffaws involuntarily. And when he blocks his mouth with his fists, you can hear him chortle through his nose. (in Schmitt 1990, 137)

Seemingly an insignificant example, it nonetheless shows how the monastic ethos may suddenly break down in the very body expected to bring it to life. Such troubled and troublesome laughter signals Bakhtinan freedom, even if involuntarily, as it breaks not only through the monk's nose and grinded teeth, but through the Cistercian rule of silence, through centuries of monasticism, and through the grip that monasticism aimed to have on the spirit of the time, on life itself, on nature itself. Suddenly, the organism casts Luciferian lights into the heart of the medieval embodied collective memory, the monastery. Of course, this troublesome organismic reaction can be easily banished and the monk brought back to order. Perhaps he himself will lustfully seek athletically demanding penances. But for the time being, such laughter creates a small, personal Bakhtinan carnival. It pierces through the spirit of seriousness that dominated the Middle Ages. Even such stark monastic order, such systematic institutional *dispositif*, as Foucault may say, could not simply form the body "out of formless clay." On the contrary, the process of disciplining the body involves toil, trouble, energy spent in the work of repression, and such work is often reverted, even if involuntarily, particularly when the organism itself feels the usurpatory nature of superegoic demands. Such laughter, to borrow again from George Herbert Mead, is indeed *the response of the organism itself* to these demands.

Let me also discuss a central type of organismic response, a common problem constantly besetting monastic life, sexuality, the mortal sin of fornication, the key reason for such astonishing technologies of self-submission and self-mastery. In the totalitarian order that George Orwell imagined in his famous novel, *1984*, the "thought police" targeted sexual thoughts and related "thought crimes"; and, indeed, one of Big Brother's central aims was to finally and ultimately extinguish the human orgasm; for, should this be achieved, all brothers and sisters living in this cruel Orwellian world would finally detach themselves from their ownmost wants. They would thus forsake themselves, and redirect all libidinal energies to The Party, and of course to Big Brother, the tyrannical ruler that demanded total devotion. The ultimate goal of The Party, that is to say, was not to colonize the mind of the individual but, precisely, the responses of the organism itself. Similarly, the main target for the Cistercian order was sexual desire, and the crucial battle raging within monasteries, as well as within the monk's minds and bodies, was precisely the battle for chastity. As in Orwell's dystopic fantasy, a goal that largely governed life in these holy fortresses was helping brothers finally and utterly abandon all self-centered desires — so as to be able to open their souls entirely to the will of the system, and of course to the will of the Lord who, much as Big Brother, also demanded total devotion. Theologian Peter Brown writes,

The sexuality of the [nocturnal] emission created a disjunction between [the monk's] public, daylight self and a last oasis of incommunicable, privatized experience. When such dreams ceased, the last fissure between the private person and his fellows could be assumed to have closed . . . The total expropriation associated with the life of the desert had begun, as in the case of Antony, with the surrender of private wealth. It ended with the surrender of the last traces of sexual fantasy. (in Coakley 1997, 201)

Yet, God granted perfect "purity of heart" only to a few saints. Such is the lesson that these monks teach to theorists of embodiment: the organism can respond on its own terms to external circumstances. As Freud may agree, the organism, often beyond the conscious ego, is in fact constantly trying to appropriate for itself elements of the world, and it is only through hard work that it may be rendered quiescent. And then, lower and conflict-prone claims, the "indestructible demand of human nature," as Peter Brown said, tend to return yet again.

NOTES

1. http://www.nytimes.com/2006/07/30/health/30age.html?scp=3andsq=bodily%20sizes%20civil%20warandst=cse. Last visited: 11/01/11.

2. See, e.g., http://www.cdc.gov/cdctv/ObesityEpidemic/ Last visited: 8/16/2011.

3. Bear in mind as well that throughout pre-modern, mostly agricultural history, bodies were in constant movement; and that today the environment in general allows for less physical activity (ibid.).

4. Hence, Botox injections, as they inhibit conscious control of facial expression, may lead to decreased emotional experiences and responses (Davis et al 2010; Havas et al 2010).

5. Famously depicted by François Truffaut's film *l'Enfant Sauvage,* which I recommend to interested readers. Relatively faithful to the medical record, the film illustrates the extent to which we are encultured, even when even at the level of affects, gait, and capacity to recognize ourselves in a mirror.

6. Tears thus "cannot be measured," Heidegger suggests, precisely insofar as they contain objective and subjective elements. This discussion is amplified in the appendix.

7. It is worth noting, as well, that identical states of physiological arousal may be interpreted and experienced differently according to setting; such that adrenaline injections, for example, may be experienced as euphoria, anger, or joy, depending on experimentally manipulated settings (Schachter and Singer 1962). Affect has roots in physiology but also in circumstance.

8. Pre-modern women often lived to age 30, peasants, in particular. Even up to the nineteenth century, most children experienced the death of at least one sibling. About one every two children under twenty-one saw the death of at least one parent.

9. Hence, El Quixote, the mad "Knight" Errant invented by Cervantes centuries later, fell in love with Dulcinea simply because being in love is a necessary mandate of knighthood. And he fell in love not with the real Dulcinea, but with the pure, platonic form of the "lady," with the concept of the lady, which he loved more than life itself.

10. When his first wife died Rubens said, "I have no pretention about ever attaining a stoic equanimity" (Schama 1999, 144-145).

11. The ruler of the Knights Templar, the main force of the Second Crusade, Clairvaux was arguably the central religious and political figure during his time (and the prime theological and political rival of humanist Peter Abelard, tragic lover of Heloise). Clairvaux was perhaps the most prominent representative of the radical orthodoxy that characterized the High Middle

Ages, in general. Monasteries grew under his rule and the monastic ethos spread outside the monastery, managing to have a significant hold on everyday life, on the medieval zeitgeist. Monastic life, bear in mind, was meant to be, and often was, an example for life in general.

12. Clairvaux denounced the "opulence" of Benedictine monasteries (which were opulent indeed, as their abbots often had a keen interest in art, especially if lavishly ornamented with precious stones). But Clairvaux's rules nonetheless had roots in those originally scripted by Saint Benedict of Nursia (480-547 BC). Indeed they go back to Cassian in the fourth century BC.

Chapter Thirteen

External Features of ECMs

GESTURES AND MANNERS

The history of gestures, as we saw, is as old as the species, and gestures have always been important for us, a profoundly social species that has evolved to be keenly attuned to the movements of others (Iacoboni 2009). But if gestures are extensions of our species memory, they also extend from historical memories. They also speak the sign languages of various histories. These most visible and external features of embodied collective memories, gestures, punctuate and underpin the meanings of everyday life, as we previously saw; and they, in fact, are important mechanisms of social ordering, because they often demarcate social boundaries and hierarchies, as I will argue below. In this chapter, focusing primarily on monasteries and courts, two main centers from which ideas and gestures have historically spawned into the larger domain of life, I provide some fragments from the history of gestures to show how a gestural collective memory developed in the West. Here I show that this development progressively demarcated, precisely, social boundaries and naturalized social ranks; boundaries and ranks that, however, can be affected by changes in gestural collective memories.

Late Rome and the Middle Ages

Many "insignificant" bodily movements, positions of hands but also of facial muscles, for example, are often laden with culture and history. From Cicero to Ambrose (Augustine's teacher) patrician gestures were largely governed by the classical Roman notion of the golden mean, as historian Jean-Claude Schmitt observes (1990). *Mediocritas optimum est,* "nothing in excess" was the adage of the day, not even excess in the movements of the hands, legs or indeed brows or lips. Cicero, arguably the embodiment of the Roman republican spirit, sees excellence "in every movement and attitude of the body," "in standing or walking, in sitting or reclining, in our expression, in our eyes or the movement of our hands." "Gait," Cicero says, "must not be 'too animated' nor yet 'overly nice' or 'effeminate'" (in Schmitt 1990, 132). This originally Delphic idea, Schmitt argues, was bequeathed by Roman grammarian "Macrobius, taken up by Saint Augustine, then by Alcuin [Charlemagne's advisor] ... and has been with us ever since" (ibid., 132).

By the end of Classical Rome, at the beginning of the Middle Ages, gestures became the "outward (*foris*) physical expression of the inward (*intus*) soul" (ibid., 131); and membership in the higher social orders demanded a degree of control in movements; movements that were largely governed by notions such as *temperantia* or *modestia*. With Saint Ambrose, one of the original Doctors of the Church and a pillar of Christianity, these ideas came to underpin the training of the clerics. But unlike the Roman consul, Cicero, Ambrose was more interested in *verecundia*, a self-conscious sense of balance between the impulses of the self and the needs of the other, mixed with the sense of knowing one's place, and the willingness to collaborate with the other to help him maintain face, as Robert Kaster explains (2007.) (This was the kind of emotion and disposition that, if excessive, the hardier Romans often associated with femininity.) *Verecundia*, Saint Ambrose said, had to show in the clerics' "movements, gestures, and gait"; for in "the movement of the body," he says, "is the voice of the spirit" (in Schmitt 1990). The cleric's gestures had to give no offence to others, but without being entirely self-effacing.

Such was the gestural memory that Ambrose aimed to cultivate. During the Early Middle Ages, Schmitt continues, "gesture is no longer object of serious thought." To be sure, for members of the higher orders, corporeal movements are not a trivial matter but, particularly among clerics, contemplation, with its disembodied connotations and implications, gains an upper hand over *gestus*. This is so, perhaps because of the "suspicion with which the body was regarded had increased during [these] years," Schmitt says; or perhaps because God came to play a stronger causal role in the life of men (these precepts applied to men); men who, thus in the hands of God, lost a degree of control over their own actions and movements. During this period, prescriptions about proper gesturing moved from monasteries to the courts, from the clerics to the princes; so that counselors to princes, such as Isidore of Seville in Hispania (Spain and Portugal) and Alcuin in the Carolingian Empire, included gesture advice in their treatises. Saint Isidore, for example, tells the young Visigoth ruling Spain that he must keep the "movements of the body full of constancy and gravity, with no vain fickleness or disorderliness, and a gait which does not by its extravagance imitate the contortions of actors and the gestures of clowns who run hither and thither" (in Schmitt 1990, 135). Alcuin tells the son of Pepin the Short, Charlemagne, that his "head should be held up straight, the lips uncurled, the mouth not immoderately open, not looking behind one, or turning the eyes to the ground, neither bending the neck, nor rising or lowering the eyebrows" (ibid.).

Importantly, such front stage specialists, as Erving Goffman may call them, these learned ecclesiasts in the business of providing counsel on manners and movements, were relatively less important during the Early Middle Ages, if compared to any of the subsequent periods. (As Norbert Elias may agree, complexity in gestural patterns often reflects complexity in social structures, so that when social structures expand, gestures tend to became more important as markers of social location and as tools of social control. Hence, front stage behaviors and front stage specialists are often more prominent in complex societies.) The twelfth century, however, the Age of Chivalry, saw a Renaissance of gestures, as Schmitt also says, due in part to "the recovery of the ancients" (Schmitt 1990). Bear in mind that the chivalric code was very gestural, and that these men endeavored to be *visibly* chivalrous, deploying, for such purpose, coded rhythms of hands, feet, lips, brows, precisely to state their social standing.[1] Proper ladies, in their turn, often saw Chastity as the ideal to be enacted, expressed, and performed by their bodies. Bear in mind, again, that, at this historical juncture, women were increasingly seen not only through the filter of Eve, the cause of the Fall, but through the filter of Mary, the emerging icon of purity. This newfound sense of purity was expected not only in the souls of women, in their thoughts and emotions, but also in their bearing, garments, speech, movements, in their corporeal memory.

With the recuperation of the ancients, *temperantia* and *modestia* also begin to advance with firmer steps during this period. *Modestia*, "gives [man] his bearing," Alain de Lille says, "tempers his actions, measures his speech, weighs his silences, balances his gestures" (in Schmitt 1990, 141). *Modestia*, de Lille continues, "dresses him with propriety, curbs his senses . . . She outlines the correct gesture of the head . . . and gives the proper balance to the face, lest with face aloft, turning toward the beings above, he seems to spurn our mortal race and disdain to look upon our type of life, or with the face turned overmuch to the earth, show the signs of an inactive and vacant mind" (ibid.).

The paintings of the period, particularly those from the Middle Byzantine era (i.e., eleventh century), are also instructive from the point of view of the dominant gestural codes. Save exceptions, these images often depict the wooden quality of *temperantia* and *modestia* — even in the gestures of those holy men and women undergoing torture. As Janson and Janson tell us, these faces, though presumably in pain, nonetheless convey the sense of "restrained and noble suffering" (2003). *The Martyrdom of the Twelve Apostles* by Stefan Lochner (1410-1451), for example, shows various scenes of torment: apostles are boiled, flayed alive, crucified ("in a variety of imaginative ways," as Linda Nochlin observes [in Siri 2005, 31]) while, however, still complying with the gestural code.

These "saints neither wince nor flinch nor grimace," Nochlin says. "Rather, crouch or crawl though they may, they maintain a steady calm. Instead, it is their torturers — in their vile snarls, low jeers, and effortful stabs — who express emotion, who are abject" (ibid.). We have to wait until the Renaissance, perhaps until Giotto, the painter who opened the door to the Renaissance, for such holy scenes of suffering to betray the gestures of agony and sorrow. (But even in 1475, Antonio Pollaiuolo's *The Martyrdom of Saint Sebastian* conveys a serene man who endures torture with temperate, saintly gestures.) It is only with painters such as Matthias Grünewald, and particularly with Michelangelo da Caravaggio, in the sixteenth century, that the sense of bestiality underneath a face in pain is finally and unreservedly released onto the canvas. Grotesque grimaces, fingers contorted and palsied by pain, upturned and demented eyes begin to return the observer's gaze. Grünewald's *The Crucifixion* "left nothing undone to bring home to us the horrors of this scene of suffering," as Gombrich explains. "By His features and the impressive gesture of His hands, the Man of Sorrows speaks to us of the meaning of His Calvary" (2002, 351).

Norbert Elias: Fragments from the History of Manners

Importantly, "propriety," in the sense used by de Lille above, was not "propriety" in the sense in which we understand it today (similarly, *verecundia, modestia*, etc. need to be rendered in Latin to avoid, back to Hegel, "mediating" these concepts through contemporary discourses and perspectives). In general, medieval manners, if measured against manners today, "were relaxed in all senses of the word," Elias explains (1978, 91). Medieval gestural memory was different. To illustrate, let us consider, for instance, commensality and behavior at the table.

The conventions that governed this sphere of gestures during the twelfth century would have seemed not only "unpolished" or "naïve" from our perspective, but extraordinarily "improper." Throughout the Middle Ages, a set of precepts only begin to roughly outline our contemporary standards of behavior and their attendant gestures, particularly at the table. Here is the embryonic advice that medieval front stage specialists provided for members of the feudal nobilities: do not "slurp from the same spoon with somebody else," because this is "coarse" (in Elias 1978, 55); do not "gnaw a bone and then put it back in the dish"; do not "throw gnawed bones back into the communal dish," or on the floor; do not blow your nose on the tablecloth: "one who blows his nose in the tablecloth [is] ill-bred, I assure you" (ibid., 74) (But "to use the hand to wipe one's nose was a matter of course," Elias explains [ibid., 56]). When you blow your nose do not examine the results, as if "jewels" had come out of your head. Do not "poke your fingers into your ears or eyes, or pick your nose while eating." Do not "loosen [your] belt at the table," or scratch yourself at the table. Do not "fall greedily on the food," or fall upon the food "like swine while eating, snorting disgustingly and smacking [your] lips" (ibid., 73); do not "fall asleep at the table," or bulge your cheeks with food, "like bellows." Do not pull apart your lips while eating "like a pig" (ibid., 73). "Do not clean your teeth with your knife [or with the tablecloth]. Do not spit on or over the table" (ibid., 129) or against the wall or "out of the window or onto the fire" (ibid., 131).

(These injunctions, incidentally, were necessary because the techniques and the technology of eating, forks, spoons, dishes, were different than those common today. During the Middle Ages everyone "helps themselves from communal dishes," Elias explains. "Solids [above all, meat] are taken by hand, liquids with ladles or spoons. But soups and sauces are still very frequently drunk. Plates and dishes are lifted to the mouth. For a long period, too, there are no special implements for different foods. The same knife or spoon is used. The same glasses are drunk from. Frequently two diners eat from the same board." . . . This was "the standard eating technique during the Middle Ages" [Elias 1978]. "The inventory of Charles of Savoy, which is very rich in opulent table utensils, counts only a single fork" [ibid., 59]).

Even by the sixteenth century, Italian Giovanni della Casa marvels at the notion that "whole peoples sometimes lived so moderately and conducted themselves so honourably that they found spitting quite unnecessary" (Elias 1978, 130). In 1530, Erasmus of Rotterdam still suggests that "some people put their hands in the dishes the moment they have sat down. Wolves do that" (ibid., 76). It was only, "From the sixteenth century on [when the feudal nobility was already in decline], at least among the upper classes, [that] the fork came into use as an eating instrument, arriving by way of Italy first in France and then in England and Germany, after having served for a time only for obtaining solid foods from the dish" (ibid., 60). Indeed, as "late as the seventeenth century the fork was still essentially a luxury article of the upper class, usually made of gold or silver" (ibid.).

Only by the eighteenth century does the generic use of the fork begin to become self-evident; though in 1774 La Salle still makes a point of explaining that "the spoon is intended for liquids, and the fork for solid meats" (ibid., 83). "At the end of the eighteen century," Elias continues, "shortly before the Revolution, the French upper class attained approximately the [modern] standard of eating manners" (ibid., 89). And of course, later on, civilized modernity will introduce specialized utensils, the use of which, rather than being self-evident, involves yet more specialized precepts and training, which added yet new features to the gestural memories of (some) members of the emerging upper classes.

Outside the Dining Hall

Gestures, and gestural collective memory, are of course not limited to the table. Historian Michael Camille tell us of an earlier 1394 book of instruction for married women, the *Ménagier de Paris,* which instructs a young wife thus: "if you are walking out go with your head straight forward, your eyelids low and fixed, and to look straight before you down to the ground and twelve yards without turning your eyes on man or woman, to the right or to the left or staring upward or moving your eyes from one place to another, or laughing or stopping to talk to anyone in the streets" (in Camille 1998, 35). In 1606, Della Casa advises noblemen that, when walking, it is improper to either run like "a lackey" or, by contrast, to "walk unduly slowly," like a matron or a bride (in Elias 1978, 66).

Shakespeare's *The Winter's Tale,* is also informative here (it is not situated in an actual historical period, but deals with these class-based ideologies and related gestures). Recall, for example, Autolycus, the peddler and pickpocket who at the end of the story helps Princess Perdita. Disguised in courtly clothes, Autolycus speaks to a shepherd who is in the company of a simpleton known as "Clown." To foist himself off as a courtier, Autolycus superciliously approaches and addresses them in his better courtly voice: "Whether it like me or no, I am a courtier. Seest thou not the air of the court in these enfoldings? hath not my gait in it the measure of the court? receives not thy nose court-odour from me? reflect I not on thy base-ness court-contempt? . . . I am courtier, cap-a-pe, and one that will either push on or pluck back thy business there: whereupon I command thee to open thy affair" (Shakespeare 1623). The lowly peddler is bizarrely trying to convey a "higher nature": the courtiers' gait, smell, and speech. "How bless'd are we," he continues, "that are not simple men! Yet *nature* might have made me as these are, Therefore I'll not disdain" (ibid., my emphasis).

Autolycus hopes, of course, that the "measure of the court" should have been clearly visible in his mincing, leisurely, "princely" gait, in the self-styled *sprezzatura* that would correspond to virtuosi of gentlemanliness (which, given his upbringing, he cannot quite convey). By contrast, expected from someone in Autolycus' position would be either a tired stroll befitting a peddler or a wanderer, or back to Della Casa, a focused gait, befitting those whose time is owned and limited by labor, and whose gait is therefore nudged by haste. "Disguised" by Autolycus are aspects of embodied memory that pertain to the laboring classes, which, back to Bourdieu, are often understandable "from body to body," and indeed from unconscious to unconscious: others can read them "intuitively," particularly those who, sharing the same socio-symbolic universe, also share features of the embodied collective memory that brings this universe to life. Foolish Clown is fooled by the ridiculous pantomime: "This cannot be but a great courtier," he says, "He seems to be the more noble in being fantastical: a great man, I'll warrant; I know by the picking of one's teeth." But the wiser shepherd wonders: "His garments are rich, but he wears them not handsomely": clothes aside, he doesn't move like a courtier; he doesn't seem to bear a courtly bodily memory.

Gestures Today

Norbert Elias' research on the history of manners speaks of an organic entwinement connecting evolving class ideologies to evolving mental and bodily schemata, a European process that, we saw beyond Elias, spanned from at least the Classical Age to modernity. The ideologies transmitted by front-stage experts such as Della Casa, eventually became more visible, particularly through the movements and gestures of courtiers and burghers. Eventually, such prescriptions about commensality, movement (and even scatological behavior, as we will see in the next chapter), became detached from front stage experts such Erasmus or Della Casa; and later generations are simply "born" bearing a set of "appropriate" gestural techniques. They are born into a certain embodied collective memory.

By the seventeenth century, these "well-born" individuals begin to appear everywhere; and they naturally begin to expect certain movements and behaviors from their equals. They begin to demand clear visibility — gestural visibility — to confirm the status of those in their midst, and the status of those outside such social borders; borders that are now "innate" and that naturally mark their social and existential standing. Social equality among members of the upper classes now involves, in general, the ability to mirror a set of rhythms and movements, which eventually become inherited components of class-based embodied collective memories.

Today, notions such as courtesy have lost their historical context (the court); but they have been in-corporated, in varying degrees, into modern cultural life, where they have become second nature, for the most part. For example, today most people simply do not spit on the table, or aimlessly against the wall, or randomly out of the window, or leisurely onto the fire, simply because these behaviors are not "natural." In an almost Aristotelian sense (recall the notion of *hexis*, in the connotation of virtuosity) *we do not refrain*, consciously, from spiting on the table. Such a thing merely doesn't occur because it is no longer part of our embodied collective memories.

But beyond such behaviors, more specialized gestural techniques, particularly among members of polite society, are bequeathed from one generation to the next, as natural markers of class consciousness, the sign language of "high culture." So that, much as in the past, class-based aspects of embodied memories are today also naturally opposed to loud, Pantangruelian, Rabelaisian, full-mouthed natures that befit "others." To be sure, front stage specialists today often expect that such things as walking techniques, gestures — movement in general — will vary across classes. For example, John Molloy, author of *Dress for Success* (1975), explains that "Upper-middle-class and lower-middle-class people not only stand and sit differently, they move differently. Upper-middle-class people tend to have controlled precise movements. The way they use their arms and where their feet fall is dramatically different from lower-middle-class people, who tend to swing their arms out rather than hold them closer to their bodies" (in Fussell 1991, 35). Journalist Vance Packard says that "A now famous Hollywood actor still reveals his lower origins every time he sits down. He pulls up his trousers to preserve the crease" (ibid., 59). Paul Fussell adds that

> The Chris-Craft mail-order catalogue will show you the look to imitate [a yachtsman, for example], but classes much below the upper middle should take warning that they're unlikely to affect this yachtsman's look with much plausibility. A lot depends on a certain habitual carelessness in the carriage, a quasi-windblown calculated sloppiness. It's almost impossible to imitate. (ibid., 66)

Or recall what John Berger says about August Sander's well-known photograph of three German peasants on their way to a wedding. The young men, as the occasion demands, wear suits and hats with brims slanting akimbo over their brows, and walking sticks — which they use, Berger says, "as though they were driving cattle" (Berger 1980). They return the camera's gaze with a certain rustic dignity but, their clothes and posed panache notwithstanding, "[b]y no stretch of the imagination can you believe that these bodies belong to the middle or ruling class," Berger says (ibid.). On the contrary, the suits only underscore the sense that these bodies belong to the lower classes. "[F]ar from disguising the social class of those who wore them [the suits] underlined and emphasized it." The clothes in fact "deform" these well-formed men. "Wearing them they look as though they were physically misshapen" (ibid.). Again, this example also illustrates class-based features of embodied memories. Bear in mind that the suit — "developed in Europe as a professional *ruling class* costume in the last third of the 19th century [to] idealize purely sedentary power" (ibid., my emphasis) — calls for a repertoire of naturalized movements that are not part of the peasants' embodied memory. "Because of the very varied hard physical work they do," Berger says, peasants have a certain physique and a certain "physical rhythm … directly related to the energy demanded by the amount of work which has to be done in a day [which] is reflected in typical physical movements and stance. It is an extended sweeping rhythm. Not necessarily slow. The traditional acts of scything or sawing may exemplify it." "In addition, peasants possess a special physical dignity: this is determined by a kind of functionalism, a way of being fully *at home in effort*" (ibid. original emphasis).

As suggested, socioeconomic location is often reflected by bodies such that hands, feet, corporeal rhythms, facial muscles — are themselves class barriers. It would not be exaggerated to say that impression managers today typically expect that *bodily memory in general* — not only gestures and rhythms but also bodily sizes, expressions of affect, scatology, etc. — will vary with class. (Some empirical measurements have provided partial support to this idea: Sanchez-Vaznagh et al. [2009], for example, report a negative correlation between socioeconomic status and body mass index, which is mediated by covariates such as gender, ethnicity, education, and income.) The assumption of these front stage experts is that class involves not only material, economic resources but also, and fundamentally, immaterial resources: a certain "nature," "quasi-windblown," which "has nothing to do" with the mere possession of economic capital.

In a strict sense, these assumptions are pre-modern, naïvely seigniorial. But embodied collective memories do have class-based features that are in fact important for class positioning and class mobility. (It seems to me that ECMs have in fact always reflected, in different ways and degrees, socioeconomic hierarchies. Patricians and plebeians, lords and serfs, the bourgeois and the proletarian have been separated not only by material resources but also by aspects of embodied memory rooted in them.)

Hence, via a process that Antonio Gramsci may characterize as hegemonic, some members of the middle-lower sectors also seek to adopt and deploy such upper gestural markers ("borrowing status," in the phrase by C. Wright Mills). And indeed, front stage specialists target not the gentry, as Della Casa and Erasmus did, but audiences motivated by class anxiety. It should be clear that today the audiences for etiquette manuals and related advice columns come from the middle-lower and lower socioeconomic sectors, in general. (A manual of manners self-published in rural Texas, for example, speaks not to "the ambassador of Sweden," but to "us worker bees" [Middleton 2006; see also Fussell 1991]). To be sure, in part because of this downward drift in gesture, some members of the upper-classes may disclose their status via "negligence" in gesture, through a more or less backstaged gestural language that expresses social ease, the prerogative of the leisure class, as Thorstein Veblen may agree. Today, front-staged self-awareness at the table, for example, or self-consciousness in movement, in general, is often an indicator of class anxiety and of membership in the lower or "middling orders," as Tocqueville called them. Today, proper manners and movements may broadcast the signals of the lower classes. But manners and movements, in general, continue to reflect external, social feedback, the socioeconomic order, and the position that social actors occupy within it.

Conclusion

Gestures, these most visible and external aspects of embodied collective memories, change with what Hegel called "the spirit of the time" (Zeitgeist), and reflect it. In this chapter I have focused primarily on class but other aspects of the spirit of the time as race and gender, for example, involve specialized gestural memories of their own, as I previously argued. Genders and races also speak the sign language of the zeitgeist, and related gestural memories are also mediated by dominant consensuses, by ideas that emerge to "phenomenologize" themselves through bodily movements, the rhythms of hands and feet, the movements of the brows and lips.

Indeed observing how gestures change over time — what gestures emerge, what gestures become impossible — is perhaps the easiest way to see changes in the zeitgeist. Embodied collective memory provides a good barometer for it. El Quixote embodies a dead zeitgeist and his "knightly" gestures clearly point to this. Of course, anyone today can deploy chivalric gestures, but these gestures would be dead, already inscribed by current scripts, killed by them. Such incongruous gestures would not only mean altogether different things today, but in fact would be very difficult, if not impossible, for us to fully grasp, beyond our mediating notions and stereotypes about the past.

Halbwachs said that history is dead collective memory if it is not organically entwined with the world and with life as lived. Similarly, such Quixotic gestures are dead embodied collective memory. But when alive, shared gestural memories provide a shared phenomenology of mutual recognizability for social actors, so that, beyond cognition, individuals can *sense* how they stand with respect to others and with respect to the larger social sphere. The Roman patrician, the chivalrous knight, the courtier, the burgher and the peasant, the bourgeois and the laborer generally gestured within certain parameters that brought their time and social location to life, and that mediated their interactions. But importantly, the zeitgeist that lives in, and to an extent reproduces itself through, the movements and rhythms of social actors, can change as people begin to broadcast different gestures, as I suggested in the chapter on race. And the idea is that, if gestural memories are fraught with history, with class boundaries, with ideas and hierarchies pertaining to gender and race, they are also fraught with possibilities, as the previous chapter also suggests. In the next chapter, we turn toward scatology and other internal aspects of embodied memory to further illustrate both the conservative and the resistive aspects of embodied memory.

NOTE

1. This is not to say that these men were "courteous" in the contemporary sense. As we will see below, the domain of gestures during the twelfth century was, in general, much less "polished" than anything that we associate with "courtesy" today.

Chapter Fourteen

Internal Features of ECMs

SCATOLOGY AND EMBARRASSMENT

Civilization, Elias shows, progressively advanced "the frontiers of shame, the thresholds of repugnance" and embarrassment (1978). More and more, scatological functions became miasmal, violative, and thus retreated to the backstages of everyday life. Most people in the ancient world and throughout the Middle Ages, gentry included, fell free to urinate, burp, fart, pick their noses, blow their noses in their fingers with relative impunity and without much shame or guilt. And today, these things have lost this aura of normality, and occur mostly among small children, whose bodies are not quite tied to external conventions; children who thus "encroach again and again on the adult threshold of repugnance," Elias says.

Psychoanalyst Sándor Ferenczi explains that "the education of a child presupposes a psychic control of certain organ-activities which later apparently occur 'automatically' or as 'reflexes,' but which are really command-automatisms active since childhood; for example the regular functioning of the sphincter and expulsive muscles of the bowel and bladder" (2008, 92). Of course, such pedagogical techniques are not exclusive to modernity, but in modern times these requisites became more important, and more enforced. In this chapter, I provide a historical perspective on how such command-automatisms, particularly those related to scatological function, became invested by culture, and thus attached to the embodied collective memories of the modern period. These developments, I also show, were not without consequences for modern societies.

Internal Embodied Memory

In the ancient world, in general, excreta did not elicit the images of pollution, danger, or indeed immorality and even profanity that they elicit today. Of course there were exceptions, prominent among them was, for instance, the Hebrew tradition, which had relatively strict codes governing things that issue from the body (so that "Some rabbis believed," for example, "that a man should not pray within four cubits of excrement or urine," as Colleen Bryant explains [2000, 10]). And to be sure, some pre-modern cultures were quite phobic when it came to these things. As Mary Douglas has observed, spit, blood, tears, semen, urine, etc. were sometimes seen as being imbued with malefic powers (see also Durkheim 1912, 338). The Coorgs, for example, "treat the body as if it were a beleaguered town, every ingress and exit guarded for spies and traitors. Anything issuing from the body is never to be re-admitted, but strictly avoided" (Douglas 2002, 152). "The Trickster of primitive mythologies," Douglas also says, is often "surrounded by unsublimated and undisguised anality" (ibid.). Others indeed saw the *body itself* as a site of pollution, and Porphyry and the classical Gnostics, for example, were embarrassed by carnality itself.

Yet, what I want to emphasize in this chapter is that such phobic concerns about excreta, so common today, were not so common in the ancient world, and that this way of thinking and feeling expanded and became normalized only with modernity. Let us begin by considering, for example, one of the mythological versions referring to the birth of Orion, the huntsman after whom the constellation was named. The particular version that I have in mind tells us that King Hyrieus of Boeotia[1] had provided proper hospitality (*xenia*) to Zeus, Poseidon, and Hermes, who visited him disguised as human beings. *Xenia*, a system of reciprocity at the center of Greek culture, obliged the guest to reciprocate, so that, in return, Zeus granted the king a wish. Hyrieus asked for a son and, obligingly, the gods urinated on a bull's hide and asked their host to bury it. A child grew nine months later in the ground, and was named Orion, precisely after the urine of the Gods (though this name could connote "semen," as well). The child was often referred to as the Handsome Earthborn Orion, the Handsome Earthborn Urine, a boy who grew to become the great hunter after whom the constellation is named. The Greeks did not foster the phobic notions of excreta that Douglas describes and that are so common today. On the contrary, they knew the benefits of excreta in agriculture (Bracken et al. 2007), used excreta as means of divination, and Paulus of Aegineta even prescribed urine to color and treat hair (Aegineta 1833). Indeed, as we will see below, these practices were common throughout the ancient world (and some cultures, we will also see, indeed ascribed benefic, and even talismanic meanings to urine, feces, and flatulence).

These Greek agricultural practices, as Bracken and colleagues explain, were probably passed on to the Romans, who were also "well aware of the cleaning power of urine, and also used it for washing clothing, developing the logistics to collect larger volumes of urine in settlements. Fullers, who worked in laundries, would install amphorae in streets and alleyways as public urinals passing regularly to collect the urine, and transporting it back to the laundry for washing" (Bracken et al. 2007, 220). Saint Augustine reports that, indeed, the Romans "thought divine honors [were] due to the discoverer [of the agricultural uses of excreta], Stercutio, from whose name the word for dung [*stercus,* the politer version of *merda*, shit] is derived" (Augustine 1872, 59). "In India," Bracken and colleagues say, "ancient Sanskrit texts outlined the medicinal use of urine through shivambu (auto-urine therapy), which still has a popular following today" (Bracken et al. 2007, 220). The Celts used urine for dyeing and washing cloth. Ancient China (500 BC) also had systems for collecting excreta from cities, transporting it to the fields, and selling it to farmers for crop production. In Japan, 23,950,295 tons of excreta were used as fertilizer in 1908 (King 1911). "The reuse of excreta was however not only limited to China and Japan, and was and continues to be practiced right across Asia" (Bracken et al. 2007, 220). Similarly, ancient Peruvian, Mexican and Arab cultures knew of the agricultural benefits of reusing nutrients from faeces. In Europe, such uses were known and used throughout the Middle Ages: "the use of excreta and greywater [as agricultural nutrients] was the norm," a practice that "clearly continued in Europe into the middle of the 19th Century" (ibid., 222).

Other cultures saw excreta — beyond their agricultural or practical uses — as entirely benefic. Some pre-Colombian peoples, for example, ascribed magical powers to flatulence, assigned curative properties to faeces and urine, and decorated their prodigious art with demiurgic personages from whose heads *and* tails emanate cosmological representations, theogonic and cosmological forces (Narvaez 2003). As archeologist Alfredo Narvaez explains, excreta, "are [and have been] of great value in the Andean world (urine, faeces, gasses)" (ibid., 7). Here are two examples:

> It is interesting to note [Narvaez says] that among traditional Andean cultures, the bad smell produced by the digestive system has magical powers: flatulence . . . is used to get rid of evil spirits in desolate places. One of the most well known cases is that of the *Casharaca,* a woman with thorns in her vulva who lures and tries to seduce the lonely wanderers of the northeast Peruvian sierras. Farting and screaming the highest-caliber insults are the only two elemental remedies to ward off such a dangerous personage and thus free oneself from certain death. (Narvaez 2003, 26, my translation)

Similarly,

> Tales from the Amazonian oral tradition [also] make reference to the creative and productive powers of flatulence: the Toad Woman, although "a bit ugly," was able to make the Sun Family quite happy. She became the wife of the Sun's Son. She cultivated the land by herself, prepared *masato* [yucca beer] and provided victuals for the family. "She lived for years and years. It was because of her that the lands of the Sun, her father in law, were bountiful. Such was the life of the Toad Woman. When she went to bed with her husband at night, she would fart, and thus a portion of peanuts would appear at the crack of dawn. For all this her father and mother in law loved her with much tenderness." (ibid., my translation)

Another tale from the Amazonian tradition speaks of another goddess, the Star Woman, who urinated valuable beads. In the northern Peruvian sierras, urine is also used to neutralize witchcraft and avert bad luck (Narvaez 2003). Snakes, for example, were seen as portending evil, and after killing a snake, the person had to urinate over the dead animal to conjure evil away. Or when beholding the rainbow, which could dangerously penetrate the entrails through the nose, the person had to cover his/her nostrils with a mixture of urine and soil. Indeed, faeces from infants were similarly used in the Andean world, and still are used in some regions, for their curative or magical properties (ibid.). Among the Aguarunas, also in the Amazonian region, defecating was seen as the gift of a civilizing hero: "once upon a time," Narvaez writes,

> human beings had no digestive system and these primitive people therefore had no anus. They could not eat food, and nourished themselves only by smelling food. A myth tells the story of an otherworldly and civilizing hero, who knew about fire, was able to cook food *and as also able to defecate*, something quite extraordinary. This ancient humanity had to learn to cook their food. And to allow them to defecate, this hero made an anus for each one of them, with a sharp stick. The civilized world is thus conceived on the basis of the integration of all the capacities of head and the 'tail,' which together [are vital parts] of a biological unity. (Narvaez 2003, 21, my emphasis and translation)

The Development of a Modern Scatological Habitus

Back to Bracken and colleagues, they show not only that pre-modern peoples were familiar with excreta, but that this situation changed only in the twentieth century, particularly as water-rich countries developed flushed sewerage technologies for growing cities. [2] "Viewing faeces, urine and grey water as a worthless waste to be disposed of is a *modern concept*," the say, "which ignores . . . the obvious benefits to be had from closed-loop systems — which was clearly recognised in the past" (Bracken et al. 2007, 225, my emphasis). "'[F]aecophobic' thinking," the researchers conclude, is modern. (And though such modern thinking has helped improve some health standards, it has "also drained economies, polluted and squandered fresh water resources, broken nutrient cycles and impoverished soils" [ibid.].)

Likewise, with the normative, indeed moral reasoning that often accompanies faecophobic thinking: scatological habits "become associated with embarrassment, fear, shame, or guilt, even when one is alone" particularly with modernity, as Elias explains. They have become polluted and profane, particularly among the emerging polite societies, as we will presently see. "Much of what we call 'morality' or 'moral' reasons," Elias says, "has the same function as 'hygiene' or hygienic reasons: to condition children to a certain social standard. Moulding by such means aims at making socially desirable behavior automatic, a matter of self-control, causing it to appear in the consciousness of individuals as the result of their own free will, and in the interests of their own health or human dignity . . . which gained predominance with the rise of the middle classes" (Elias 1978, 127). The development of these aspects of embodied collective memory, insignificant as it seems, was not without consequences for the social order.

Below, I provide some historical detail and show how, as such feelings of revulsion and embarrassment became culturally and socioeconomically mediated, the social order was transformed in significant ways. As we saw in the previous chapter, from the Classical Age to the Middle Ages, social expectations targeted outward gestures (*gestus*, again, was the *foris,* "outward," expression of the *intus*, the "inside"). By contrast, particularly from the Renaissance on, social expectations increasingly begin to target internal, scatological habits. So that, by the fifteenth century, Erasmus of Rotterdam, for example, writes a treatise on human conduct, on "seemly and unseemly conditions of the whole body" and on "bodily culture," which provides proto-modern prescriptions to those aspiring to politeness. Expanding and updating the ethos of gesture with an emphasis now on *civilitas*, Erasmus says that, "It is impolite to greet someone who is urinating or defecating." It is "dangerous . . . to retain wind by compressing the belly." If possible, "withdraw," for this "should be done alone. But if not, in accordance with the ancient proverb, let a cough hide the sound." Even moving back and forth from one's chair was not proper, because "it gives the impression of constantly breaking or trying to break wind." "Act," in any case, "according to the suggestions in Aethon's epigrams: Even though he had to be careful not to fart explosively in the holy place, he nevertheless prayed to Zeus, though with compressed buttocks. The sound of farting, especially of those who stand on elevated ground, is horrible. One should make sacrifices with the buttocks firmly pressed together" (in Elias 1978, 71 and 110).

In 1570, a courtly book of conduct from Wernigerode, Germany, asks males not to relieve themselves "without shame in front of ladies, or before the doors or windows of court chambers or other rooms" (in Elias 1978, 111). Also in the sixteenth century, Della Casa suggests that a "modest, honorable" man should not "relieve nature in the presence of other people." He advises those aspiring to politeness that when sharing the same bed with others (a common occurrence in an era unconcerned with privacy), they should not hold any "stinking thing" that they may find "for the other to smell, as some are wont, who even urge the others to do so, lifting the foul-smelling thing to his nostrils and saying, 'I should like to know how much that stinks'" (ibid., 111). In general, the emerging gentry were increasingly expected to (retentively) conform to the requisites of *civilitas* and then of *urbanitas* during the Enlightenment. Gail Paster (1993) argues that in fact a different, "internal habitus" was progressively formed:

> Bourdieu [speaks of a] silent and invisible formation of the external habitus . . .
> But we can reasonably infer an equal or even greater hiddenness and efficacy
> in the social formation of the internal habitus, in, as Mary Douglas says, the
> "continual exchange of meanings between the two kinds of bodily experience
> [namely, experience associated to the social and physical demands on the
> body]." Society's cumulative, continuous interpellation of the subject includes
> an internal orientation of the physical self within the socially available dis-
> courses of the body. (Paster 1993, 6)

If Elias shows the development of the external features of modern embodied collective memories, Paster shows the development of internal features. She lets us see that modern history not only grafted itself at a "capillary" or "surface" level, as Foucault would say, but that it in fact pierced the viscera of the social actor, to the hilt, so to speak. Thus we see that these processes involved a transition between more or less expulsive embodied memories to more "polite," "urbane" and retentive ones; again, a modern development that had consequences for modern life.

Politeness and Urbanity

Politeness and urbanity are etymologically related to the word "city": *urbanitas*, roughly means "citification" in Latin, and "politeness" stems from the Greek *polis*, the city. These urbane and polite aspects of embodied collective memories grew with cities, and with the burghers, the "city dwellers." The requisite to commit excretory functions to the backstages grew as city crowds grew. It grew with the need for privacy; it surfaced as a demand for interpersonal boundaries. Thus, the command-automatisms that regulate ex-cretory processes became more firmly embedded within embodied collective memories. Significantly, "politeness" is also related etymologically to "poli-tics" and to "citizenship" (Greek politics was the domain of citizens, to the exclusion of slaves or women, for example; similarly with *civility*, from the Latin *civilitas*: "citification," "citizenship," politics). And it is not a coinci-dence either that these politer dimensions of embodied memory grew in importance particularly among the emerging bourgeoisie, the dominant classes that had a greater degree of control over politics and over the lives of citizens. Members of this rapidly emerging social class were, after all, the ones who could afford privacy, the novelty of private bedrooms and private water closets, for example (which the crowds couldn't). Thus being able to afford a measure of privacy, they were also able to afford such standards of politeness. Soon enough, the good bourgeois expected these standards from others, so that these embodied markers of urbanity became basic markers of social membership.

Note, as well, that politeness is also etymologically related to "police" and "policing." These polite expectations, which policed the orifices of the lower bodily stratum, emerged in fact to police the lower social strata, the growing crowds. Self-monitoring implied monitoring of others; it was a mechanism of social ordering, used in particular to separate those who did not police their own bodies, to thus keep them firmly in their place. To be sure, in contrast to the Middle Ages, when bodily functions, and bodily odor in general, generally *did not* elicit the "natural" feeing of revulsion that they do today, these second class citizens became polluted, polluting, and "revolting," in the double sense of the word (regardless of their virtues and vices). Bear in mind that, "Up until the end of the nineteenth century the dominant theory on the spread of illness was the miasma theory. This theory, with its roots in classical times, held that illness was caused by inhaling volatile substances. As bad smells were thought more likely to contain illness, everything that smelled had to be gotten rid off" (Bracken et al. 2007, 223). "Impoliteness," in the sense above, was easily seen as miasmatic.

Such retentive features of embodied memory, in any case, more than other outward gestures, became visceral markers of social location. As historian E.M Collingham suggests, "[p]ersonal cleanliness," in general, became "a major force in the formation of the European bourgeois private sphere" (Collingham 2001, 174).[3] These impolite and thus second-class citizens "naturally" belonged to the underbelly of the polis. As suggested, embodied collective memory can provide firm mechanisms of social control. Yet, as we will see below, such mechanisms are not always stable or secure.

OLFACTORY COLLECTIVE MEMORY

"Most ancient civilizations," Katherine Ashenburg notes, "matter-of-factly acknowledge that, in the right circumstances, a gamy, earthy body odour can be a powerful aphrodisiac" (Ashenburg 2007, 6). The Hadza in northern Tanzania — who live "a hunter-gatherer existence that is little changed from 10,000 years ago," as journalist Michael Finkel reports (2009) — "have a word for body odor," Finkel says, but "the men tell me that they prefer their women not to bathe — the longer they go between baths, they say, the more attractive they are. Nduku, my Hadza language teacher, said she sometimes waits months between baths, though she can't understand why her husband wants her that way." Seneca preferred the company of men who smelled "of the army, of farm work, and of manliness!" Napoleon peremptorily ordered Josephine not to wash in anticipation of his arrival.

In general, "The scent of one another's bodies," Ashenburg says, was in fact "the ocean our ancestors swam in, and they were used to the everyday odor of dried sweat. It was part of their world, along with the smells of cooking, roses, garbage, pine forests and manure" (2007, 2). We may argue, with Saint Bernard, that at a time when everyone smelled, no one actually smelled, and that smell, when it became conspicuous, did not have the profane connotations that it has today. Today, by contrast, odors (and bodily functions) are of course naturally and automatically confined to the back-stages of everyday life, as Erving Goffman argued (1971a). But, again, it was only with modernity, its flushing sewage systems and its massive odorizing and deodorizing industry, that such olfactory "intrusions," as Goffman says, became the "territorial violations" that assault us today. Indeed, it is only since the nineteenth century (Hoy 1995) that the smell of sweat, for example, became conspicuous, as the dominant semiotics of scents changed in response to health concerns as well as to the needs of a growing market; a market that in the U.S. alone grew to involve about $50 billion annually as it does today (Ashenburg 2007). Today, this is a massive industry that encourages olfactory meanings, images — motives — in consumers, which are necessary for it to function. It is owing in part to the size of this business that many Americans today experience the olfactory territorial violations mentioned above, and see dirt, in general, as an obvious offence and indeed as a synonym of immorality, as we will see below. By contrast, for "hard working New England or midwestern [sic] farm families, dirt was seen as something positive, even healthy" [Hoy 1995, 4]).

Naturally, an argument could be made that the modern semiotics of scents (and, as we saw, the politics and economics of scents) are healthier than those of pre-modernity, an advancement somehow. Perhaps. But I want to underscore the idea that, beyond health concerns, many Americans, as Ashenburg notes, have been "thoroughly . . . conditioned [to expect that others] smell like an exotic fruit (mango, papaya, passion fruit) or a cookie (vanilla, coconut, ginger). The standard we read about in magazines and see on television is a sterilized and synthetic one" (2007, 8). Let me highlight, as well, the idea that infractions often involve degrees of exclusion. A time when Botox injections have become "proper grooming for the twenty first century," actual body odor is an increasingly important marker of social exclusion. Back to Ashenburg,

> In my generation, standards reached . . . absurd levels. The idea of a body ready to betray me at any turn filled the magazine ads I pored over in *Seventeen* and in *Mademoiselle* in the late 1950's and early 60's. The lovely looking girls in those pages were regularly baffled by their single state or their failure to get a second date or their general unpopularity, and all because their breath, their hair, their underarms or — the worst — their private parts were not "fresh." A long-running series of cartoon-style ads for Kotex sanitary napkins alerted me to the impressive horrors of menstrual blood, which apparently could announce its presence to an entire high school.
>
> The most menacing aspects of the smells that came with poor-to-middling hygiene was that, as we were constantly warned, we could be guilty of them *without even knowing it*! There was no way we could ever rest assured that we were clean enough. For me, the epitome of feminine daintiness was the model who posed on the cover of a Kotex pamphlet about menstruation titled *You're a Lady Now*. This paragon, a blue-eyed blond ... had clearly never had a single extraneous hair on her body and smelled permanently of baby powder. I knew I could never live up to her immaculate blondness, but much of my world was telling me that I had to try. (Ashenburg 2007, 5-6 original emphasis)

Today, bodily scents in general, much as bodily functions, have also been firmly pushed beyond the threshold of embarrassment, and indeed they have become stamped not only by aesthetic but also by moral considerations, and, again, by related practices of exclusion. The word "dirty," bear in mind, today has clear moral connotations, as in "dirty business," "dirty old man," etc. The "morality" of cleanliness, as Ashenburg notes, is indeed firmly built in our very language. And it is also built in our schemata of perception, into our perceptual collective memory. At least in part, we see and smell through certain systems of meaning, including those sponsored by the market.

"Freeing of Potentialities"

Let us finally consider Mikhail Bakhtin's insightful analysis of the carnival during the Middle Ages and the Renaissance (1984), which provides a point of contrast with respect to the foregoing discussion. Bakhtin shows that whereas the court increasingly demanded continence and pushed scatology to the backstages, the peasants, by contrast, often deployed scatological behaviors to demarcate their own existential territory, and to defend their own political ground. Around the sixteenth century, the Rabelaisian reveler not only freely deployed the lower body, but in fact used it in mocking opposition against the retentive spirit of the political and ecclesiastical powers that yoked his everyday existence (ibid.). "For thousands of years," Bakhtin says, "folk culture strove at every stage of its development to overcome by laughter, render sober, and express in the language of the material bodily lower stratum . . . all the central ideas, images, and symbols of official culture"; thereby reversing the "up" and the "down," the king and the cleric with the peasant, the head with the tail, voice with flatulence, the spirit of seriousness and retention with the spirit of laughter, release, and relieving expulsion (ibid., 394).

The medieval carnival was a feast of the lower body, a ritual mechanism that exploded the court's expectations about bodily as well as social and political control. Bear in mind that, as we saw, political control often succeeded by means of controlling and policing the potentially revolting body of others, a body that, however, at times revolted nonetheless. While the aristocracies undertook the front stage task of subduing the increasingly embarrassing humors of the body, as Elias has shown, the popular classes exuberantly deployed the lower stratum as a weapon against dominant rules. The Pantangruelian belly of laughter, public defecation, drunkenness, and fertility thus became an odd locus of dissent through which the popular classes attempted to devitalize the dominant seriousness. Much as the wild parties of the Dionysian maenads, which deployed a bodily counteroffensive against the laws of Apollo, these carnivals, full of sound, smell, sight, and intoxication, also involved "unconscious hopes" of "free[ing] human consciousness, thought, and imagination for new potentialities" (Bakhtin 1984, 49). "Gay matter," Bakhtin says, has been a popular weapon against the dominant "spirit of seriousness."

Bakhtin, I should finally note, is sometimes criticized for "romanticizing" medieval popular forms, such as the carnival, purportedly overlooking the negative, dark and brutish aspects of medieval life. However, I would argue that he neither romanticized the obviously horrible aspects of the Middle Ages, nor the obviously horrible problems that constantly beset the life of medieval peasants. He only suggests that the laughter of the people, obscured by medievalists who focused on the toils and troubles of the time, simply existed; and that it was deployed, along with the lower stratum, precisely as a locus of dissent. This was a form of dissent that, even if it often involved mere *"unconscious hopes,"* was nonetheless not without consequences. If anything, it helped alleviate the peasant's toils, gave him a measure of revenge against those who yoked him — helped her survive. But more than that, Bakhtin also suggests that these deployments ultimately demarcated a different aesthetic domain, which not only informed the Rabelaisian aesthetic, but also aspects of the Renaissance. Such "gay" insistence on combating the many slings and arrows of life eventually influenced new voices and symbols as those that characterize, for example, Shakespeare's work. The bard's humor, though often having the court as its target audience, nonetheless includes the festive, lower elements of the carnival that Bakhtin studied.

And the idea is that not only the carnival, but the body itself provided scaffolds for a different cultural narrative that, again, weakened aspects of the dominant spirit of seriousness also during the Renaissance (much as comedy today also reveals that Rabelaisian humor is still deployed against the dominant "high culture"). Bakhtin, in summary, lets us see that the body in general, and the lower stratum in particular, have not been fully colonized, and that they have in fact provided alternative aesthetic and indeed political parameters. (It is worth noting that, coincidentally or not, some sexual minorities today also often deploy the body as a weapon to devitalize dominant norms and to free "human consciousness, thought, and imagination." For example, in New York, a gay leather club, the L.U.R.E., forbade patrons wearing "Cologne or other odors, scents, soaps, or fabric softeners that hide one's manly scent." This is the Rabelaisian norm among so-called leather men. "Sports" in this "leather scene" include "scating," blood sports, golden showers: a carnivalesque deployment of the lower stratum against the dominant spirit of seriousness.) The body, we saw, is a device whereby dominant ideologies are channeled, vivified, and in which they are in fact policed. Bakhtin let us see that dominant discourses can, however, be diverted, in the double sense of the word, and inverted, at least by degrees. Again, precisely because the body helps sustain the social order, social hierarchies can be disrupted by embodied practices. Such disruptions may become more durable if they result in new features of ECMs.

NOTES

1. A character depicted as a demigod in other versions, or a peasant according to Ovid.

2. Cities grew to the point of making the collection of excreta unfeasible. Chemists also developed cheap artificial fertilizers.

3. Of course I am not reducing citizenship and politics to these aspects of ECM. Rather, I am arguing that these embodied processes, inserted within a larger historical process, were not without consequences in their own right. The contributions of these particular variables need to be understood within, so to speak, a much larger regression model.

Chapter Fifteen

Perceptual Collective Memory: The Eye

OPTICS AND VISION

Perception itself, which may seem to be a fundamentally biological function, is also encultured, as we will see in this chapter. Heidegger says that, "We never . . . originally and really perceive a throng of sensations, e.g., tones and noises, in the appearance of things . . . ; rather, we hear the storm whistling in the chimney, we hear the three-engine aeroplane. . . . Much closer to us than any sensations are the things themselves. We hear the door slam in the house, and never hear acoustic sensations or mere sounds" (Heidegger 1977, 156; quoted in Smith 2002, 105). We do not hear like an oscilloscope. Heidegger would also agree with the idea that, in general, we do not just see throngs of colors and shapes either, like a scanner. Any phenomenologist would in fact agree with the idea that, more generally, we don't perceive like machines (as we saw, we do not detect pain in that manner, either). Of course the perceptual act involves objective physical factors; for example, at the level of physics and neurochemistry; but, when perceived, the throng of physical factors generally becomes invested with cognitive, affective, cultural contents. These contents are usually present in the perceptual act. This does not mean that our minds simply create our perceptual reality as, for example, the radical idealism of Bishop Berkeley proposes. It means that, as I will discuss below, seeing involves an ontological complicity connecting objective external facts, excitation of cones and rods, nerve firing, *and* cognitive and affective memories, the person's identity which, as we saw, is attached to history, and to class, gender, race, to culture, in general.

As Hermann von Helmholtz argued, the percipient usually deploys "unconscious inferences," visual templates that, gathered through life and consigned to memory, help her read the environment and quickly retrieve the information that is necessary at that moment. Perceiving, Antonio Damasio explains, now from the point of view of contemporary neurobiology, "is as much about acting on the environment as it is about receiving signals from it" (2005, 225). In her obituary for Franz Boas, anthropologist Ruth Benedict similarly said that "if we were to understand human behavior we must know as much about the eye that sees as about the object seen. [Boas] understood once and for all that the eye that sees is not a mere physical organ but a means of perception conditioned by the tradition in which its possessor has been reared" (in Jacobson 1998, 10). Taking now a historical perspective, Walter Benjamin also notes that, "During long periods of history, the mode of human sense perception changes with humanity's entire mode of existence. The manner in which human sense perception is organized, the medium in which it is accomplished is determined not only by nature but by historical circumstances as well" (Benjamin 1968, 222). Back to the Wild Boy of Aveyron, if perception is linked to history, a human being who lacks history in such a dramatic way should have *sui generis* schemata of perception. The order of importance of his senses seemed reverted, with smell being first in importance followed by taste, sight, hearing and touch (Benzaquén 2006, 158). Whereas we often approach the world eyes-first (the visual cortex is the largest neural system), this child, whose perceptual reality was not mediated by culture, often approached the world nose-first.

The notion that the perceptual act carries a history, aspects of the collective memory, is not new. This is at least the near-consensus in the subdisciplines mentioned above, those in the business of studying the percipient. We can safely say, in any case, that any radical form of perceptual realism, the notion that we perceive reality directly, veridically, and without the mediation of subjectivity, has disappeared from the purview of science. Yet, we haven't fully explored the implications of this idea, the idea that the percipient is encultured, and that therefore we may, perhaps, speak of histories of perception. In this chapter, I discuss the notion of perceptual collective memories: collectively relevant perceptual structures that in some ways follow the flow of history, while in other ways resisting historical mediation. Below I argue that these perceptual structures, much as other social or political structures, can mark the life of the percipient and the life of the group.

Optics is outside history, but vision is biological, physical, *as well as* historical. History always addresses the gaze, and often charges it with collective expectations, with ideologies and myths, with the spirit of the time, which can claim aspects of the act of seeing. Let us begin by considering the famous Aphrodite of Cnidos (the "Knidian Goddess"), the first monumental nude carved around 360 BC by Praxiteles and placed in the sanctuary of Eros, in the ancient city of Thespiae. Optically, Greek and contemporary eyes would see the same thing, of course. But, from the point of view of vision, our perceptions diverge. I will talk about the ways in which we perceive this image, but let me first provide a few contrasting examples that illustrate how the Greeks perceived it.

In general and save exceptions, the Greeks saw an object of veneration (*Venere,* related to "veneration," "venereal" and "Venus," is the name of the goddess herself, in its Italian version). Notice, however, that this was not Judeo-Christian worship.[1] Notice that the contours of the marble, belonging to the goddess of sexual passion as they did, aroused the sexuality of many worshipers. "There are stories of men crying over it, having sex with it and staining it with semen," as classicist James Davidson reports (1998). Pseudo-Lucian, for instance, tells the story of a devotee who, one "night that cannot be spoken of," violated the marble to then, after leaving a stain of semen on her thigh, and maddened by the deed, cast himself into the sea, the cradle from which the goddess had emerged (in Nasrallah and Schüssler Fiorenza 2010, 69-70). This icon was invested by a particular aura, as Walter Benjamin says, which also rendered some visitors "more motionless than statues," as a Lykinos, a tourist to the "otherwise not worth seeing city of Thespiae," reports (ibid.). This aura was not merely an effect of Praxiteles' astonishing ability. Venerable yet vulnerable, venereal and venal (the model for the statue was a prostitute named Phryne), the arresting image of the Venus was invested also by a very singular theology. It indeed contained an entire zeitgeist, an ethnicity, which often returned the worshiper's gaze. By contrast, today we see the statue primarily as a piece of marble from which, as Hegel might say, "the living soul has flown" ("just as the hymns are words from which belief has gone" [in Žižek 2008]). And the idea is that this object's aura has disappeared not only from our conceptual register but from our *perceptual* register (Benjamin 1968), as we will see below.

The idea, furthermore, is that, as Benjamin argues, it is not just the Venus that somehow emerges in a different light today. Rather, visual reality, in general, emerges in new ways today, bearing new phenomenal contents, associations and meanings. In "the age of mechanical reproduction," as Walter Benjamin called it, not only this image — but images in general — tend to lose their aura: a sense of intrinsic singularity, their identity, their "living soul," ritual functions and iconic statuses formerly attached to them. These qualities tend to become diluted in an increasingly massive stream of reproductions. Here, images tend to become detached from the singular piece of reality they represent, and from particular cultural meanings and beliefs, so that, instead of fulfilling their function as representatives of reality, they come to form a massified, artificial, and indeed ersatz reality of their own. It is not that this particular image of the Venus has become souvenirized and thus emptied of original contents. Rather, by flooding the world with images repeated again and again, the age of mechanical reproduction has emptied *images*, in general, of a former force often attached to them. To be sure, the very definition of art, as Paul Valery says, is at stake in this particular historical period that has superseded the "ancient craft of the Beautiful."

To further illustrate these ideas, it is worth discussing how, in their turn, Medieval and Renaissance eyes saw this venerable/venereal image. Mediated in their own ways, the eyes of the Renaissance also saw the statue from their own vantage point. Behind these eyes were optimism and nostalgia about the Classical Era, which in general the percipient projected onto this particular image. In turn, the Middle Ages, busy destroying things pagan and the old cult of pleasure and beauty, likewise saw what they themselves projected onto it: danger, a malefic idol, as Walter Benjamin also reminds us. (The original Aphrodite seemingly did not survive the iconoclastic, "image-breaking" period. By means of a pagan miracle only some fragments remain [Gombrich 2002].) And to insist on an important point, these anxieties and notions projected onto to the statue *were not merely "belief."* They were aspects of the perceptual act. Seeing, again, is not merely a retinal event.

Here are other examples: just as we do not hear mere sounds but "the train," "the creaking door," we generally do not see, for instance, skin pigmentation either. Instead, we generally see the auras that have become attached to pigmentation. As suggested in Chapter Eleven we see "races": historical and ideological constructs projected onto skin colors. As W.E.B DuBois reported, it was in fact difficult for him to see *his own skin color* beyond the ideology of race (2011); it was hard to see his own image in the mirror beyond the historical frame. Arguably the most important theorist of race in the U.S., DuBois describes how, as a Black man growing up in a Jim-Crowed and officially racist country, he often saw himself not only through the filter of racial ideology, but through the specific standards and stereotypes that his peers had about black people. Growing up he experienced the peculiar sense of "always looking at one's self through the eyes of others" (ibid.). He saw himself and others through ideological, political systems, through a particular zeitgeist. Perception, and even self-perception, is, in various degrees, othered (and eyes can become, we may say, alienated, depersonalized).

It is worth considering, as well, other, less fraught aspects of perception. As Bourdieu shows, the perception of the sunset, for instance, is sometimes mediated by socioeconomic position (1987), which can intervene within the perceptual act. The perceived beauty or ugliness of the sunset, Bourdieu also shows, may vary with class, where "class" involves objective as well as subjective conditions that the percipient projects onto the object of perception. Class may sediment scopic habituses in people.

Thus, much as memory, and much as the self, vision is also individual and individuating, but is never separate from the social context. History enables but also frames and constraints vision. It enables it because it helps us see beyond the mere throng of shapes and colors, but it constraints it because it provides a point of view for us to see these things. Husserl says that perception implies a "turning-toward" (Zuwendung) the world. Perception does not end in the body but already implies a particular preoccupation with the world, a turn from protention toward projection, he says, whereby the world is had, is understood, and is indeed created. Back to DuBois, in a sense he *creates* his skin color, beyond the color itself. Seeing, in any case, is not a Cartesian event, a "distancing," a mediation that separates the percipient from the world. Rather, it is like a string that, twined with biological and historical strands, separates and unites the subject and the object, erasing their double structure. Inasmuch as sense perception erases this double structure, the object of perception becomes subjectified, and the percipient is thrown into particular states of subjectivity, which this object nudge into being. The gaze, in other words, often releases a relational structure: the meeting of opposites: an uncanny separation-with-union, so that we become, as Paul Valery says, our "we of the moment."

Note also that, much as memory, the perceptual act also links the person to time, particularly to the past. Recall, again, Proust. The tasting of the madeleine did not end in the tongue. It was irretrievably attached to the narrator's memory, to his childhood, to the town of Combray, and to what those things represent culturally, historically. He tasted the madeleine as a bearer of a particular history. Vision, similarly, not only involves an active openness to the lifeworld (Lebenswelt), as Merleau-Ponty argued, but also an active openness to shared pasts, as the act of seeing is already mediated by a tradition. It indeed involves a sense of enacting tradition. It involves, in sum, a (perceptual) memory attached to common pasts.

Example: The Medieval Eye

There is a sense in which the world is thus seen with epochal eyes. In a sense time and place are in the eyes. Let me go back to the Middle Ages to further illustrate this idea. During that period, the forests, for instance, did not have the contemplative attraction that they acquired during the modern Romantic Period, when nature suddenly became "innocent." (It is not by coincidence that Dante finds the way to Hell through a *"selva selvaggia,"* through untamed woods, "astray in the dark wood/where the straight road had been lost sight of.") The idea is that, in the Husserial sense, the medieval eye, particularly the eye of the peasant, turned-toward medieval things when it beheld the forest. Though the eye of the knight was, to an extent, mediated by proto-romantic ideas about nature, the eye of the peasant generally turned-toward danger and magic when beholding the forest, the domain of witches, werewolves, magical creatures, brigands — all of which made their natural appearance in the eye (as well as in the "I"). Back to Valery, such was the peasant's "we of the present moment": the perceptual "we" that connected the subject and the object, and the subject and his/her history.

But of course the forest doesn't have a privileged ontological status for this medieval percipient, and what I argue is that the medieval world, in general, was perceived by medieval eyes — charged in particular ways by the mythos of an era. Importantly, these eyes were bearers not only of ideas, but also of collectively relevant sentiments, affects, of a libidinal economy that was also attached to this particular world. Influenced by Platonic, Aristotelian, and Arabic science, the medieval person thought that the gaze was a beacon, a purveyor of forces; that it was capable of transmitting temptations, and casting malefic powers. On the other hand, the Middle Ages also saw the eye as a sponge-like receiver of external forces; so that pregnant women, for example, were warned not to gaze at pictures of monsters (Camille 1998), lest their wombs be polluted by demonic forces channeled in precisely through the mother's gaze (hence their uneasiness with pagan icons). And thus, throughout the Middle Ages the very act of looking was an act charged with dangers and also with pleasures, as Camille also says (ibid.). Seeing involved wants, fears, affects attached to the period. Medieval eyes, for example, saw through the libidinal economies that regulated the interactions between sexes, privileging the male point of view, of course, charging it with a sense of power that was generally foreign to the eyes of women.

In summary, the medieval wisdom was thus correct in assuming that the eye is a purveyor of powers and energies. But these energies are those of the zeitgeist. They are associated with gender, race, class, social positioning, in general, an idea that can be applied to any other historical circumstance beyond the Middle Ages. Below we will see that our contemporary gaze purveys and absorbs the energies and interests — political, libidinal, scientific, technological — that emanate from our world.

The Gaze and the History of Representation

Let me go back in time and briefly peek into the history of visual representation, particularly the history of the technologies of visual representation. This quick historical excursus is needed to add an important layer to the foregoing discussion: the idea that, beyond ideology and politics, *technology itself* also stirs the eye in ever new and unexpected ways, installs new features of visual memory, a process that is not without consequences for the social order.

Ernst Gombrich (2002) suggests that the history of Western representation began in Egypt, after a long launching period, since Egyptian art remained more or less unaltered for about 3,000 years, from the Early Dynastic Period, 3000 BC, to the Late Period, about 400 BC. Though the Egyptians launched this history, they did little to expand it. Their paintings and reliefs had forever clear outlines, nothing was foreshortened, every human part was represented from its most characteristic angle. All this, however, changed with the Greeks, who indeed initiated a new and decisive period in the history of representation. By 500 BC, Gombrich says, we find "the greatest discovery of all, the discovery of the foreshortening technique," "a tremendous moment in the history of art when . . . artists dared for the first time in all history to pain a foot as seen from in front" (Gombrich 2002, 81). And of course, not only feet, but the world as such had never been foreshortened. It took thousands of years for us to conceive such visual daring. But from 500 BC on, we became not only able to represent the world in this way, but we were able to finally *see,* as a culture, tridimensionality within a bidimensional space. A transformation in the domain of visual memory had occurred.

Yet, back to Benjamin, today this visual trick has lost its aura. We can't quite see this as a visual revolution (though a revolution it was). Another 25 centuries have passed in the history of visuality and today we grow experiencing a different visual order, with naturalized features of its own, with a technological background of its own. Susan Sontag notes that "Through photographs [for example], the world becomes a series of unrelated, free-standing particles; and history, past and present, a set of anecdotes and faits divers. The camera makes reality atomic, manageable and opaque. It is a view of the world which denies interconnectedness, continuity, but which confers on each moment the character of a mystery" (Sontag 2001). Taking a Heraclitean stance, photographer Henri Cartier-Bresson tells us that in the world there *are no forms but processes,* flux, movement, growth, decay; and that photography, by freezing the flux of things otherwise not available to the naked eye — *released a heightened sense of form* into our modern lives. [2] Thus, a new world emerged *before* the eye. And a new world emerged *from* the eye that purveyed new visual habits and new visual memories.

Because photography plunges its flashing hand into the flux of time to dig something discrete out, our mode of relating to the world has been altered. Our relationship with processes was altered. Altered was in fact our relationship to time itself. Today we can preserve moments in time; we can save the past, shot by shot, as a series of "stills." These stills invoke absences, perhaps familial absences filled with a sense of domestic or melancholic sweetness, which, though ordinary for us, become precisely "moments," fixed aspects of our past, parts of who we are. By contrast, such mode of self-perception hardly existed in the days when the past was linked primarily to storytelling. Such "moments," such ocular proofs of our past, hardly existed when our personal histories were verbal and not visual. When we sat around the fire, as Benjamin says, fixed images of course existed, paintings, in particular (the oldest image made by human beings, geometric patterns on a small stone discovered by Christopher Henshilwood, is at least 70,000 years old). But, as suggested, these early images were invested with different qualities, with a very different aura. They were often charged with ritual, and even monumental and magical and sacred qualities. (Again, this is why the Middle Ages engaged in this systematic campaign to destroy ancient images). This pre-photographic epoch was in part propped by different technologies, including technologies of visual representation. And these, in turn, propped different visual habituses (that also contributed to propping the epoch).

The idea is that, as Marshall McLuhan would say, media should not be understood as mere perceptual prosthetics, as though photographic cameras and videos, for example, were external with respect to the percipient, as if these devices were mere recorders of time. On the contrary, the capabilities and limitations of media tend to become part of the percipient's structures of cognition and perception. Media tend to become part of the act of perception itself. As Nicholas Carr, says, the invention of the map, for example, located us within visual and bidimensional coordinates in space that hitherto did not exist. Henceforth we began to see space in a much more abstract manner. The invention of the internet provided windows into distant worlds. The world became smaller; the exotic became more and more mundane. Media encroaches upon our nature, and contributes to our mode of being.

Let me go back to Bourdieu again. As suggested, he shows that members of the French middle classes are more likely to see the sunset as "beautiful" than members of the upper classes, who are more likely to see it as uninteresting or ugly. The latter may see it as ugly because there is photography in the world, and because the sunset has therefore lost its powers, its aura in the Benjaminian sense. Only with the invention of photography, the image of the sun could become cliché. Writing before George Eastman popularized photography, Walt Whitman sang to the "Splendor of Ended Day" with "unmitigated adoration." We respect this locution today, largely on account of Whitman's own aura, but during Whitman's time, this locution also carried the aura of the pre-photographic sun. By contrast, today we see the sunset — and the world, in general — through the filter of photography, and through the filter of technology in general. We relate to the world the way we do in part because visual technologies mediate our perceptual memory.

Of the introduction of filmmaking, Walter Benjamin (1968) tells us that "with the close-up, space expands; with slow motion, movement is extended. The enlargement of a snapshot does not simply render more precise what in any case was visible, though unclear: it reveals entirely new structural formations of the subject. So, too, slow motion not only presents familiar qualities of movement, but reveals in them entirely unknown ones"; things that are not available to the pre-filmic eye (ibid., 236). "Evidently," Benjamin continues, "a different nature opens itself to the camera than opens to the naked eye."

THE EYE AND LIBERAL CAPITALISM

Debord Revisited

The historical circumstances surrounding contemporary visual memories have been a matter of debate. Guy Debord, a Marxist theorist of visuality whose work addresses the explosion of new media in the 1960s and 1970s, is at the center of these debates, particularly because, today, we face a new stream of images through the internet. His *The Society of the Spectacle* (2010) pioneered a critique of modern visuality, speaking of the "imperiousness" of the modern technologies of visual representation, and how they have delivered the scopic apotheosis of modern capitalism. As noted in a previous chapter, Americans, for example, spend roughly two (some researchers say three) years of their lives watching only commercials on TV. They watch more than four hours of TV each day. In a sixty-five-year life, the average American will have nine years of continuous TV exposure. Children watch 1,680 minutes of TV per week, and about 20,000 commercials per year. In a lifetime (sixty-five years) they will see two million of them. Experimental data suggests that media exposure can have powerful effects. Marco Iacoboni says, for example, that,

> The results of . . . controlled experiments with children in laboratory settings could not be more clear and unequivocal: exposure to media violence [for example] has a strong effect on imitative violence . . . a consistent finding is typically observed in these experiments. The children who watched . . . violent short movies display much more aggressive subsequent behavior toward both people and objects than the children who watched nonviolent short movies. This effect of media violence on imitative violence is observed in children from pre-school to adolescence, in both boys and girls, in both naturally aggressive and non aggressive children, and in different races. [T]hese findings [violence associated to media exposure] are highly reproducible across studies and even across countries. (Iacoboni 2009, 206)

These findings, furthermore, also hold for longitudinal studies:

> [Such studies] demonstrated that watching media violence in early childhood was correlated with aggressive and antisocial behavior after high school graduation. These findings are already impressive, but there is more: the same boys were followed for more than another decade, for a total of twenty two years of follow up since initial enrollment in the study, and again the results were clear cut: both early viewing of media violence and early aggressive behavior correlated with criminality at age thirty! (ibid., 207)

As Nicholas Carr argues (2010), neurological research suggests that media can indeed affect brain processes at various levels, including synaptic interactions and neuromodulation. And importantly, though this neurological capacity for adaptation may have beneficial effects, it can also have detrimental effects, as the brain adapts without "thinking" about the moral, existential, normative, aesthetic implications of such adaptive processes.

Back to Debord, he argues that today, and more than ever before, life has indeed become almost purely scopic or spectacular, much more attuned to technologies of representation. And this, he adds, is not without consequences for modernity as a whole. In modernity, he says, presence and the present have largely become re*present*ation. The present is not really a point of action. It is already interpreted; it largely is re-present-ed; it is presented to us as a series of "readymades," in the coinage of Marcel Duchamp. Increasingly, lived *moments* cease to be invitations for critical analytical exchange. Activity — the actual, the present — has been largely supplanted by mostly passive contemplation. We are not only addressed by a continuous stream of readymades broadcasted by the new media, but these images are in fact in the business of cajoling us, convincing us of something, seducing us. And inasmuch as they do, they not only create aspects of our perceptual memory but also aspects of our reality. Indeed, the idea is that this vast simulacrum has largely *displaced* reality, and that it has displaced the bearer of reality herself, as Jean Baudillard also argued. Debord implies, perhaps exaggerating, that life, in our intensely scopic times, has in fact lost out to inertial life. Life has become lifeless: inertial, *inert*. "All that was once directly lived," he says, "has become mere representation" (2010).

Consider military actions. They are an important aspect of reality today but, As Paul Virilio has suggested, wars take place out of sight. War is very visible; it is only a matter of turning the TV on. And yet "war" involves edited visual fragments in a continuous stream of news, entertainment, and infotainment, with the protagonists of war often appearing as protagonists in yet another hyperreal, spectacular stage provided by the media. "War," back to Benjamin, has been divested of its aura. And thus, precisely because it has been rendered more and more spectacular, it has become more and more invisible. Freud, a witness to the events leading to WWII, said that on account of modern wars, "life has, indeed, become interesting again; it has recovered its full content [because] death is no longer to be denied; we are forced to believe in it. People really die" (quoted in Whitebook 1996, 72). But times are different and today this stark statement is less applicable. Today, war no longer forces us to believe in death. Today, victims of war generally die spectacular, "collateral" deaths that are largely diluted in a massive stream of images and sound bites, of cognitive and affective associations that often render death irrelevant and even entertaining. The meaning of death is thus recast. The larger point, however, is that the spectacle recasts the meaning of life, and the experience of being alive.

Debord argues that, inasmuch as we live through spectacular images chosen by others, we learn to imagine and speak the language of the spectacle, to think spectacular thoughts, and to thus reinforce "spectacular power," the political and economic sources that sustain these pervasive images. Furthermore, the human body as such, a central motif of this modern spectacle, is also fettered to the eye of liberal capitalism, and has begun to partake from the logic of the spectacle. As a commodity inserted in a scopic economy, the body is encouraged to move, gesture, and even desire in certain ways, a process that is also driven by pre-given images, by the readymades that are necessary for this economic system to function. Again, today some consumers see Botox injections as "proper grooming" for the twentieth-first century. (Even though this toxin has been linked not only to medical outcomes, such as respiratory failure, speech disorders, and even death, but also to psychological outcomes such as decreases in emotional experiences and responses, which results from extended periods of involuntary facial expression [Davis et al 2010; Havas et al 2010].)

Debord argues that, for all these reasons, spectacularization is a crucial weapon in the arsenal of capitalism. And the collective visual memory, he may agree, is thus an important target and an important tool for this economic system to function; a system that bespeaks a culture of images that constantly reinforce the conditions that engender "lonely crowds" (Debord 2010). (And thus, we may extrapolate, the arts have an important role as they may be able to provide alternatives to these Duchampian visual patterns, restoring our ability to connect to reality by injecting different visual memories within the larger domain of embodied memory. Pessimistic as he seems to be, Debord nonetheless argues that it is possible to restore the capacity of images to express authenticity, to nurse critical thinking, to bring us closer to presence.)

Michel Foucault and Nicholas Carr

In this last part I want to consider, briefly and critically, the work of Foucault (which will lead us to the work of Nicholas Carr). It is important to note, first, that, formerly considered one of the most important theorists of the twentieth century, Foucault has fallen out of favor today. (To be sure, he is often ridiculed, dismissed as a "charlatan" as Vargas Llosa says [2011a]. Camille Paglia [1992], for example, never found one "single line" of interest in the writings of Foucault. She "hates" his "pretentious," "verbose," "mendacious," and "ignorant" scholarship.) One may grant that his model has flaws, as I discuss later, but his ideas about modern visuality have contributed to the conversation outlined above, about how capitalism relies on a scopic economy to fulfill its goals, and they can contribute, as well, to a theory of collectively relevant visual memories. Let us briefly recall some of his central ideas. Foucault argues that this economic system feeds from a "panoptical" logic: the Panopticon, a prison designed by one of the fathers of utilitarianism, Benjamin Bentham, was designed not primarily to punish or inflict pain, but to observe the prisoner, and to observe him all day and every day. In contrast to prior designs (e.g., the dungeon), the modern Panopticon was meant to be an all-powerful observer — the eye of the law, in the biblical idiom, a gigantic superegoic mechanism (not Foucault's term). And the logic here is that if the prisoner is *super*vised, he will be more likely to comply; and that, if he is always under *super*vision, compliance will become habitual, part of habitus. Panoptical surveillance, Foucault says, hoped to become self-surveillance. By means of sheer observation this powerful eye should be able to transform the relation of the prisoner to himself, thereby transforming his relationship to the world. (This is why, incidentally, Sartre was Foucault's natural enemy: Sartre's theory of responsibility argues that *we have* to internalize the gaze of the world and live accordingly.)

Importantly, the Panopticon, for Foucault, was not merely a prison but a metaphor for modernity, the entrance door to the scopic logic that governed modernity, and capitalism, in particular. He argues that, today, the supervised, over-seen lives of social actors face a panoptical scopic regime and, for this economic system to function, the eye of schools, factories, sciences — of the institutional order — has to fall upon life. This includes not only cameras in factories and other systematic technologies of surveillance, as the stereotype goes, but primarily the theoretical surveillance of the "disciplines": sociology, statistics, genetics, psychology, etc, which are important components of this disciplinary eye.

Foucault suggests that, thus super*vised* more than ever before, the modern social actor, much as the prisoner of the Panopticon, is more likely to defer, and even to submit to the systemic eyes that purvey the interests and powers dominant today. Think of market surveillance, for example, of the massive tracking of consumers' trends, preferences, and demographics (level of education, pet ownership, sexual orientation, etc.). Market surveillance aims to "capture" market segments: to cajole the affective and libidinal investments of consumers. It tries to gently and seductively "discipline" them, Foucault would say, particularly through images that, addressing the eye of the consumer, convey primarily the needs of the panoptical market and of those who vie to control it. Back to Dubois, we sometimes see the self and the world with borrowed eyes. The larger point that Foucault helps us understand is that, perhaps, we unwittingly see with borrowed eyes that are in fact interested, and that have been designed by increasingly massive and sophisticated technological, ideological, scientific, and economic apparatuses.

It is often remarked that both, Foucault's panoptical theory and Debord's Situationism exaggerated the role of representation and apperception. After all, even the mythological Panopticon, the thousand eyed monster that never slept and was thus used by the gods to surveil potential enemies, was in the end defeated, put to sleep by the sweet music of an artist, Pan. Perhaps the panoptic, spectacular nature of capitalism can be contested by new visual aesthetics, by new discourses emerging with globalization (gay, environmental, "ethnic," young), or by the human spirit, in general. Perhaps, back to Debord, some people watch a lifetime of commercials and develop not a passive but a critical eye. But these theories, in any case, help us better see that the eye, in general, easily bears the gazes of others: of history, of ideologies, of technologies of representation, of the market and of marketers.

Furthermore, these critiques of modern visuality help us see that these ideologies and technologies tend to encroach upon life itself, precisely through the eye that grasps related images and symbols; and that, inasmuch as ideology and technology do encroach upon life, they are not without consequences for individuals, for groups, for the global order, in general. As suggested, sense perception involves different ways of turning-toward the world, in the Husserlian sense — but, importantly, it also involves different ways in which the world turns toward us. Through the senses, we often enlist various aspects of the world; but through the senses the world can also enlist us, and certain imaginations, feelings, ideas, and actions, individual and collective. It is thus important to lend a critical eye to the images and technologies that characterize modernity. It is important to consider, theoretically and empirically, the phenomena that are encompassed by visual collective memories.

Finally, let me speak about the internet. Back to Nicholas Carr (2011), he argues that the complex visual and cognitive environment provided by the internet, which today is very deeply inserted within everyday life, is likely to produce fundamental changes in aspects of perception, cognition, in our ability to contemplate, to remember, to concentrate, to follow extended linear arguments (e.g., from books), in our capacity for solitary and self-reflective thought — in these most valuable ways of engaging with the world. Carr is neither proposing a return to nature, which is impossible, nor suggesting that this new technology is entirely negative. He also sees the obvious advantages of the internet, which indeed are too obvious for discussion. Nonetheless, much as Sontag, Benjamin, Debord and others above, Carr conveys a mood of anxious foreboding. He indeed seems very worried. It seems to me that he is worried about the historical direction that *human nature itself* is presently taking. Vargas Llosa has provided a useful summary of Carr's central ideas:

> The most recalcitrant defenders of [the internet] argue that it is a tool, and that it serves those who use it, and of course, there are abundant experiments that seem to corroborate this . . . . Who could deny that today it is almost a miracle that, in a few seconds, and only by virtue of clicking with the mouse, the internet user may retrieve information that a few years back would have de-

manded weeks or months, [and trips] to the library, and consultations with specialists. Yet, there is also conclusive proof showing that when memory is not exercised because the person has an infinite archive [connected to] his computer, it is stiffened and weakened, much as a muscle that is not used. . . . It is not true that the internet is only a tool. It is an apparatus [*utensilio*] that becomes an extension of our own body, of our own brain, which . . . in discreet ways adapts, little by little, to this new system of information . . . renouncing, little by little, to the functions that this system performs in its stead, and sometimes better than it. It is no mere poetic metaphor to maintain that the "artificial intelligence" at its service bribes and sensualizes our thinking organs, which progressively become dependent on such tools, and in the end become its slaves. (2011b, my translation)

A key principle of evolution is this: if an organ is not used, it tends to become vestigial. Birds that have no need to fly will lose their wings and, speaking metaphorically, their capacity to soar. Thus one may argue that, insofar as the internet becomes a prosthetic memory, aspects of memory, this center of the self, may become vestigial as well. After all, the difference between our memory and that of a computer is that the latter "stores" information accumulatively and permanently. By contrast, our memory is alive, and it is constantly in the process of being made and unmade (Carr 2011, 191). I now quote Carr:

Those who celebrate the 'outsourcing' of memory to the Web have been misled by a metaphor. They overlook the fundamentally organic nature of biological memory. What gives real memory its richness and its character, not to mention its mystery and fragility, is its contingency. It exists in time, changing as the body changes. Indeed the very act of recalling a memory appears to restart the entire process of consolidation, including the generation of proteins to form new synaptic terminals . . . . Biological memory is in a perpetual state of renewal. The memory stored in a computer, by contrast, takes the form of distinct and static bits. (ibid., 191)

Another difference between human and digital memory is that the latter may become full, and thus inoperative. Our memory, by contrast, is "virtually boundless," Carr explains, and the fuller it becomes "our minds become sharper" (ibid.). Hence, though the Web "provides a convenient and compelling supplement to personal memory . . . when we start using the Web as a substitute for personal memory, bypassing the inner process of consolidation, we risk emptying our minds of their riches" (ibid., 192).

Much as every other technological innovation, the internet, in any case, is also contributing not only to our way of thinking but to our way of being, in general. And it seems that, for better or for worse, new aspects of nature are encroaching upon life, precisely through the eye that serves as a link to the web. Back to Marshall McLuhan, visual media *themselves* are the message.

Again, these media broadcast not merely messages (e.g., news, commercials) but their own nature. If, as Carr says, the invention of the map located us within abstract, bidimensional, visual coordinates that helped us relate differently to space, the internet is locating us within cybernetic coordinates. It is inserting life within a different dimension of space. It is providing different coordinates for various aspects of embodied memory. This will not be without consequences for human nature.

NOTES

1. The classical idea of "veneration" was different than ours. The word "god" (*theos*) meant different things for the Greeks. "Immortals" were neither "good" in the modern sense, nor omniscient or omnipotent. Contemporary gods generally don't have the attributes of old gods either, such as sexual prowess, as was the case of many Olympians. Venus was neither the virginal Christian female deity, nor the goddess of "love," as the Victorian translators made us believe. She was a teenage goddess who governed primarily over sexual passion (her biological development fixed at a halfway point of her pubescence), which the Greeks saw as a temporary form of madness, which not even Zeus was capable of dispelling (especially not Zeus). Heeding her whim and oblivious to the consequences, she often used her powers to grant vengeance, to appease petty jealousies, hatreds, vanities, including petty jealousies and vanities of her own. Thus, the Classical Age saw things in this statue that we can neither see nor feel, and only hardly understand. The kinship between "veneration" and "venereal" is lost to those raised under asexual gods.

2. Heraclitus (about 540-480 BC) was the Presocratic philosopher of becoming (as opposed to *Being*) and spoke of the fluid nature of the cosmos, which, he thought, is like a river where we cannot step in twice, as the river of the first step will not be the same as that of the second step. Likewise, I am not the same today as the one I was yesterday; there are never two *identical* "yous."

Chapter Sixteen

The Role of Institutions

"[T]he world of institutions," Berger and Luckmann say, often "appears to merge with the world of nature" (1967). What these authors mean is that social actors often adopt and pre-reflectively enact arrays of institutionalized, commonly accepted meanings conferred by a common past. Recall, for example, our chapter on race: beliefs about race generally do not afford themselves as products of history, of human decisions, actions and struggles. Instead, they merely seem to speak on behalf of nature. They seem to extend from an elemental order "endowed with an ontological status independent of human activity and signification" (ibid.). These beliefs, and institutionalized beliefs in general, often appear to be the natural and indeed *necessary* outcomes of what Max Weber called the "eternal yesterday."

In this book, I have argued that the world of institutions merges not only with a mythical world of nature, but with very concrete aspects of human nature. Eyes, noses, palates, ("ethnic") ears, motor mechanisms, fat tissue, cortex activity, scatological thresholds of embarrassment, affects and desires, sensations and perceptions, hairstyles and sartorial standards, intonation and gestures, gestures of subordination and of superordination are marked by systems of meaning, by the technologies and the interested institutions associated with them. And such processes, much as those that underpin the construction of social meaning, also encourage the illusion that the embodied experience belongs to an order that is endowed, as Berger and Luckmann say, "with an ontological status independent of human activity and signification." Of course, the body stands upon a biological, universal, phylogenetically crafted, and relatively fixed substratum — but it is not this substratum. The body, much as the meanings that become attached to it, is constantly affected by ongoing human actions and struggles. The embodied experience is natural but not merely natural. It is also arbitrary. It responds to variable circumstances that, back to Heidegger, are not of our choosing. The very organs of the body, as I have also argued, provide a haven for fictions and errors, which are important components of the embodied experience. Race, once again, illustrates this idea. Race is an ongoing fiction that, for the time being, is securely consigned to the domain of embodied collective memory.

Thus, racial, but also sexual, economic, political, religious notions — even if arbitrary and capricious — can penetrate the texture of everyday life. To be sure, "the imaginations of the dead," in Rorty's denuded phrase, not only merge with the world of nature, but steer it in various directions and with various consequences. But precisely because human nature is fluid, these processes are not permanent. If institutions and social actors themselves work to uphold and maintain the inherited symbolic orders that become attached to the body, they also work to produce deviant and resistive symbols that sponsor new features of ECMs, as we saw in the foregoing. Democratic or undemocratic institutions, in summary, contribute to form, reform, and deform aspects of embodied collective memory. Individuals themselves participate in these processes, strategically or pre-reflectively, at the level of the ego or at the level of the drive, at the level of play or of work, and defending their own interests or going against them.

In this last chapter, I discuss various ways in which the imaginations of the dead, as well as those of the living, contribute to steer the world of nature in directions that may result in advantages and disadvantages for individuals and groups.

A Classical Political Ontology

The idea that institutions, including those of the state, can and ought to target human nature to pursue ideological goals is almost as old as political philosophy itself. This notion is already implied by Plato's *"The Republic"* (1987), which suggests that the guardians of the state should concern themselves not only with norms, values, and laws but also with such things as gymnastic exercises and music. These things, Plato says, can create not only good or bad habits, the habitus that Aristotle theorized, but ultimately good or bad citizens. Via the senses and the body, such things as music reach not only the ear but the "corners of the soul," and they can also contribute to the nature of the citizen and thus to the nature of the polis. They therefore ought to be managed by the state. Following this logic, Aristotle in fact thought that "hubristic" music can encourage hubristic habituses, dispositions antithetical to the Greek ideal of moderation. Such hubristic rhythms, Aristotle thought, abet the wrong passions, the undesirable element of excess in the body, the tendencies of the lower strata, which, if eventually ingrained in habitus, could turn a citizen into a slave (of his own appetites), thus upsetting the very order of the world. (Significantly, the early Athenian and Spartan constitutions, probably inspired by Pythagoras who thought that music was a medium of the divine, regulated music, prescribing some instruments and proscribing others, so that no orgiastic or hubristic rhythms would distort the ears — and thus the habits, minds and virtues of the citizens.)

This aristocratic political ontology was designed to guide institutional mechanisms to control, in particular, the Dionysian portion of nature, the "unruly horse," Plato says, tied to the chariot of life. This political program involved programmatic ascetic practices (*aeskesis*: "training") that citizens had to impose upon their bodies to remove, precisely, the elements of excess in nature and to therefore bring out the natural wisdom latent in nature's design (in the body). As "free men" thus learn to master their own instincts, they become masters in the political and domestic senses. They become "ideal" citizens: the media that organically connect the city to The Good; the principle that governs over the domain of pure (platonic) ideas, the platonic heaven. Everyday life, *la vie vivante* as Dostoyevsky may say, thus becomes "ideal" in the double sense of the word: it becomes good and also ruled by universal ideas and ideals.

Via the citizen, these ideal ideas descend from the platonic heaven to encroach upon the material aspects of life. In an Aristotelian sense, these "ideal" citizens would not weigh all their everyday actions according to hypothetical or categorical imperatives (as in Christianity or as in Kant), but would simply *be* good citizens, ontologically. They would carry and sustain a good civic order much as one carries an accent, a bodily rhythm. Civility and virtue would be embodied, something relatively inertial, a question of temperament. Thus, life's mundane, material impermanence would acquire qualities associated with the eternal. The city and the citizen would partake from the quiddity, the "whatness" of Being. In an almost Hegelian manner, The Good would become phenomenologized through the daily actions of the citizens, through daily exercises of virtue.

Gilles Deleuze and Félix Guattari, after Antonin Artaud, worried about the extent to which bodies can become "organ-ized" according to the colonizing needs of the institutional order (2001). By contrast, this ancient political ontology says that a systematic process of organ-ization is necessary for a good polis. It teaches that political organs, such as the state, ought to organize bodily organs: the ear, the eye, the lower stratum. It argues that institutional organs, in general, ought to organize individual and social bodies. Indeed, there is a sense in which this form of Platonic idealism aimed to provide a philosophical and political framework for an effective life-reform. This ancient form of bio-politics, to twist Foucault's term, aimed to manufacture an "ideal" (that is: aristocratic) nature, an "ideal" embodied collective memory.

This idealistic model is utopian, to be sure. As we saw, the social actor is a social but also a biological creature pushed by higher and by lower claims.

The first person is agonistically constituted by norms that speak on behalf of gregariousness and by raw and egotistical impulses that are biological in origin. And this economy of forces also facilitates the development of the embodied memory through which personhood is experienced and enacted. Thus, ideas and institutions will never steer nature toward the platonic archetype of The Good, as if through a linear teleological pathway. Yet, utopian as it is, this Platonic schema helps us consider an important question: to the extent to which the institutional order does mold aspects of ECMs, can it be crafted to steer "nature" in ways that render democratic ideas and ideals *organic*, more or less "natural," Aristotelian?

We saw that the processes whereby institutions merge with nature often create "natural" advantages and disadvantages for individuals, as well as for classes, genders, "races," generations. The theory of symbolic violence suggests, we also saw, that embodied memory is not only an important channel of social control, but also an obstacle for the person, for the group, and arguably for the nation (some citizens of poor countries such as mine, Peru, often take all the necessary pains when it comes to making the series of "normal" choices that again and again go against their very own interests, which, as Vargas Llosa as argued [1993], is one of the factors that contribute to their economic and cultural stagnation). Bourdieu, in any case, shows that obstacles that extend from objective conditions and from collective meanings sometimes become encysted in the very bodies of social actors, in the general domain of "nature," the "nature" of the disadvantaged. Yet, embodied memory is not only a site of resistance, as already suggested, but it can also be a pragmatic factor of development.

Let me offer an example to illustrate this idea: the social order in the early North American colonies. Fiercely organized around a set of (puritan) meanings, principles and laws, this institutional order contributed to aspects of ECM that, I argue, provided a ground for the development of the U.S., as Alexis de Tocqueville (2000) and Max Weber (1858) would probably agree. There is a sense in which the U.S. and its achievements are rooted in naturalized dispositions, in features of ECMs that have provided some of the bases for development. Bear in mind that these early colonies, which drew from Leviticus and Deuteronomy to establish their laws and institutions, aimed to "penetrate the consciousness" of social actors (Tocqueville 2000); and that, as argued in Chapter Eleven, they could do so only by first encroaching upon the body: its desires, gestures, rhythms, sartorial standards, hairstyles, speech, the ratio of rest to labor, drinking, smoking, etc. It is not by coincidence that, for example, when a New Englander girl allows herself to be given a kiss she is punished with a fine (Tocqueville 2000); or that "simply keeping company among unmarried people [was] severely repressed" (ibid); or that adultery was punishable by death (ibid); or that one "sees a solemn association being formed in Boston having for its purpose to prevent the worldly luxury of long hair" (ibid), etc. A myriad of examples can be supplied to illustrate how these colonies attempted to mold even minute aspects of ECM. But the general idea is that this everyday "petty, intrusive, mild despotism," as de Tocqueville says, emerged from a social apparatus, from an efficient *dispositif,* as Foucault would call it: from an ideological, juridical, and institutional matrix that aimed to *organize* individual as well as social bodies.

Naturally, one may note that the history of these "ardent sectarians" and "exalted innovators," as Tocqueville calls them, is neither ideal in the platonic sense above, nor devoid of disadvantages. The story of these "heroic entrepreneurs," in Weber's phrase, went hand in hand with the Native American holocaust. It bespoke a slave-based economic development, class fractures and related anxieties, gender disparities, elements of symbolic violence that have punctuated the development of the country, and still do. But this country nonetheless provides examples that illustrate the idea that the ECMs can be, as suggested, factors of development for social groups and even for countries.

Michel Foucault

The platonic model, aristocratic as it is, helps us consider the relationship between embodied memory, development, and democracy, and the notion that not usurpative but democratic ideas and ideals may also mold features of ECMs. But on the other hand, this model also helps us think, by contrast, about the extent to which even democratic institutions may play, in Foucaultian terms, a "pastoral" and undemocratic role in the domain of embodied memory. Let me finally recall, briefly and critically this time as well, some of the ideas provided by Michel Foucault, which can cast some light on this important point.

Foucault's polemic is well-known, but let me recall the key points. He says that, with the demise of the Monarchical system and the rise of liberal capitalism, modern institutional orders ceased to rely on physical suffering as the main locus and signifier of power. (By contrast, monarchical systems redeemed infractions against the King primarily through a body in pain, through the suffering body of the condemned, so that torture and death were in fact the main organizing principles of monarchical law.) With democracy and modern capitalism, Foucault says, power ceased to present itself "in its murderous splendor" (1984a), and increasingly became a "positive [i.e., productive] influence on life, that endeavors to administer, optimize, and multiply it, subjecting it to precise controls and comprehensive regulations" (ibid.). Modern law became organized around "technologies of subjectivation," which, at least in principle, aimed to change the *nature* of the infractor.

By the seventeenth and eighteenth centuries, capitalism in fact depended on a "bio-politics, "bio-power" (ibid.), on "techniques for achieving [the] subjugation of bodies and the control of populations" (ibid.). This was "without question an indispensable element in the development of capitalism. The latter would not have been possible without the insertion of bodies into the machinery of production" (ibid). To be sure, in liberal capitalism "*the life of the species* is wagered on its own political strategies" (Foucault 1979, my emphasis), so that we may speak of a "bio-history" to designate the "pressures through which the movements of life and processes of history interfere with one another [and] one could [also] speak of bio-power to designate what brought life ... into the realm of explicit calculations and made Power/knowledge an agent of transformation of human life" (1984a 256). Modernity thus arose "centered on the body as a machine: its disciplining, the optimization of its capabilities ... its docility ... all this was ensured by the disciplines: an anatomo-politics of the human body. The second ... focused on the species body ... propagation, births and mortality [etc.]" (ibid.).

This sort of modern "power/knowledge" is a fluid and ubiquitous energy at once localized and deployed from innumerable points. It flows through the social fabric in many guises and through many techniques, "heteromorphously," perpetually producing features of embodied memory that can hardly be outside its domain of influence. "Danger," Foucault says, "is everywhere." Yet, power is particularly concentrated in institutional apparatuses, prisons, barracks, schools, each of which has its "own history, [its] own trajectory, [its] own techniques and tactics" (1980), each with its own normalizing and disciplining effects. (Foucault, by the way, says that he doesn't study institutions but "regimes of practice," which, however, emerge particularly through institutions.) Hence, by the end of the eighteenth century,

> [T]he soldier [for example] has become something that can be made; out of formless clay, an inapt body, the machine required can be constructed; posture is gradually corrected; a calculated constraint runs slowly through each part of the body, mastering it, making it pliable, ready at times, turning silently into the automatism of habit...one has "got rid of the peasant" and given him "the air of a soldier"... *The classical age discovered the body as a target of power.* (Foucault 1984a 179-180, my emphasis)

Foucault also theorizes resistance, and he says that wherever power is deployed, a reactive resistance is set in motion. "Suddenly, what made power strong becomes used to attack it. Power, after investing itself in the body, finds itself exposed to a counterattack in that same body" (1980). But almost as in Bourdieu, he is mostly interested in the idea that the modern social order is "the effect not of consensus but of the materiality of power operating on the very bodies of individuals" (ibid). In these brave new Foucaultian worlds, dominant discourses seem fundamentally designed to organ-ize

ECMs as if "out of formless clay." Foucault in fact feared that modernity as a whole was constituted as an apparatus of "docilization." Thus, if the Greek philosophers bespoke a utopian institutional order that aimed to empower life itself, Foucault bespeaks a dystopian order that aims to mold life so as to extract power from it.

Again, important portions of Foucault's theory have been effectively questioned (e.g., Hoy 1986) and, indeed, the critical corpus is too large for treatment, here. But it is worth considering a brief and telling example that highlights some of the limits of his model. Classrooms, part of the Foucaultian disciplinary "apparatus," also discipline students and channel a truth-consensus that speaks on behalf of power and those in power. But as Vargas Llosa has suggested (2011a), even a glimpse at school systems in Europe and the U.S. today reveals that, in general, they are not Foucaultian disciplinary agents with their "own techniques and tactics" of subjection. The atmosphere of violence that often hangs over some high schools in the U.S., and shootings and indeed massacres perpetrated by students, seems to suggest that a quota of "disciplinary power" may be actually needed in the modern school system. In the U.S. in 2009, "31.5% of high school students had been in a physical fight ..., 6.3% had attempted suicide ..., 34.2% were currently sexually active, and 2.1% of students had ever injected an illegal drug" (Eaton et al 2010). Perhaps schools are channels of truth-consensus, and in this sense of discursive power, but they are unlikely candidates for the sort of "disciplinary," bodily power that Foucault seems to have in mind. They don't seem to have "discovered the body as a target of power." More generally, Foucault's notion that modernity operates primarily as a disciplinary apparatus (*dispositif*) is also difficult to generalize. Again, human nature is fluid and conflicted, an idea that this philosopher under-theorized.

Yet, much as the utopian Greek model above is limited but helpful, in that it allows us to consider a potentially positive role for the institutional order, Foucault's hermeneutics of suspicion helps consider the idea that that even democratic institutions, practices, and discourses may affect ECM in ways that create disadvantages for groups. As suggested, "bio-politics" helps us see that elements of (racialized) embodied memories, for example, were organ-ized according to utilitarian, parasitic ideologies stemming from institutions organized according to "democratic" ideals, including the state, the market, the church, the law. "Bio-politics" is not very useful when it is a question of understanding "race" as a structure of possibilities that is potentially resistive and innovative, but it does provides an angle from which to see that democratic systems can and have historically had an usurpative and, I insist, parasitic role in the domain of nature.

A final reflection, to conclude: as I suggested in the introduction, ECMs are not structures that can be easily crafted so as to deliver either good or bad outcomes, dichotomously. Yet, embodied memory can lead to good or bad

outcomes for individuals and groups. In the West, questions about the potential role of the body have been discussed for about twenty five centuries.
(Arguably it was Xenophanes [570–475 BC], the Greek poet-philosopher,
who set in motion this millennial concern with the body, as he began to think
about the differences between mortals and immortals, and how our fate is
marked by the finitude of our bodies.) But today, more than before, the body
ought to be of central concern, as Foucault correctly argued. Recall, first, that
post-industrial bodies have changed in ways that have no parallel in the
history of the 7,000 generations that have inhabited the earth. And that in the
Digital Age very different systems of meaning and exponentially evolving
technological networks are merging with embodied collective memories;
such that the "nature" of the person is today increasingly connected to new
images, sounds, symbols, meanings *and to the interests* that are broadcasted
by these media. How will these rapidly emergent processes affect human
nature? What advantages and/or disadvantages will result from them, and for
whom? Nietzsche thought that philosophy, broadly conceived, must help
culture produce a "healthy body," to thus help produce a healthier culture and
a worthwhile history. Philosophy, Nietzsche says, has to be "medicine" for
history. This Nietzschean idea has not lost its relevance. And indeed Nietzsche's questions will become increasingly important. At stake, I have argued
in this book, are the contents of human nature and the historical directions
that these contents will facilitate.

Psychoanalysis as a "Failed Science"

A PSEUDO-SCIENCE

This appendix aims to clarify the scientific and epistemological status of psychoanalysis, and to underscore its advantages and weaknesses. It is not possible to provide, here or in any other single volume, a comprehensive review of the critical appraisals leveled against the discipline; and below I try to cover only the main areas of criticism against psychoanalysis. Bear in mind that, as Hans Lowenthal says, from the very beginning it has been "a despised and scorned science" (in Whitebook 1996, 1); and that for over a century psychoanalysis has therefore amassed an impressive collection of criticisms, perhaps the largest of any discipline. "To my knowledge," Louis Althusser writes, "in the course of the nineteenth century, two or three children were born who were unexpected: Marx, Nietzsche, Freud. . . . A child without a father, Western Reason makes him pay dearly for it. Marx, Nietzsche, Freud had to pay the price, sometimes terrible, of survival: a price counted in exclusions, condemnations, insults, miseries, hungers and death, or madness" (in Borch-Jacobsen and Shamdasani 2008, 9).[1]

Indeed, criticisms against psychoanalysis, as Freud predicted, have steadily increased; and, as psychoanalysis extended its influence into all disciplines in the human sciences and the humanities — every expanding discipline has had, by turns, critical assessments to make. In fact, as psychoanalysis itself progressively branched out into various schools, perhaps the most serious, and at times most severe, critics of psychoanalytical theory have been psychoanalysts themselves. To be sure, every major contributor to Post-Freudian theory has provided corrections, pleas for purging some of the concepts or techniques.[2] The late Freud was in fact an enthusiastic critic of some of the concepts from the early Freud.[3]

Freud himself was the target of innumerable diatribes. Diatribes that, however, were as numerous as the accolades that he also received, including, for instance, the commendatory correspondence from Albert Einstein who praises Freud's "irresistible lucidity" and his "passion to ascertain the truth."[4]

In general, it is also easy to see that the critics have not confined the discipline to a fringe; and that psychoanalysis has in fact expanded in a Julianic fashion across languages, disciplines, movements, schools. And, as suggested, a pleiad of writers across the disciplines have been directly influenced by psychoanalysis. The odd language of psychoanalytical theory has in fact, in an almost Jungian, archetypical fashion, encroached upon our collective imagination, the everyday language, even upon popular culture. As we will see, it is difficult to deny that Freud's ideas touched the world because they touched on important aspects of human nature. There are legitimate reasons that explain its influence.

The Hydrodynamic Model

To outline some of the major concerns often leveled against psychoanalysis, I will start by enlisting the scholarship of Emanuel Peterfreund and Jacob Schwartz, and their old but often quoted book, *Information, Systems, and Psychoanalysis* (1971). These writers, who pioneered the notion that psychoanalysis partakes from vitalistic biases, accept some of the clinical aspects of the discipline, but their goal is to move the discipline away from its "anachronistic vitalistic position," to shake it from its foundations, and to discard its pseudo-scientific constructs. The main problems outlined by their influential investigations can be summarized as follows: First, they are concerned about the "pseudo-biologism" surrounding the theory, perhaps the major area of anti-psychoanalytical critique that is in general leveled against the discipline. Secondly, and all the problems derive from the first problem, they discuss purportedly profound deficits besetting Freud's "hydraulic model," another major problem pointed out again and again by critics. And thirdly, they discuss the discipline's "primitive anthropocentrism" and how the dynamic forces and agencies of the Freudian mental apparatus are ultimately products of Freud's anthropocentric and anthropomorphic habits of thought (these agencies, the authors suggest, as they are divorced from physiology and neurology, resemble in fact mystical forces, mystical entities and energies that simply reveal Freud's naïve and pseudo-biological view of human nature, a worldview wedded to the crypto-vitalistic zeitgeist of the nineteenth century).

These conceptual inadequacies, the authors suggest, impoverish not only this and that concept, but the conceptual apparatus of the discipline, including its key building blocks, such concepts as *energy, ego, cathexis*, and *instinct*.

All these problems, one gathers from their critique, are organically entwined and stem from a general lack of scientific insight. Indeed, the basic problem from which many shortcomings stem, Peterfreund and Schwartz imply, is the elemental problem of operational definition. They ask us to consider, for example, the psychoanalytical notion of "energy," this dynamizer of the entire psychosomatic apparatus. Energy, the authors explain, is a "qualitative" construct in psychoanalysis and as such is "quite alien to the rest of the scientific world" (Peterfreund and Schwartz 1971, 49). For the rest of the scientific world, energy obeys the laws of thermodynamics. By contrast, energy in psychoanalysis is a vitalistic, almost mystical entity endowed with anthropomorphic motives of its own (e.g., psychoanalysts speak of "aggressive" energies). "Physical energy concepts," Peterfreund and Schwartz say, "do not exist" in psychoanalysis (ibid., 51): "There are no concepts . . . that can explain any aspect of the existence of the world of physical and organic entities" (ibid., 52)

The model, we are told, involves anthropomorphic energies and fluids, which psychoanalysis uses as pseudo-causes explaining motivation, thought, behavior, etc. "In psychoanalysis, the anthropomorphizations are considered to be explanatory; the theory goes no further" (ibid., 73). "Psychoanalysis views the world of biology, neurophysiology, and evolutionary time from a completely anthropocentric standpoint . . . Psychoanalysis is still attempting to force the world of biology, physiology, and evolutionary time into a world at the center of which is the mind of man [*sic*]. This has been the pitfall of a theory which remains on psychological ground" (ibid., 40).

Of course, if one puts this "host of internal difficulties and contradictions" together, one gets a parallel array of pseudo-theoretical constructs, such as the ego, another central aspect of the theory which, the authors explain, is like a little mind within the mind, an entity that has no connection to biological or neurological processes. Because "psychological observables [i.e., behavior, etc.] are assigned to an agent [the ego] whose nature remains unknown and unexplained," the ego is not even useful as a "generalization or an abstraction" (ibid.). This notion, the ego, is "grossly inadequate" and it misleads us into thinking that the mind is a controlling entity that, like a little homunculus in the head, is separate from the body but somehow inserted in it, after a naïve Cartesian fashion. Thus we arrive at what would seem to be the major problem of the model (which has been pointed out by many other critics as well): "Clearly," the authors say, "psychoanalytical theory has *separated the mind from the body*." "Mind [in psychoanalysis] *is not viewed as a manifestation of biological activity*; it is not viewed as subject to universal biological law. Instead it *is seen as controlling biological attributes* that have actually evolved through eons of evolutionary time" (Peterfreund and Schwartz 1971, 67, my emphases).

Perhaps there is no need to belabor the point that Peterfreund and Schwartz are making: they try to convey the idea of a general domino effect, where elemental difficulties naturally lead to higher and higher levels of failure, to systemic error and basic misconceptions. For them it is clear that psychoanalytical theory is similar to the mind of a small child for whom it is "apparently easier to think in an anthropocentric way, in concrete terms that are close to one's experience than to think in more abstract terms necessary for the advancement of scientific theory" (ibid., 53). Naturally, then, "Fundamental fallacies [have to] result when this kind of thinking is used to devise acceptable scientific explanations" (ibid., 54). Hence,

> Current psychoanalytical theory essentially represents a hydrodynamic model. Uniting the anthropomorphic entities in the mind are psychic energies with fluid properties and with anthropomorphic qualitative characteristics, e.g., sexual and aggressive qualitative characteristics. These qualitative characteristics or identities can be transferred or transformed . . . . Because of its basically anthropocentric position, its hydrodynamic character, its primitive anthropomorphism, and its fundamental conceptual divorce from biology and from all of evolutionary time, current psychoanalytical theory is a very limited theory. It cannot develop an adequate learning theory nor an adequate theory of the psychoanalytic process, and it cannot be meaningfully linked to modern neurophysiology. (ibid., 85)

The view that emerges from their critique, in summary, brings to mind what Lakoff and Johnson, quoted above, had to say about the "Society of the Mind": in psychoanalysis, it would seem, obscurities, stereotypes and contrived metaphors come to inhabit a Vitalistic Society of the Mind. According to this perspective, shared by many writers, such a failed science cannot possibly provide an adequate framework for a theory of the subject as it in no way complies with the requisites of theory itself, falsifiability, in particular. Furthermore, this sort of critical assessment implies that psychoanalytical theory can only obscure our understanding of embodiment, and that it cannot come to the aid of a discipline such as phenomenology, a discipline that, post-Husserl, is concerned with what lays *between* subject and object, with the connection between body and mind — all of which would therefore appear to be antithetical to the naïve Cartesian ontology that Freud supposedly conceived.

Yet, as I will argue hereafter, psychoanalysis is in fact an *indispensable* point of connection linking sociology and phenomenology (and critical for the problem of embodied memory).

Peterfreund and Schwartz are not entirely mistaken. They have given us, in any case, an opportunity to see how psychoanalytical thinking can, and to some extent has, drifted into various forms of mysticism, which, it seems to me, is an effect of the rapid and uncontrolled expansion of the discipline. In addition, their strong language notwithstanding and apparently forgiving the theory for its mistakes, they are not interested in discarding the theory or practice. They want to revamp it, and have in fact suggested helpful conceptual avenues for it.[5] Their task, then, has not been, as sometimes is the case, that of deaf "debunking" and can therefore be helpfully discussed and debated. But beyond these contributions, it is also easy to see that these authors' assessment has mistakes of its own, as we will see below (mistakes that have contributed to the crudely stereotypical idea that psychoanalysis it provides a hydraulic model riddled with crypto-vagueness).

The Project

A main point of contention for these authors, and arguably for the larger number of critics, is the "lack" of biological foundations, the lack of neuroscience, which, hand in hand with anthropocentrism, leads to the host of problems above, particularly to the notorious "hydrodynamic model." However, searching as they were for the neurobiological underpinnings of the theory, Peterfreund and Schwartz failed to take into account Freud's *Project for a Scientific Psychology* (1895), where he provides, precisely, the neurobiological foundations that gave the initial momentum to the discipline. The *Project,* this cornerstone that haunts Freud's subsequent theorizing, is bizarrely absent from their list of references. In the following passage from the *Project,* Freud describes the main principles governing the dynamics of the nervous system:

> The principle of [neuronal] inertia finds its expression in the hypothesis of a current [not fluid but electrical] passing from the cell's paths of conduction or processes [dendrites]* to the axis-cylinder [axon]. A single neurone is thus a model of the whole nervous system with its dichotomy of structure [discharge vs. accumulation of electrical energy], the axis-cylinder being the organ of discharge. The secondary function [of the nervous system],* however, which calls the accumulation of Qṅ [neuroelectric manifestation], is made possible by the assumption of resistances which oppose discharge; and the structure of neurones makes it probable that the resistances are to be located in the contacts [between one neuron and another, synapses], which in this way assume the value of barriers (in Pribram and Gill 1976, 33. Asterisked brackets theirs; non-asterisked brackets mine; original italics).

Let us begin outlining this model by enlisting now the help of Karl Pribram and Merton Gill (ibid.). Referring to the passage above they ask, "Can anyone really maintain in the face of these quotations that Freud the neuroscientist was developing a hydrodynamic model? Can anyone really doubt that

Freud was referring to ordinary, garden variety neurophysiology?" (ibid., 33).

This "garden variety neurophysiology" could not — and did not — provide the only causal framework for Freud's theory of the mind. But it did launch a discipline that rested upon the most advanced neurobiological hypotheses that could have been conceived at the time. Rather than hydrodynamics, Freud's model rested on neuroelectrical (not fluid) currents at the dynamic and economic origins of the nervous system; currents that he attempted to measure with a galvanometer, as Pribram and Gill also explain, an instrument measuring amperes that had been in use since the first quarter of the nineteenth century, and which was relatively common in Freud's milieu. (Luigi Galvani and his associate Alessandro Volta already knew, as of the middle of the eighteenth century, that nervous impulses were electrical in nature.) Pribram and Gill suggest that, when assessing the Freudian model, one should proceed assuming that,

> Freud did mean what he seems to mean — that *current* means not a current of fluid but action currents of electrical nerve impulses . . . that when he speaks of *Niveau* [cautiously translated in the Standard Edition as "level"] he means level of *potential*; that when he speaks of *resistance* he means resistance to passage of nerve impulse. In short we subscribe to the idea that Freud the physicalist was in fact attempting an Ohm's Law of neural function but since the quantitative data to do so was not available he refrained from actually writing the equation (Pribram and Gill 1976, 43, original emphases).

In short,

> Contemporary neurophysiology could find little to fault in [Freud's] outline of the nervous system function. Thus the *Project* contains exactly what the critics of the current mélange of psychoanalytical dogma are seeking [cf. Peterfreund and Schwartz]: a biological (physical) definition of the *energy concept* which can be 'meaningfully linked to modern neurophysiology.' (ibid., 34)

The foundational psychoanalytical picture of the mind involves neither hydraulics, with pipes embedded in the mind, nor anthropomorphic (good and bad), ghostly fluids running through them. If this initial model might be simplified for the sake of brevity, it would involve two main functions or postulates, which can provide a first window onto the analytical structure of the model. First, the theory postulates a primary function of neural discharge of electrical excitations, a function associated with the overall flow of electrochemical energy within the nervous system. The secondary function is related not to excitation and discharge, but to excitation and accumulation of energy; accumulation that Freud described as *Besetzung* ("*cathexis*": "holding onto," "occupation," from the Greek *Kathexis,* etymologically akin to "cathode, a negative potential," Pribram and Gill explain). This secondary function, related to neuromodulation, is responsible for higher processes as memory, and is the focus of Freud's attention. It points toward mechanisms of synaptic resistance to discharge (though the term "synapse" was coined after the Project; Freud, instead, speaks of "contact barriers"). According to this second postulate, repeated transmission of electrochemical impulses (repeated excitation) lowers synaptic resistance, which results from reinforcement (repetition of particular stimuli). Reinforcements open the way to neuronal plasticity and adaptation: repetition of stimuli leads to neuromodulation. Hence, these secondary neural functions are associated with memory — cellular memory and, in the end, personal memory — and are therefore associated with motive, affect, higher processes — consciousness, in general.[6] Back to Pribram: "garden variety neurophysiology." But let Pribram provide the technical summary. An extended quotation is needed:

> For the uninitiate it comes as an almost bewildering realization that in this document of 1895 [the Project] Freud emphasizes the same vital distinction made by contemporary neurophysiology between impulse transmission and graded potential change, the first referring to rapid discharge along a nerve and the other referring to slow changes in potential differences in the nervous tissue, especially in its dendritic portions. The basic distinction is that between a quantity of excitation which moves rapidly along the axon [primary function] — the usual nerve impulse discharge phenomenon — and a cathexis [secondary function] which is a quantity that is held in the neurons, biases (tunes) their activity, and is usually related to the dendrites. The understanding of this meaning of cathexis is vital to [various functions of the model, including Freud's understanding of] consciousness. (Pribram and Gill 1976, 63)

And later,

> Freud's model has often been alleged to be a hydrodynamic one. More correctly it is an energic model. But still more precisely the conception is based on the electrical concomitants of neural activity which had come to be seriously investigated in the last decades of the 19th century. Impulse transmissions (action currents) become *current* in flow. Synapses, contact barriers, interpose resistance to the flow of current. What remains is *voltage*, and the capacitance of neurons to store potential excitation. Cathexis refers to this third term in Freud's neural version of Ohm's Law. Freud was thus *not* using analogy and metaphor but talking fact. He does not suggest that water is running around in the head but rather that electricity is there . . . . This, it seems, is the aim of the *Project*, true to the Helmholtzian tradition in which Freud was steeped: to base a quantitative psychology on physical principles, on an Ohm's Law of neural function. (ibid., 66, original emphases)

Quantitative measurements in this Freudian model are given in Q, a measurable quantity of energy, explicated by Pribram and Gill above, which is further characterized as *Qṅ*, "neuroelectric manifestation, which can accrue as *potential* within a neuron, become action currents of nerve impulses, which when they overcome the resistances at contacts between neurons, discharge the neuron" (ibid., 34, original emphasis). Energy, this dynamizer of the psychosomatic system, was for Freud not a qualitative entity divorced from measurements (and thus from science). Indeed, the purported "anthropomorphic" nature of the Freudian notion of energy is less apparent still if we bear in mind that this concept was,

> [O]riginally derived from thermodynamics, where the first law deals with the conservation of energy and the second with its organization. The first law reads that every interaction among systems is constrained by the fact that any action begets an equal and opposite reaction. It is a law describing inertia, a concept which becomes the first postulate of the *Project.* The second law deals with the amount of change produced in the organization of the energy systems involved in these interactions . . . . This dissipation of organization is measured as entropy. (ibid., 25)

The neurobiological parameters of the emerging discipline, Pribram and Gill suggest, are "currently useful and truly a 'Preface to Contemporary Cognitive Theory and Neuropsychology'" (ibid., 17).

Certainly, as I will discuss shortly, aspects of the Freudian theory do not pretend to provide neurobiological explanations; and, indeed, where Freud uses a neurobiological language, he in general provides hypotheses and not explanations. These are hypotheses, he said, to be addressed in a "few dozen years" by future neuroscientists. After these few dozen years, as Antonio Damasio may agree (2005), many answers to the Freudian questions are still missing from the repertoire of biology and neuroscience. But many other answers have come forth. And as Pribram suggests, many of them are indeed supportive of foundational psychoanalytical hypotheses, of the overall conception, which thus "anticipates . . . nerophysiological inquiries by more than half of a century" (ibid., 67). Let me note also that a growing corpus of neurological research, particularly under the banner of neuro-psychoanalysis, has begun to map, precisely, the neurophysiological dynamics that may underpin psychoanalytical constructs.[7] Karen Kaplan-Solms and Mark Solms (2001) have provided a leading commentary (see also, the *Journal of Neuropsychoanalysis*; Panksepp 1999; Solms and Turnbull 2010)

Freud's neurobiology, in summary, albeit hypothetical, provided feasible scaffolding for subsequent theorizing. The often-rehearsed stereotype, which portrays an anthropomorphizing, pseudo-biological Freud hauling along a hydraulic system, is easily correctable.[8]

Post-Project

The post-project criticisms are less stereotypical and not easily dismissible, as we will see. Nonetheless, psychoanalysis has not lost its vitality because of them. On the contrary, if anything it has learned from, and become dynamized by, them. The neurophysiological model outlined above provided only the initial momentum for the discipline; and psychoanalytical theory can be divided at least into two phases. The first phase intends to model "psychical process," Freud says, "as quantitatively determinate states of specifiable material particles" (Freud 1950, 295), as described above. The second phase, discussed hereafter, purportedly abandons his scientistic goals, according to critics, and fully embraces an interpretive psychology that owes nothing to the criteria required by empirical science. Let us have a glimpse of this second phase. In his magnum opus, *The Interpretation of Dreams*, Freud suggests that, in this particular text,

> I shall entirely disregard the fact that the mental apparatus with which we are here concerned is also known to us in the form of an anatomical preparation, and I shall carefully avoid the temptation to determine psychical locality in the anatomical fashion. I shall remain upon psychological ground. (1900, 574)

This passage, particularly the last sentence, is often cited by critics as evidence that Freud the psychologist got disillusioned with neurobiology, subsequently abandoned it as a principle of explanation, and thus forsook the possibility of having a quantitative, biological — scientific — ground for later psychological theorizing; theorizing that thus was fated to remain speculative at best. I will discuss this criticism subsequently, but let me begin by pointing out that only a couple of pages after Freud promises to "remain upon psychological ground," he uses the language of neurobiology as a matter of course: he speaks of "neurones," of "facilitations," of "conductive resistances" (synaptic resistances), of the "ψ systems," etc. His "psychological ground" is not, as critics suggest, divorced from neurobiological foundations; and indeed the language of quantity and of neurobiology appears with relatively frequency throughout the post-*Project* writings. As the editors of the Standard Edition put it, "The Project, or rather its invisible ghost, haunts the whole series of Freud's theoretical writings to the very end" (in Gay 1989). To put it differently, in his subsequent writing, Freud does not rely on causal mechanisms beyond those outlined in the *Project* (Gomez 2005, 17-22). Freud the psychologist — and, more broadly, the critic of civilization and history — comes to see that human phenomena cannot be reduced to the single perspective of neuroscience. But his "psychological ground" is still rooted in the neurobiology of the Project, though not reduced to it.

"Naïve Cartesian Dualism"

Freud believes in fact that the domains of neurology and psychology (as the domains of biology and culture) can be separated only analytically. This division of labor among domains and disciplines is practical and expeditious, but empirically these phenomena form part of an encompassing and inseparable structural-functional system. They are ontologically attached. "I so rarely feel the need for synthesis," Freud says. "The unity of this world seems to be something so self-evident as not to need emphasis. What interests me is the separation and breaking up into its component parts what would otherwise revert to an inchoate mass" (Freud 1985, 32). This "world-unity," Freud would argue, encompasses biology and culture, neurology and psychology, quantities (e.g., neural) as well as qualities (e.g., sensation, awareness), internal as well as external stimuli, somatic, psychological, and environmental or cultural factors.

It is true that in 1912 the middle Freud characterized his position as "dualist": "if [I] *had* to choose among the views of the philosophers, [I] would characterize [myself] as a dualist. No monism succeeds in doing away with the distinction between ideas and the objects they represent" (quoted in Livingstone-Smith 1999, 36, emphasis mine). But it is wrong to assume that Freud therefore ended up with a naïve dualistic Cartesian split between body and mind (ibid., see also Askay and Farquhar [2006]). Again, Freud sees the use of an analytical separation between mind and body, but, as indicated, empirically "the ego is first and foremost bodily ego" (Freud 1923, 26). "The ego is ultimately derived from bodily sensations, chiefly from those springing from the surface of the body" (ibid., 26). His "dualism" is only a rejection of a monistic sense of oneness in human phenomena: it rejects any notion of humans as "*blobjects*," as Horgan and Potrč would say: it rejects the notion of part-less human phenomena. Instead, somewhat as in Bourdieu, Freud posited a functional unity encompassing the body and the ego, the organism and the environment, ideas and also the objects represented by these ideas. As we saw in previous chapters, he posited ontological linkages connecting the body (related to the id), the person (related to the ego) and culture/environment (related to superego), in a "total" Maussian sense. His "dualism" is indeed the recognition of dynamic, functional exchanges involving forces that extend in space (e.g., the body, environment), and in time (mind, ego). It assumes a related economy of energetic exchanges connecting the body and the ego, the subject and the object, the internal world and external world.

Freud's original Cartesianism notwithstanding, psychoanalytical theory, in the end, came to envision a functional unity connecting these seemingly separate Cartesian domains. Again, the baby "does not have the breast"; he, instead, "is the breast"; he is *not* ontologically separated from the object. In the end, this "total" model allowed Freudians to connect seemingly discontinuous phenomena — somatic, psychological, and cultural phenomena — under a unified theoretical perspective. (Hence they can write about a wide spectrum of seemingly disconnected things: hysterical paralyses, jokes, dreams, myths, irrational collective violence, the origin of religious phenomena, works of art, the causes of war.) Rather than abandoning neurobiology, Freud integrates it in a total epistemology and a total ontology.[9]

Popper's Critique

I have indicated that, as Freud moves from the neurobiology of the *Project* to the later psychological writings — as he moves from quantities to qualities, and from neurobiology to eventually history, culture, and civilization — he concentrates on the latter, not directly biogenetic aspects of human nature. Methodologically, this transition into the domain of qualities resulted in an *interpretative* psychoanalytical approach not limited to the hypothetico-deductive logic. Freud, again, assumes that interpersonal and cultural processes cannot be reduced to biological determinisms; and likewise he assumed that these processes cannot be reduced to the hypothetico-deductive model.

When this happens — when psychoanalytical theory becomes concerned with "the mysterious leap" whereby neural activity becomes mental phenomena, with the transformation of chemistry into personhood, and quantities into qualities — the model faces its greater methodological tests. And this theoretical leap also invites the most sophisticated critiques, including perhaps the most influential critique of the psychological model, that of Karl Popper (2003).One of the foremost humanists and activists of the twentieth century, Popper is arguably the most respected critic of psychoanalysis.

To schematically extract the basic, and relatively simple, Popperian critique it may be said that psychoanalysis, for the Austro-British philosopher, is a failed science because it provides a hypothetical model while, however, dispensing with the standards of the hypothetico-deductive method. Sciences such as physics, Popper says, have to provide testable — that is, falsifiable, refutable — theoretical statements. Psychoanalysis, by contrast, provides theoretical statements that cannot be falsified. The psychoanalytical theorist, Popper argues, can find any number of instances that can easily "corroborate" her theoretical statements, but cannot provide the possibility of falsifying such statements. And as falsifiability is the key criterion of science, psychoanalysis is therefore not only a non-science but indeed partakes from the logic of ideology and myth, which also dispense with the need for falsifiability.

In part, the problem arises because psychoanalysis does not provide a "prohibitive" epistemology, Popper would say. The idea is that to discover any laws underlying reality, sciences must prohibit certain behaviors or cases from occurring; such that, if the scientific community or the researcher her-self can eventually show that these cases occur, the theory can be falsified, its laws questioned, its foundations shown to be "doxological." Classical phys-ics, for example, prohibits all apples in gravitational range from failing to fall in the direction of the ground. Since no case has been found to contradict this theoretical statement, the law of gravity stands as a law, the theory stands as a theory. Popper suggests that, by contrast, far from using the criterion of prohibition, psychoanalysis readily allows for occurrences inconsistent with any sense of lawfulness. According to the analytical parameters of this disci-pline, any number of "apples" may fail to fall to the ground. Indeed, core hypothetical variables underpinning the discipline such as repression, the unconscious, trauma (which, Popper argues, operate as independent variables or causes), or neurosis (purportedly a dependent variable or outcome), cannot be specified, cannot be clearly and distinctly operationalized. Neurosis, for example, is not a distinct analytical category, Popper would say. Instead, there are "neurotics" of all sorts, people who exhibit a range of conditions, behaviors, impediments, advantages. "Who has ever met a prospective pa-tient," Popper asks, "who was told by his prospective psychoanalyst that he was not neurotic?" Likewise, "repression," "the unconscious," etc. cannot be clearly and distinctly operationalized and therefore cannot be tested within scientific, hypothetico-deductive parameters.

Thus, much as any myth or any ideology, psychoanalysis may provide some insights and wisdom regarding human phenomena — while, however, remaining merely pre-scientific. It remains, Popper's argument goes, perhaps one notch above pseudo-sciences such as astrology. Indeed, the student of this discipline, much as any mystagogue, is simply enlightened by "revela-tions." And once initiated, he/she finds confirmations everywhere, such that the world becomes "full of verifications of the theory" (ibid.). Let us ima-gine, with Popper, that a man wants to save a child from drowning. This Good Samaritan, the psychoanalytical theorist would say, is likely sublimat-ing repressed material. Another man wants to drown a child. He is merely expressing formerly repressed material. Thus finding confirmations in ran-dom occurrences, psychoanalytical theory grows. Unbelievers are clearly people who merely refuse to see the truth. Perhaps, Popper ironically says, they are "repressing" something. Perhaps "they are crying for treatment" (ibid.). (But never mind that: their cure is, of course, psychoanalysis.) This important critic indeed suggests that children and neurotics, especially neuro-tics, think in these terms. By contrast, abiding by the criterion of falsifiabil-ity, scientists look not for confirmations but for negations of their theories.

Popper's analysis may have an immediate intuitive appeal. It may seem to result in a very simple, logical, perhaps unassailable critique. Yet this cri-tique is not without deficits of its own, as I will presently discuss.

The Human Sciences

The hypothetico-deductive method is the key to understanding, to controlling, to predicting (and ultimately to conquering) physical, quantifiable — lawful — phenomena. This analytical strategy has opened the door to the many advantages that modernity boasts; and thanks to it, our lives are no longer so "short, brutish, and nasty," as the pre-Newtonian Thomas Hobbes would have it. But it is also easy to see that, as Aristotle says, logical deduction is better suited to some phenomena and not to others. Lavinia Gomez (2005) has suggested that the problem with critiques that focus on the hypothetico-deductive logic as the standard of scientific truth, is that they fail to see that the hypothetico-deductive method was developed by the physical sciences, "with physics as the paradigm science. [However, it] fits the human sciences less well, since human actions cannot be investigated in the same way as other happenings . . . . It was this that led Mill to advocate the inductive method for 'human' subject matter. This approach treats human actions as no different in principle from other natural events, but only as more complicated" (Gomez 2005, 22).

No theory, Freudian or otherwise, has provided laws for the human phenomenon, because human phenomena such as consciousness do not behave in a systemic, predictable, Newtonian manner. Whereas the Newtonian domain is law-abiding, a lack of systemicity is the especial characteristic of subjectivity. To be sure, this is what makes us human, the fact that we do not behave following principles akin to those that govern a hydraulic engine, nails and magnets, apples and gravity. Hence, this otherwise powerful and helpful hypothetico-deductive method shows its weaknesses when it comes to certain aspects of human life (and certain aspects of reality, in general). As Aristotle suggested, a method can provide precise answers *only to the extent to which the objects being studied allow it.* Demonstrable certainty ("apodicticity" in the Aristotelian idiom) does not depend on the efficacy of a method alone. It depends on how well an analytical method addresses or not the characteristics of the things being studied. Such things as emotions, the phenomena of dreaming, jokes, motives, interpersonal exchanges — the stuff that pertains to the human sciences — is in general less quantifiable, more fluid, less predictable, much less law-oriented — and thus much less amenable to hypothetico-deductive reasoning (Gomez 2005). When Freud fully encountered these fluid and unpredictable aspects of human nature he stumbled, and his Helmholtztian model proved to be insufficient.

Again, in the world described by classical physics, all apples are attracted to the ground. But when human phenomena are concerned, some apples will be thus attracted and others will not; and each one of them may change its likings and behaviors according to time and setting. This is why the human sciences, as Jürgen Habermas suggests (1971), cannot be limited to a positivistic, hypothetico-deductive logic. And this is why, Habermas also says, psychoanalysis, when it joins the domain of the human sciences, cannot longer rely on this sort of logic alone. Let us go back to the example of tears, which are of central importance in psychoanalysis. As we saw, Heidegger argues that tears contain not only proteins, salts, etc., but also immaterial things, events that can be conscious and unconscious, past or forthcoming, and which nonetheless are still *present* in tears. As they contain traces of biology but also traces of experience — objective and measurable properties that are intrinsically attached to subjective elements — "You can never actually measure tears," Heidegger says (Heidegger 2001, 81). For, much as the minor or major characteristics of a musical composition are larger than the sum of the notes, weeping is also larger than the sum of its component parts. Thus, resting on the logic of measurement alone, the observer of tears will be able to provide, as Nietzsche would say, only a perspective into this kind of psychosomatic expression. This perspective may be necessary and helpful, but will always remain, precisely, perspectival, incomplete.

When it comes to human phenomena, the Cartesian ideal of distinctiveness, precision, and deductive certainty is, precisely that, an ideal. We can't know human nature with the same degree of precision, distinctiveness, and certainty with which we may know a particle or mass, for example. Indeed, when it comes to human phenomena, this Cartesian ideal is potentially dangerous, as John Stuart Mill would argue. If assumed to be the only road to human knowledge, such Cartesian logic can lead the observer away from understanding the key characteristics of human beings: our capacity for spontaneity and freedom.

Of course, as Durkheim and Bourdieu have shown, human beings are not entirely free or spontaneous, but are constrained, and can even be determined, by historical forces and circumstances, such that their behaviors can be predicted in various ways and degrees. Surely, as Freud also argued, freedom is never *radical freedom*, as our will, decisions, wants, likes, and dislikes — are preceded by organic *and* cultural structures — by structures of possibilities that largely frame our lives and minds, and that have done so evolutionarily. Yet, we are not determined by pre-given laws either, like automatons are. Again, what makes us human is the fact that we do not follow laws and patterns in the same way in which lower animals or things in the inorganic world do. And thus, precisely because we are endowed with a *minimum* amount of freedom, a method that cannot grasp these human characteristics will fail to understand basic aspects of human nature. Thus, any theory dealing with freedom, desire — human nature — has to rest, as Mill argued, on flexible analytical and methodological parameters.

As Freud moved toward psychology and then culture (civilization), he came to fully understand the need for this sort of analytical flexibility, and adopted non-empiricistic, interpretive, hermeneutical approaches, which, in the end, came to sustain much of the (post-Project) psychoanalytical theory.

Back again to tears, hypothetico-deductive strategies have provided helpful measurements and insights related to tears, and their function, composition, and so on. But to understand tears fully, the observer, after specifying their measurable properties, would have to begin using the language of hermeneutics to capture the processive, qualitative dimension of tears. The same reasoning applies to human phenomena, in general. Indeed, any human science interested in a holistic approach to human phenomena has to resort to interpretative and hermeneutical approaches conversant with, but also outside of, the hypothetico-deductive method. The goal of this division of labor between hypothesis-driven and hermeneutical analyses is to provide, as much as possible, complementary, not competing, accounts of what it means to be human.

It is worth going back to Antonio Damasio's ideas about Freud's notion of superego as a mechanism of adaptation, and as a mechanism of connection between biology and culture (c.f., *Civilization and its Discontents)*. I quote Damasio:

> A task that faces neuroscientists today is to consider the neurobiology supporting adaptive [superegoic] supraregulations, by which I mean the study and understanding of the brain structures required to know about those regulations. I am not attempting to reduce social phenomena to biological phenomena, but rather to discuss the powerful connections between them. It should be clear that although culture and civilization arise from the behavior of biological individuals, the behavior was generated in the collective of individuals interacting in specific environments. Culture and civilization could not have arisen from single individuals and thus cannot be reduced to biological mechanisms and, even less, can they be reduced to a subset of genetic specifications. Their comprehension demands not just general biology and neurobiology but the methodologies of the social sciences as well. (Damasio 2005, 124, my emphasis)

This is the methodological stage at which the human sciences have arrived, a stage portended by Mauss' call for a "total" approach to human nature. The goal of this book has been to open a window onto this total domain. I have argued that psychoanalysis can help Mauss and Bourdieu and sociology in general, precisely because it attempted to connect biology to psychology and culture. Lastly, let me insist: I do not assume that the psychoanalytical model is flawless. On the contrary, I assume that it is very easy to recognize its mistakes, big and small. [10] Psychoanalytical theory is *not* a means to glean, to borrow Duchamp's coinage, readymades, final answers, dogmatic postulates. This theory is alive and well not only because it has touched upon important aspects underlying human nature, but also because it is constantly revising its hypotheses, shedding problems, incorporating new perspectives. Pribram and Gill suggest that the model is "a Rosetta Stone." Much as the Egyptian tablet, psychoanalysis can provide certain keys to make sense of the sometimes hieroglyphic, archeological, buried aspects of human nature, of life as lived.

NOTES

1. Many of these criticisms have been helpful, penetrating, sober, but not all of them. Adolf Wohlgemuth, a psychologist coetaneous with Freud, reflected on the comparisons that critics were making between Freud and Darwin: "Freud-Darwin! You may as well couple the name of Mr. Potts, of the *Eatonswill Gazette*, with that of Shakespeare or Goethe." Contemporarily, the work of Frederick Crews comes to mind in this context. An English Professor, Crews built a career largely as a critic of Freud, arguing that psychoanalysis is a vast confidence trick full of "ludicrous," "medieval" fabrications, lead by a "sham," "self-serving," "greedy," "unscrupulous," "calculating," "petty generalissimo," "the most overrated figure in the entire history of science and medicine," the founder of a bankrupt "pseudoscience," and so forth (e.g., in Borch-Jacobsen and Shamdasani 2008; Gomez 2005).

2. One my consider, for example, the work of powerful writers as John Bowlby, Medard Boss, Nancy Chodorow, Erik Erikson, Ronald Fairbairn, Sándor Ferenczi, Erich Fromm, Karen Horney, Carl Jung, Heinz Kohut, Melanie Klein, Hans Loewald, Otto Rank, Donald Winnicott and others. Perhaps Jacques Lacan may count as the most radical critic. Lacanian epistemology and practice differ substantially from, and yet are in continuity with, those proposed by Freud.

3. "I no longer believe in my neurotica," Freud wrote to Fliess as early as 1897 (1950a), before embarking upon some of the major themes, post turn of the century.

4. "You see," Einstein tells Freud, "every Tuesday I read from your works with a lady who is a friend of mine, and cannot admire enough the beauty and truth of your presentation" (in Otto and Norden 1960, 186-203).

5. I cannot discuss these here but, in general, these authors suggest that psychoanalysis ought to move in the direction of Information Systems Theory, which could reportedly enrich aspects of the discipline.

6. Volumes have been written about the neurobiological underpinnings of the model. The reader may consult Pribram and Gill, quoted above, Mark Solms and Karen Kaplan-Solm (2000), Mark Solms and Oliver Turnbull (2002), and Jaak Panksepp (1999).

7. www.neuro-psa.com provides a good bibliographical list pertaining to this line of inquiry. Last visited: 8/16/2011.

8. Indeed, it is hard to imagine how this sort of stereotypical Freud could have ever emerged from the Viennese milieu. Bear in mind that Freud's epoch, as Helen Walker-Puner says, "[W]as the age of Darwin in genetics, Mendel in heredity, Gustav Theodor Fechner in the laws of the conservation of energy. It was the age of Lord Lister and the beginnings of bacteriology; of the microscope, the test tube and the galvanometer. Those things which could not be observed, measured, weighed and tested in this age of the ascendancy of natural science were not worth considering at all" (Walker-Puner 1992, 39). Freud began his training as a neuroscientist (who, indeed, began as a histologist, as we saw). He was a physicalist who originally looked to physicists/biologists such as Ernst Mach and Hermann Von Helmholtz for guidance (Helmholtz was his "idol," the young Freud said). His training in the Helmholtzian school centered on the idea that the relatively fledgling science of biology could and ought to be in close dialogue with the methods and the concepts of the then more mature sciences: physics, in particular; and also chemistry. Recall also that his original "intention [was] to furnish a psychology that shall be a natural science; that is to represent psychical process as quantitatively determinate states of specifiable material particles thus making these processes perspicuous and free from contradiction" (Freud 1950, 295).

9. What he abandons, though, is his earlier (Helmholtzian) understanding of neuroanatomical function, which rested "almost entirely [...] on the method of *clinico-anatomical correlation*" (Kaplan-Solms and Solms 2002). According to this Helmholtzian perspective, as Kaplan-

Solms and Solms suggest, all mental functions could be taxologically assigned to corresponding brain areas, so that such functions as "reading, writing, skilled movement, and visual recognition [and] a wide range of psychological faculties were localized in a mosaic of so-called centres on the surface of the human brain" (ibid., 10), centers that were thus seen as static pieces in the jigsaw puzzle of the mind. The goal of this early neurological approach was to provide a taxological neuroanatomy, so that mental functions (and dysfunctions) could be ascribed to specific neuro-anatomical locations corresponding to mental events and mental phenomena in general. By contrast, as Freud moves away from the Helmholtzian School and continues his training at the Salpêtrière Hospital where a different neuro-anatomical approach is used — he discovers, particularly under Charcot, that mental functions could not be reduced to a of "narrow localizationism," Kaplan-Solms and Solms explain. He discovers that, instead, mental events need to be explained not by reference to static brain locations, but as effects of functional and dynamic neural interactions, continuously connecting different neuro-anatomical locations across the nervous system.

10. To borrow the phrase from Heidegger, "those who think greatly err greatly," and Freud certainly made great mistakes. To glean a small glimpse into some of the errors committed (and left uncorrected) by Freud and by psychoanalytical theory in general, one may only to consider, for instance, a quote such as the following, which many feminists have discussed at length and in more appropriate contexts: "little girls," Freud says, "notice the penis of a brother or playmate, strikingly visible and of large proportions, at once recognize it as the superior counterpart of their own small and inconspicuous organ, and from that time forward fall a victim to envy for the penis" (1925). As Totton suggest (1999), if it weren't because this sentence is invested with Freud's authority (in the Roman sense of *auctoritas*: prestige, natural ability to influence thoughts, actions, feelings) this statement, along with others throughout the psychoanalytical corpus, would be perhaps justifiably derided.

References

Abercrombie, David. 1968. "Paralanguage." *British Journal of Disorder Communications* 3: 55-59.

Abraham, Karl. 1921. "Contributions to the Theory of the Anal Character." In *Essential Papers on Obsessive-Compulsive Disorders*, edited by Dan J. Stein and Michael H. Stone, 1997. New York: New York University Press.

Abu-Lughod, Lila. 1985. "Honor and the Sentiments of Loss in a Bedouin Society." *American Ethnologist* 12 (2): 245-261.

Aegineta, Paulus. 1833. *The Medical Works of Paulus of Aegineta.* London: Cornwall Herald Office.

Alfano, Francesca. 2004. *Extreme Bodies.* Milan: Skira.

American Anthropological Association, http://www.aaanet.org/stmts/racepp.htm. Last visited: 8/16/2011.

Anderson, Benedict. 1991. *Imagined Communities.* London: Verso.

Arendt, Hannah. 1954. *Between the Past and the Future.* Cambridge: Harvard University Press.
———. 1989. *The Human Condition.* Chicago: University of Chicago Press.

Argyle, Michael. 2007. *Bodily Communication.* New York: Routledge.

Aristotle. 2003. *Metaphysics.* Translated by Richard Hope. Ann Arbor: University of Michigan Press.

Asch, Solomon. 1951. "Effects of Group Pressure upon the Modification and Distortion of Judgment." In *Groups, Leadership and Men*, edited by H. Guetzkow, 1951. Pittsburgh, PA: Carnegie Press.

Ashenburg, Katherine. 2007. *The Dirt on Clean: An Unsanitized History.* New York: North Point Press.

Askay, Richard and Jensen Farquhar. 2006. Apprehending the Inaccessible: Freudian Psycho-analysis and Existential Phenomenology. Evanston: Northwestern University Press.

Attali, Jacques. 1985. *Noise: The Political Economy of Music.* Translated by Brian Massumi. Minneapolis: University of Minneapolis Press.

Augustine of Hippo. 1872. *The Works of Aurelius Augustine, Saint Augustine (Bishop of Hippo) Volume Five*, edited By Marcus Dods. London: Murray and Bibb.

Bakhtin, Mikhail. 1984. *Rabelais and His World.* Translated by Helene Iswolsky. Blooming-ton: University of Indiana Press.

Bakker, Martijntje and Johan Mackenbach, eds. 2002. *Reducing Inequalities in Health: A European Perspective.* London: Routledge.

Bargh, John A., Mark Chen, and Lara Burrows. 1996. "Automaticity of Social Behavior: Direct Effects of Trait Construct and Stereotype Activation on Action." *Journal of Personality and Social Psychology* 71 (2): 230-244.

Bass, Alan. 2000. *Difference and Disavowal: The Trauma of Eros.* Stanford: Stanford University Press.

Battaille, Georges. 2000. *Visions of Excess: Selected Writings, 1927-1939.* Minneapolis: University of Minnesota Press.

Benjamin, Walter. 1968. *Illuminations: Essays and Reflections*, edited by Hannah Arendt. Translated by Harry Zohn. New York: Schocken Books, Inc.

Benzaquén, Adriana. 2006. *Encounters with Wild Children: Temptation and Disappointment in the Study of Human Nature.* Quebec: McGill-Queens University Press.

Berger, John. 1980. *About Looking.* New York: Vintage International.

Berger, Peter and Thomas Luckmann. 1967. *The Social Construction of Reality: A Treatise in the Sociology of Knowledge.* New York: Anchor Books.

Bergson, Henri. 1990. *Matter and Memory.* Translated by N. H. Paul N. and W. S. Palmer. Brooklyn: Zone Books.

Blackmore, Susan. 2000. *The Meme Machine.* New York: Oxford University Press.

Boas, Franz. 2001. *Changes in Bodily Form of Descendants of Immigrants.* New York: Adamant Media Corporation.

Bollas, Christopher. 1997. *The Shadow of the Object: Psychoanalysis of the Unthought Known.* London: Columbia University Press.

Borch-Jacobsen, Mikkel and Sonu Shamdasani. 2008. "Interprefactions: Freud's Legendary Science." *History of the Human Sciences* 21 (3): 1-25.

Bourdieu, Pierre. 1977. *Outline of a Theory of Practice.* Cambridge: Cambridge University Press.

———. 1987. *Distinction: A Social Critique of the Judgment of Taste.* Cambridge: Harvard University Press.

———. 1990b. *The Logic of Practice.* Stanford: Stanford University Press.

———. 1990a. *Homo Academicus.* Stanford: Stanford University Press.

———. 1991. *Language and Symbolic Power.* Cambridge: Harvard University Press.

———. 1998. *Practical Reason.* Stanford: Stanford University Press.

———. 1999. *The Political Ontology of Martin Heidegger.* Stanford: Stanford University Press.

———. 2000. *Pascalian Meditations.* Stanford: Stanford University Press.

———. 2001. *Masculine Domination.* Stanford: Stanford University Press.

Bourdieu, Pierre and Loic J. D. Wacquant. 1992. *Invitation to a Reflexive Sociology.* Chicago: University of Chicago Press.

Bracken, P., A. Wachtler, A. R. Panesar, and J. Lange. 2007. "The Road not Taken: How Traditional Excreta and Greywater Management May Point the way to a Sustainable Future." *Water Science and Technology: Water Supply* 7 (1): 219–227.

Braun, Lundy. 2002. "Race, Ethnicity, and Health: Can Genetics Explain Disparities?" *Perspectives in Biology and Medicine* 45:159–174.

Brown, Norman. 1985. *Life against Death: The Psychoanalytical Meaning of History.* Middleton: Wesleyan University Press.

Brunner, José. 2001. *Freud and the Politics of Psychoanalysis.* New Jersey: Transaction Publishers.

Bryant, Colleen. "Semen Impurity in Ancient Judaism: A Jungian Approach," MA diss., Harvard University, 2000.

Brym, Robert and John Lie. 2009. *Sociology: Your Compass for a New World.* Belmont, CA: Wadsworth Publishing.

Burke, Peter. 1989. "Memory: History, Culture and the Mind." In *A Kant Dictionary,* edited by Howard Caygill. 1995. Malden: Blackwell Publishing.

Burns, Steven. 1994. "If a lion could talk." *Wittgenstein Studien* 1 (1) http://sammelpunkt.philo.at:8080/396/. Last visited: 12/29/11.

Butler, Judith. 1993. *Bodies that Matter: On the Discursive Limits of Sex.* New York: Routledge.

Camille, Michael. 1998. *The Medieval Art of Love: Objects and Subjects of Desire.* London: Lawrence King Publishing.

Carr, Nicholas. 2010. *The Shallows: What the Internet Is Doing to Our Brains.* New York: W. W. Norton.

Cervantes, Miguel De. 1999. *Don Quixote.* New York: Oxford University Press.

Chapman, A. and M. Chapman-Santana. 1995. "The Influence of Nietzsche on Freud's Ideas." *British Journal of Psychiatry* February 166 (2): 251-3.

Chatfield, Charles and Ruzanna Ilukhina, eds. 1994. *Peace/Mir.* Syracuse: Syracuse University Press.

Chauncey, George. 1994. *Gay New York.* New York: Basic Books.

Cioran, Emil. 2004. *Tears and Saints.* Chicago: University of Chicago Press.

Coakley, Sarah. 1997. *Religion and the Body.* London: Cambridge University Press.

Collingham, E. M. 2001. *Imperial Bodies.* Cambridge: Polity Press.

Connerton, Paul. 1989. *How Societies Remember.* Cambridge: Cambridge University Press.

Crews, Frederick. 1993. "The Unknown Freud" New York Review of Books 40 (19): 55-66.

———. 1994a. "Professor Frederick Crews" http://www.pbs.org/newshour/bb/health/jan-june99/freud_crews.html. Last visited: 8/16/2011

———. 1994b. "The Revenge of the Repressed" (Part one and Two) *New York Review of Books* 41 (19): 54-60.

———. 1995. *The Memory Wars: Freud's Legacy in Dispute.* New York: New York Review of Books.

Crossley, Nick. 1997. "Corporeality and Communicative Action." *Body and Society* 3 (1): 17-46.

Damasio, Antonio. 2005. *Descartes Error: Emotion Reason and the Human Brain.* New York: Penguin Books.

———. 2006. *The Feeling of What Happens: Body and Emotion in the Making of Consciousness.* New York: Mariner.

Davidson, James. 1998. *Courtesans and Fishcakes: The Consuming Passions of Classical Athens.* New York: St. Martin's Press.

Davis, J.I., A. Senghas, F. Brandt, and K.N. Ochsner. 2010. "The effects of Botox Injections on Emotional Experience." *Emotion* 10(3): 433-40.

Davis, Wade. 1988. *Passage of Darkness: The Ethnobiology of the Haitian Zombie.* Chapel Hill: The University of North Carolina Press.

Debord, Guy. 2010. *Society of the Spectacle.* New York: Black and Red.

Deleuze, Gilles. 1983. *Nietzsche and Philosophy.* New York: Columbia University Press.

Deleuze, Gilles and Guatari, Félix. 2001. *A Thousand Plateaus* London: The Athlone Press.

Descartes, Rene. 1988. *Selected Philosophical Writings.* Cambridge: Cambridge University Press.

Dijksterhuis, Ap. 2005. "Why we are Social Animals: The High Road to Imitation as Social Glue." In *Perspectives on Imitation: From Cognitive Neuroscience to Social Science,* 2: 207-220, edited by Hurley and Chater. Cambridge: MIT Press.

Donne, John. 1991. *The Complete English Poems.* London: Penguin Books.

Douglas, Mary. 2002. *Purity and Danger.* New York: Routledge.

Douglass, Frederick. 1846. "The Relation of the Free Church to the Slave Church: An Address Delivered in Paisley, Scotland, on March 20, 1846." *Renfrewshire Advertiser*, March 28, 1846. In *The Frederick Douglass Papers: Volume 1, Series One-Speeches, Debates, and Interviews,* edited by John Blassingame. et al., 1979. New Haven: Yale University Press.

———. 2003. *Narrative of the Life of Frederick Douglass, an American Slave.* New York: Barnes and Noble Classics.

DuBois, W.E.B. 2011. *The Souls of Black Folk.* New York: Tribeca Books.

Durkheim, Emile. 1965. *The Elementary Forms of Religious Life.* New York: Free Press.

———. 1973. *Moral Education.* New York: Free Press.

———. 1982. *The Rules of Sociological Method.* New York: Free Press.

———. 1994. *The Division of Labor in Society.* New York: Free Press.

Durkheim, Emile and Marcel Mauss. 1963. *Primitive Classification.* Chicago: University of Chicago Press.

Duster, Troy. 2003. *Backdoor to Eugenics.* Second Edition. New York: Routledge.

Eaton Danice, Laura Kann, Steve Kinche, et al. 2010. "Youth Risk Behavior Surveillance — United States, 2009." *Morbidity and Mortality Weekly Report, Surveillance Summary, Jun 4,* 59 (5): 1-142.

Einstein, Albert. 1931. "Letters to Sigmund Freud, April 29." Library of Congress, Manuscript Division, Sigmund Freud Collection.

Elam, Harry. 2010. "We Wear the Mask: Performance, Social Dramas, and Race." In *Doing Race: 21 Essays for the 21ˢᵗ.* Edited by Hazel Markus and Paula Moya. New York: Norton and Company.

Eliade, Mircea. 1961. *The Sacred and the Profane.* Translated by Willard Trask. New York: Harper Torchbooks.

———. 1967. *Myths, Dreams and Mysteries: The Encounter Between Contemporary Faiths and Archaic Realities.* Translated by P. Mairet. New York: Harper and Row.

Elias, Norbert. 1978. *The Civilizing Process: Sociogenetic and Psychogenetic Investigations.* Translated by Edmund Jephcott. Massachusetts: Blackwell Publishers.

England, Paula and Reuben Thomas. 2006. "The Decline of the Date and the Rise of the College Hook Up." In *Families in Transition.* Fourteenth Edition. Edited by Arlene Skolnick and Jerome Skolnick. Upper Saddle River: Allyn and Bacon.

Eyal Press. 2012. *Beautiful Souls: Saying No, Breaking Ranks, and Heeding the Voice of Conscience in Dark Times.* New York: Farrar, Straus and Giroux.

Fausto-Sterling, Anne. 1992. *Myths of Gender.* New York: Basic Books.

Ferenczi, Sandor. 2008. *Further Contributions to the Theory and technique of Psychoanalysis.* New York: Ford Press.

Finkel, Michael. 2009. "The Hadza." *National Geographic Magazine.* http://ngm.nationalgeographic.com/2009/12/hadza/finkel-text/1.

Floud, Roderick, Robert W. Fogel, Bernard Harris, and Sok Chul Hong. 2011. *The Changing Body: Health, Nutrition, and Human Development in the Western World since 1700.* Cambridge: Cambridge University Press.

Foucault, Michel. 1979. *The History of Sexuality, Volume 1: An Introduction.* Translated by Robert Hurley. New York: Vintage.

———. 1980. *Power Knowledge: Selected Interviews and Other Writings.* Edited by Colin Gordon. Translated by Colin Gordon, Leo Marshall, John Mepham, and Kate Soper. New York: Pantheon.

———. 1984a. *Foucault Reader.* Edited by Paul Rabinow. New York: Pantheon.

———. 1984b. *The History of Sexuality Volume III: The Care of the Self.* Translated by Robert Hurley. New York: Vintage.

———. 1990. *The History of Sexuality Volume II: The Use of Pleasure.* New York: Vintage. Translated by Robert Hurley. New York: Vintage.

———. 1995. *Discipline and Punish.* Translated by Alan Sheridan. New York: Vintage. New York: Vintage.

Freud, Sigmund. 1900. "The Interpretation of Dreams." *The Standard Edition of the Complete Psychological Works of Sigmund Freud,* 4-5: 1-625. Translated and edited by James Strachey. New York: W. W. Norton.

———. 1907. "Delusions and Dreams in Jensen's Gradiva." *The Standard Edition of the Complete Psychological Works of Sigmund Freud,* 9: 48-49. Translated and edited by James Strachey. New York: W. W. Norton.

———. 1925. "Some Psychical Consequences of the Anatomical Distinction Between the Sexes." *The Standard Edition of the Complete Psychological Works of Sigmund Freud,* 19: 241-258. Translated and edited by James Strachey. New York: W. W. Norton.

———. 1926. "Inhibitions, Symptoms and Anxiety." *The Standard Edition of the Complete Psychological Works of Sigmund Freud,* 20: 145-146. Translated and edited by James Strachey. New York: W. W. Norton.

———. 1927. *The Ego and the Id.* Translated by J. Riviere. Hogarth Press and Institute of Psycho-analysis; 1961. Revised for *The Standard Edition of the Complete Psychological Works of Sigmund Freud,* translated and edited by James Strachey. New York: W. W. Norton.

————. 1940. *An Outline of Psychoanalysis. The Standard Edition of the Complete Psychological Works of Sigmund Freud*, 9: 48-49. Translated and edited by James Strachey. New York: W. W. Norton.

————. 1941f [1938]. "Findings, Ideas, Problems." *The Standard Edition of the Complete Psychological Works of Sigmund Freud*, 23: 299-300. Translated and edited by James Strachey. New York: W. W. Norton.

————. 1950 [1895]. "Project for a Scientific Psychology." *The Standard Edition of the Complete Psychological Works of Sigmund Freud*, 281-391. Translated and edited by James Strachey. New York: W. W. Norton.

————. 1950a [1887-1902]. "Extracts From the Fliess Papers." *The Standard Edition of the Complete Psychological Works of Sigmund Freud*, 1: 173-280. Translated and edited by James Strachey. New York: W. W. Norton.

————. 1961. *Beyond the Pleasure Principle*. New York: W. W. Norton.

————. 1985. "Sigmund Freud and Lou Andreas-Salome, Letters." New York: W. W. Norton.

————. 2002. *Civilization and Its Discontents*. Translated by James Strachey. New York: W. W. Norton.

————. 2003. *The Psychopathology of Everyday Life*. Translated by Anthea Bell. London: Penguin Classics.

Friedan, Betty. 2001. *The Feminine Mystique*. New York: W. W. Norton.

Fullilove, M.T. 1998. "Abandoning 'Race' as a Variable in Public Health Research — an Idea Whose Time has Come." *American Journal of Public Health* 88: 1297–1298.

Fussell, Paul. 1983. *Class: A Guide through the American Status System*. New York: Touchstone.

Fussell, Samuel. 1991. *Muscle: Confessions of an Unlikely Bodybuilder*. New York: Avon Books.

Galeano, Eduardo. 1985. *Genesis*. Translated by Cedric Belfrage. New York: W. W. Norton.

————. 1991. *The Book of Embraces*. Translated by Cedric Belfrage. New York: W. W. Norton.

————. 2008. *Espejos, Una Historia Casi Universal*. Madrid: Siglo.

Gallup, Gordon. 1970. "Chimpanzees: Self Recognition." *Science* 167 (3914): 86–87.

Garry, Stephanie. 2007. "In Defense of His Confederate Pride." *The St. Petersburg Times*, October 7, 2007.

Gay, Peter, ed. 1989. *The Freud Reader*. New York: W. W. Norton.

Giddens, Anthony, Mitchell Duneier, Richard Appelbaum, Deborah Carr. 2010. *Essentials of Sociology*, Third Edition. New York: Norton and Company.

Gino, Francesca, Michael Norton, and Dan Ariely. 2010. "The Counterfeit Self: The Deceptive Costs of Faking it." Psychological Science. May 21 (5): 712-20.

Gergen, K., M. Gergen, and W. Barton. 1973. "Deviance in the Dark," *Psychology Today*, May: 129-30.

Goffman, Erving. 1971. *Relations in Public*. New York: Basic Books.

————. 1971a. *The Presentation of the Self in Everyday Life*. New York: Penguin Books.

Gogarten, Peter. 2000. "Evolutionary Theory: An Esalen Invitational Conference November 5-10." www.esalen.org. Last visited: 8/16/2011.

Goldfarb, Jeffrey. 2006. *The Politics of Small Things*. Chicago: University of Chicago Press.

Gombrich, E.H. 2002. *The Story of Art*. London: Phaidon Press.

Gomez, Lavinia. 2005. *The Freud Wars: An Introduction to the Philosophy of Psychoanalysis*. New York: Routledge.

Goodman, Alan. 2012. *Race: Are We So Different*. New Jersey: Wiley-Blackwell.

————. 2000. "Why Genes don't Count (for Racial Differences in Health)." American Journal of Public Health 90: 1699–1702.

Gould, Stephen Jay. 2002. *The Structure of Evolutionary Theory*. Cambridge, MA: The Belknap Press of Harvard University Press.

Grosz, Elizabeth. 1994. *Volatile Bodies: Toward a Corporeal Feminism*. Bloomington: University of Indiana Press.

Grout, Donald and Claude Palisca. 1996. *A History of Western Music*. New York: W.W. Norton.

Habermas, Jurgen. 1971. *Knowledge and Human Interest*. Translated by Jeremy Shapiro. Portsmouth: Heinemann.

———. 1973. *Theory and Practice*. Translated by John Viertel. Boston: Beacon Press.

———. 1991. *The Philosophical Discourse of Modernity*. Cambridge: MIT Press.

Halbwachs, Maurice. 1980. *The Collective Memory*. New York: Harper and Row.

———. 1992. *On Collective Memory*. Chicago: The University of Chicago Press.

Haney Lopez, Ian. 2006. *White by Law*. New York: New York University Press.

Hariri, Ahmad R. and Paul H. Whalen. 2011. "Face to Face with the Emotional Brain." *The Scientist Magazine of the Life Sciences* 25 (2): 30.

Hatfield, Elaine, John Cacioppo, and Richard Rapson. 1993. *Emotional Contagion*. Cambridge: Cambridge University Press.

Havas, D.A., A.M. Glenberg, K.A. Gutowski, M.J. Lucarelli, and R.J. Davidson. 2010. "Cosmetic Use of Botulinum Toxin-A Affects Processing of Emotional Language." *Psychological Science* 21(7): 895-900.

Heidegger, Martin. 1991. *Nietzsche: Volumes One and Two*. New York: Harper Collins.

———. 1996. *Being and Time*. Albany: SUNY Press.

———. 2001. *Zolikon Seminars*. Translated by R. Askay and Franz Mayr. Evanston: Northwestern University Press.

Herr, N. 2008. *The Sourcebook for Teaching Science*. San Francisco: Jossey-Bass. See also, http://www.csun.edu/science/health/docs/tvandhealth.html#tv_stats. Last visited: 8/16/2011.

Hobsbawm, Eric. 1983. *Mass-Producing Traditions*. Cambridge: Cambridge University Press.

———. 1996. *The Age of Revolution: 1789-1848*. New York: Vintage.

Hochschild, Arlie. 1979. "Emotion Work, Feeling Rules, and Social Structure." *American Journal of Sociology* 85: 551-575.

———. 2003. *The Managed Heart: Commercialization of Human Feeling*. Berkeley, CA: University of California Press.

Hoy, David. ed. 1986. *Foucault: A Critical Reader*. San Francisco: Blackwell Publishing.

Hoy, Suellen. 1995. *Chasing Dirt: The American Pursuit of Cleanliness*. New York: Oxford University Press.

Hume, David. 1757. "Of the Standard of Taste" http://www.mnstate.edu/gracyk/courses/phil%20of%20art/hume%20on%20taste.htm. Last visited: 8/16/2011.

Husserl, Edmond. 1973. *Experience and Judgment*. London: Routledge and Kegan Paul.

———. 1999. "Material Things in Their Relation to the Aesthetic Body" In *The Body* edited by Don Welton. San Francisco: Blackwell Publishing.

Hutton, Patrick. 1993. *History as an Art of Memory*. Boston: New England Press.

Iacoboni, Marco. 2009. *Mirroring People: The Science of Empathy and How We Connect with Others*. New York: Picador.

Jablonski, Nina. 2004. "The Evolution of Human Skin and Skin Color." *Annual Review of Anthropology* 33: 585-623.

Jacobson, Matthew Frye. 1998. *Whiteness of a Different Color: European Immigrants and the Alchemy of Race*. Cambridge: Harvard University Press.

James, William. 1884. http://psychclassics.asu.edu/James/emotion.htm.

———. 2000. *Pragmatism and Other Writings*. New York: Penguin Classics.

Janson, H. and Anthony Janson. 2003. *History of Art*. Upper Saddle River: Pearson.

Janssen, Jacques and Theo Verheggen. 1997. "The Double Center Gravity in Durkheim's Symbol Theory." *Sociological Theory* 15 (3): 295-307.

Jenkins, Jenkins, Keith Oatley, and Nancy Stein eds. 1998. *Human Emotions: A Reader*. Massachusetts: Blackwell Publishers.

Jostmann, Nils, Daniel Lakens, and Thomas Schuber. 2009. "Weight as an Embodiment of Importance." Psychological Science 20 (9) 1169-1174.

Kahn, Jonathan. 2004. "How a Drug Becomes 'Ethnic': Law, Commerce, and the Production of Racial Categories in Medicine." *Yale Journal of Health Policy Law, and Ethics* 4:1–46.

Kant, Immanuel. 1965. *Critique of Pure Reason*. New York: St. Martin's Press.

Kaplan-Solms, Karen and Mark Solms. 2001. *Clinical Studies in Neuro-Psychoanalysis: Introduction to a Depth Neuropsychology*. New York: Other Press.

Kaster, Robert A. 2007. *Emotion, Restraint, and Community in Ancient Rome*. New York: Oxford University Press.

Kawachi, Ichiro, S. V. Subramanian, Brisa N. Sanchez, and Dolores Acevedo-Garcia. 2009. "Do Socioeconomic Gradients in Body Mass Index Vary by Race/Ethnicity, Gender, and Birthplace?" *American Journal of Epidemiology* 169 (9): 1102-1112.

King, F. H. 1911. *Farmers of Forty Centuries*. Emmanus: Rodale Press.

Kishiyama, Mark M., W. Thomas Boyce, Amy M. Jimenez, Lee M. Perry, Robert T. Knight. 2009. "Socioeconomic Disparities Affect Prefrontal Function in Children." *Journal of Cognitive Neuroscience* 21 (6): 1106-1115.

Klossowski, Pierre. 1969. *Nietzsche and the Vicious Circle*. Chicago: University of Chicago Press.

Kofman, Sarah. 1983. *Nietzsche and Metaphor*. Translated by Duncan Large. Stanford: Standford University Press.

Krafft-Ebing, Richard. 1998. *Psychopathia Sexualis*. New York: Arcade Publishing.

Kristeva, Julia. 1986. "The System and the Speaking Subject." *The Kristeva Reader* edited by Toril Moi. New York: Columbia University Press.

Kurlansky, Mark. 2002. *Salt: A World History*. New York: Walker and Company.

Lacan, Jacques. 1977. *Écrits*. New York: W. W. Norton.

La Capra, Dominick. 1972. *Emile Durkheim, Sociologist and Philosopher*. Ithaca: Cornell University Press.

Lakoff, George and Mark Johnson. 1999. *Philosophy in the Flesh: The Embodied Mind and Its Challenge to Western Thought*. New York: Basic Books.

Lancaster, H. O. 1990. *Expectations of Life: A Study in the Demography, Statistics, and History of World Mortality*. New York: Springer.

Lanzetta, John T., Jeffrey Cartwright-Smith, and Robert E. Eleck. 1976. "Effects of Nonverbal Dissimulation on Emotional Experience and Autonomic Arousal." *Journal of Personality and Social Psychology* 33 (3): 354-70.

Laplanche, Jean and J. P. Pontalis. 1973. *The Language of Psychoanalysis*. New York: W. W. Norton.

Lautenbacher, Stephan and Roger B. Fillingim, eds. 2004. *Pathophysiology of Pain Perception*. New York: Plenum Publishers.

Lee, Soo-Jin, Joanna Mountain, and Barbara Koenig. 2001. "The Meanings of 'Race' in the New Genomics: Implications for Health Disparities Research." *Yale Journal of Health Policy, Law and Ethics* 1:33–75.

Le Goff, Jacques. 1992. *History and Memory*. New York: Columbia University Press.

Lewontin, Richard. 1993. *Biology as Ideology: The Doctrine of DNA*. New York: Harper Perennial.

———. 2000. *The Triple Helix: Gene, Organism and Environment*. Cambridge: Harvard University Press.

Livingstone-Smith, David. 1999. *Freud's Philosophy of the Unconscious*. New York: Walter Kluwer Academic Publishers.

Lutz, Catherine A. 1988. *Emotions: Everyday Sentiments on a Micronesian Atoll and Their Challenge to Western Theory*. Chicago: University of Chicago Press.

MacIntyre, Alasdair. 1988. *Whose Justice? Which Rationality?* Notre Dame: University of Notre Dame Press.

Mahler, Margaret S. 2000. *The Psychological Birth of the Human Infant*. New York: Basic Books.

Marcuse, Herbert. 1962. *Eros and Civilization*. New York: Vintage.

Marks, Johnathan. 2002. *What it Means to be 98% Chimpanzee: Apes, People, and Their Genes*. Berkeley: University of California Press.

Markus, Hazel and Paula Moya, eds. 2010. *Doing Race: 21 Essays for the 21st Century*. New York: Norton and Company.

Mauss, Marcel. 1921. "The Mandatory Expressions of the Sentiments." Translated by Loic Wacquant. Unpublished, n.d.

———. 1923. "Total Man." Translated by Loic Wacquant. Unpublished, n.d.

————. 1928. "Joking Kinship Relationships." Translated by Loic Wacquant. Unpublished, n.d.

————. 1973. "Techniques of the Body." *Economy and Society* 2 (1): 70-88.

————. 1953. "Techniques of the Body." Translated by Loic Wacquant. Unpublished, n.d.

Max, D.T. 2005. "National Smiles." *The New York Times*, December 11, 2005.

Mazzocchi, Fulvio. 2008. "Complexity in Biology: Exceeding the Limits of Reductionism and Determinism Using Complexity Theory." *European Molecular Biology Organization Science and Society*, Rep. January 9 (1): 10–14.

McNeill, William H. 1999. "How the Potato Changed the World's History." *Social Research* 66 (1): 67-83.

Mead, George Herbert. 1934. *Mind, Self, and Society.* Edited by Charles W. Morris. Chicago: University of Chicago Press.

Meltzoff, Andrew N. and M. Keith Moore. 1977. "Imitation of Facial and Manual Gestures by Human Neonates." *Science* 198: 75-78.

Melzack, R. and K Casey. 1968. "Sensory, Motivational and Central Control Determinants of Chronic pain: A New Conceptual Model." In *The Skin Senses: Proceedings of the first International Symposium on the Skin Senses, Florida State University* edited by Dan R Kenshalo. Springfield: Charles C. Thomas Publisher.

Melzack, Ronald and Patrick D. Wall. 1996. *The Challenge of Pain.* London: Penguin Books.

Merleau-Ponty, Maurice. 1964. *The Primacy of Perception.* Edited by John Wild. Evanston: Northwestern University Press.

————. 2002. *The Phenomenology of Perception.* Translated by Colin Smith. New York: Routledge.

Meyer, Ilan. 2003. "Prejudice, Social Stress and Mental Health in Lesbian, Gay, and Bisexual Populations." *Psychological Bulletin* 129: 674-97.

Middleton, H. 2006. *Best Foot Forward.* Self published: Abilene, Texas.

Milgram, Stanley. 1975. *Obedience to Authority: An Experimental View.* New York: Harper Perennial.

Mintz, Sidney W. 1984. *Sweetness and Power: The Place of Sugar in Modern History.* New York: Penguin Books.

————. 1999. "Sweet Polychrest." *Social Research* 66 (1): 85-101.

Molloy, John T. 1975. *Dress for Success.* New York: Wyden Books.

Mundy, Jennifer, ed. 2001. *Desire Unbound.* Princeton: Princeton University Press.

Narvaez, Alfredo. 2003. "Cabeza y Cola: Expresión de Dualidad, Religiosidad y Poder en los Andes." Edited by L. Millones, H. Tomoeda, and T. Fujii. *Senri Ethnological Reports*, National Museum of Ethnology, Osaka Japan.

Narvaez, Rafael. 2006. "Embodiment, Collective Memory, and Time." *Body and Society* 12 (3): 51-73.

————. 2009. "The Situation of Smiling." http://thesituationist.wordpress.com/category/cultural-cognition/page/2/. Last visited: 12/12/11.

Nasrallah, Laura and Elisabeth Schüssler Fiorenza, eds. 2010. *Prejudice and Christian Beginnings: Investigating Race, Gender, and Ethnicity in Early Christianity*. Minneapolis, MN: Fortress Press.

Nathan, Otto, Heinz Norden, and Albert Einstein, eds. 1960. *Einstein on Peace.* New York: Simon and Schuster.

Nietzsche, Friedrich. 1978a. *The Gay Science.* New York: Penguin Books.

————. 1978b. *Thus Spoke Zarathustra.* New York: Penguin Books.

Nora, Pierre. 1989. *The Realms of Memory.* Berkeley: University of California Press.

Odgen, C., C. Fryar, M. Carroll, et al. 2004. "Mean Body Weight, Height, and Body Mass Index, United States, 1960-2002." *CDC Division of Health and Nutrition Examination Surveys* N. 347.

Olick, Jeffrey and Joyce Robins. 1998. "Social Memory Studies." *Annual Review of Sociology* 24: 105-40.

Olick, Jeffrey, Vered Vinitzky-Seroussi and Daniel Levy. 2011. *The Collective Memory Reader.* New York: Oxford University Press.

Oliver, K. 2005. *Edinburgh Dictionary of Continental Philosophy.* Edited by John L. Protevi. Edinburgh: Edinburgh University Press.

Orwell, George. 2003. *1984.* New York: Plume.

Otto Nathan and Heinz Norden, eds. 1960. *Einstein on Peace.* New York: Schocken Books.

Paglia, Camille. 1992. "Junk Bonds and Corporate Raiders: Academe in the Hour of the Wolf." *Arion* 1 (1991): 139-212.

Panksepp, Jaak. 1999. "Emotions as Viewed by Psychoanalysis and Neuroscience: An Exercise in Consilience." *Neuro-Psychoanalysis* 1: 15-38.

Paster, Gail Kern. 1993. *The Body Embarrassed.* Ithaca: Cornell University Press.

Paz, Octavio. 1993. *The Double Flame: Love and Eroticism.* Orlando: Harcourt Brace and Company.

Peterfreund, Emanuel and Jacob T. Schwartz. 1971. *Information Systems and Psychoanalysis.* Madison: International Universities Press.

Piaget, Jean. 1977. *The Essential Piaget.* Edited by Howard E. Gruber and J. Jacques Voneche. Jason Aronson Publishers, Inc.

Plato. 1953. *Collected Works.* Translated Benjamin Jowett. New York: Oxford University Press.

———. 1987. *The Republic.* New York: Penguin Books.

Pohl, Frances K. 2002. *Framing America: A Social History of American Art.* London: Thames & Hudson.

Popper, Karl. 2003. *Conjectures and Refutations: The Growth of Scientific Knowledge.* New York: Routledge.

Poyatos, Fernando, ed. 1996. *Nonverbal Communication and Translation.* Philadelphia: John Benjamins Publishing Co.

Pribram, Karl H. and Merton M. Gill. 1976. *Freud's Project Reassessed.* London: Hutchinson and Company.

Provine, Robert. 2000. Laughter: A Scientific Study. New York: Penguin Classics.

Rees, Jonathan L. 2003. "Genetics of Hair and Skin Color." *Annual Review of Genetics* 37: 67–90.

Reich, Wilhelm. 1972. *Character Analysis.* New York: Farrar, Strauss and Giroux.

Reichert, Tom. 2002. "Sex in Advertising Research: A Review of Content, Effects, and Functions of Sexual Information in Consumer Advertising." *Annual Review Sex Research* 2002; 13: 241-73.

Renan, Ernest. 1882. 'Qu'est-ce qu'une nation?' Internet, http://ourworld.compuserve.com/homepages/bib_lisieux/nation01.htm. Last visited: May 9, 2005.

Rideout V., D. Roberts, U. Foehr. 2010. "Generation M²: Media in the Lives of 8-18 Year-Olds." Menlo Park, CA: Kaiser Family Foundation.

Roubal, Petr. 2003. "Politics of Gymnastics: Mass Gymnastic Displays under Communism in Central and Eastern Europe." *Body and Society* 9 (2).

Russell, Bertrand. 1972. *A History of Western Philosophy.* New York: Simon and Schuster.

Sanchez-Vaznaugh, Emma V., Ichiro Kawachi, S. V. Subramanian, et al. 2009. "Do Socioeconomic Gradients in BMI Vary by Race/Ethnicity, Gender and Birthplace?" *American Journal of Epidemiology* 169 (9): 1102-12.

Sankar, Pamela and Mildred K. Cho. 2002. "Toward a New Vocabulary of Human Genetic Variation." *Science* 298: 1337–1338.

Schachter, Stanley and Jerome E. Singer. 1962. "Cognitive, Social, and Physiological Determinants of Emotional State." *Psychological Review* 69: 379–399.

Schachter, Stanley and Ladd Wheeler. 1962. "Epinephrine, Chlorpromazine, and Amusement." *Journal of Abnormal and Social Psychology* 65: 121-128.

Schama, Simon. 1999. *Rembrandt's Eyes.* New York: Knopf.

Schmitt, Jean-Claude. 1990. "The Ethics of Gesture." In *Fragments for a History of the Human Body, Part Two.* Edited by Michel Feher. New York: Zone Books.

Seaford, Henry. 1978. "Maximizing Replicability in Describing Facial Behavior." *Semiotica* 24:1-32.

Shakespeare, William. 1623. *The Winter's Tale.* Electronic Text Center, University of Virginia Library. Last visited: 12/01/11.

Simmel, M. L. 1958. "The Conditions of Occurrence of Phantom Limbs." *Proceedings of the American Philosophical Society* 102: 492-500.

Siri, Engberg. 2005. *Kiki Smith: A Gathering, 1980-2005*. Minneapolis: Walker Art Center.

Slepian, Michael, Max Weisbuch, Nicholas O. Rule and Nalini Ambady. 2011. "Tough and Tender: Embodied Categorization of Gender." *Psychological Science* 22(1) 26–28.

Smith, A. D. 2002. *The Problem of Perception*. Cambridge: Harvard University Press.

Solms, Mark and Oliver Turnbull. 2010. *The Brain and the Inner World: An Introduction to the Neuroscience of Subjective Experience*. New York: Other Press.

Sontag, Susan. 2001. *On Photography*. New York: Picador.

Spitz, Rene. 1946. "Hospitalism: A Follow-Up Report on Investigation Described in Volume I, 1945." *The Psychoanalytic Study of the Child* 2: 113-117.

Sroufe, Alan L., Byron Egeland, Elizabeth Carlson, and Andrew Collins. 2005. *The Development of the Person: The Minnesota Study of Risk and Adaptation from Birth to Adulthood*. New York: The Gilford Press.

Stearns, Peter. 1994. *American Cool: Constructing a 20th Century Emotional Style*. New York: New York University.

———. 1999. *Battleground of Desire: The Struggle for Self-Control in America*. New York: New York University.

Stern, Daniel. 1984. *The Interpersonal World of the Infant*. New York: Basic Books.

———. 1990. *Diary of a Baby*. New York: Basic Books.

Stevens, Jacqueline. 2003. "Racial Meanings and Scientific Methods: Changing Policies for NIH-Sponsored Publications Reporting Human Variation." *Journal of Health Political Policy Law* 28: 1033-1087.

Sturm, Richard A., Rohan D. Teasdale, Neil F. Box. 2001. "Human Pigmentation Genes: Identification, Structure and Consequences of Polymorphic Variation." *Gene*. 277: 49-62.

Tocqueville, Alexis de. 2000. *Democracy in America*. Evanston: University of Chicago Press.

Tomatis, Alfred. 1991. *The Conscious Ear*. Barrytown: Station Hill Press.

Totton, Nick. 1999. *The Water in the Glass*. New York: Other Press.

Vargas Llosa, Mario. 2011a. "Prohibido Prohibir." *El País*, October, 17.

———. 2011b. "Más Información, Menos Conocimiento." *El País*, July, 31.

———. 1993. *El Pez en el Agua*. Madrid: Alfaguara.

Wacquant, Loic. 1995. "Why Men Desire Muscles?" *Body and Society* 1 (1): 163-179.

Walker Puner, Helen. 1992. *Freud: His Life and His Mind*. New York: Grosset Dunlap Publishers.

Wall, Patrick. 2002. *Pain: The Science of Suffering*. New York: Columbia University Press.

Weber, Max. 1958. *The Protestant Ethic and the Spirit of Capitalism*. Translated by Talcott Parsons. New York: Scribners.

West, Cornel. 1999. *The Cornel West Reader*. New York: Basic Civitas Books.

Whitebook, Joel. 1996. *Perversion and Utopia*. Cambridge: MIT Press.

Williams, Lawrence and John Bargh. 2008. "Experiencing Physical Warmth Promotes Interpersonal Warmth." *Science* 322, 606-607.

Winnicott, Donald W. 1986. *Holding and Interpretation: Fragment of an Analysis*. London: The Hogarth Press and the Institute of Psycho-Analysis.

———. 1989. *Psychoanalytic Explorations*. Edited by Claire Winnicott, Ray Shepherd, and Madeleine Davis. Cambridge: Harvard University Press.

———. 1991. *Playing and Reality*. New York: Routledge.

Wittgenstein, Ludwig. 1958. *Philosophical Investigations* 3rd edition. Translated by G.E.M. Anscombe. Upper Saddle River: Prentice Hall.

Zahavi, Dan. 2001. "Beyond Empathy. Phenomenological Approaches to Intersubjectivity." *Journal of Consciousness Studies* 8 (5-7): 151-167(17).

Zimbardo, Philip G. 1971. "The power and pathology of imprisonment." Congressional Record, Ninety-Second Congress, *First Session on Corrections, Part II, Prisons, Prison Reform and Prisoner's Rights: California*. Washington, DC: U.S. Government Printing Office.

Žižek, Slavoj. 2008. *The Sublime Object of Ideology*. New York: Verso.

Index

Index

www.ingramcontent.com/pod-product-compliance
Lightning Source LLC
Chambersburg PA
CBHW070409270326
41926CB00014B/2766